Left Turn

Left Turn

HOW LIBERAL MEDIA BIAS DISTORTS THE AMERICAN MIND

Tim Groseclose

ST. MARTIN'S PRESS NEW YORK

 For information, address St. Martin's Press, 175 Fifth Avenue, New York, N.Y. 10010.

www.stmartins.com

Book design by Richard Oriolo

Library of Congress Cataloging-in-Publication Data

Groseclose, Timothy.
Left turn : how liberal media bias distorts the American mind / Tim Groseclose.—1st ed.
p. cm.
ISBN 978-0-312-55593-1
1. Journalism—Objectivity—United States. 2. Journalism—Political aspects—United States. 3. Press and politics—United States. 4. Liberalism—United States. 5. Conservatism—United States. I. Title.
PN4888.O25G76 2011
302.230973—dc22 2011005975

First Edition: July 2011

10 9 8 7 6 5 4 3 2 1

CONTENTS

PREFACE

IN AT LEAST one important way journalists are very different from the rest of us—they are more liberal. For instance, according to surveys, in a typical presidential election Washington correspondents vote about 93–7 for the Democrat, while the rest of America votes about 50–50.

What happens when our view of the world is filtered through the eyes, ears, and minds of such a liberal group?

As I demonstrate, using objective, social-scientific methods, the filtering prevents us from seeing the world as it actually is. Instead, we see only a distorted version of it. It is as if we see the world through a glass—a glass that magnifies the facts that liberals want us to see and shrinks the facts that conservatives want us to see.

The metaphoric glass affects not just what we see, but how we think. That is, media bias really does make us more liberal.

Perhaps worst of all, media bias feeds on itself. That is, the bias makes us more liberal, which makes us less able to detect the bias, which allows the media to get away with more bias, which makes us even more liberal, and so on.

All of this means that the political views that we currently see in Americans are not their natural views. We see only an artificial, distorted version of those views.

Main Conclusions of the Book

In this book I calculate the precise degree to which those views have been distorted. Specifically, I answer the question: What if we could magically remove the metaphoric glass and see, face-to-face, the average American, *once his political views were no longer distorted by media bias*? What would we see?

The answer, basically, is Ben Stein.

Yes, the actor, author, commentator, and former host of *Win Ben Stein's Money*. More specifically, the person whom we'd see would be anyone—like Ben Stein—who has a political quotient near 25. The political quotient is a device I've constructed to measure political views in a precise, objective, and quantitative way. A person's PQ indicates the degree to which he is liberal. For instance, as I have calculated, the PQs of Barney Frank (D-Mass.) and Nancy Pelosi (D-Calif.) are approximately 100. Meanwhile, the PQs of Michele Bachmann (R-Minn.) and Jim DeMint (R-S.C.) are approximately 0.[1]

Two other people whose PQs are approximately 25 are Bill O'Reilly and Dennis Miller. O'Reilly and Miller are significantly more conservative than the average American voter, whose PQ is approximately 50. But they are significantly more liberal than politicians such as Michele Bachmann or Jim DeMint.[2]

As my results show, if we could magically eliminate media bias, then the average American would think and vote like Stein, Miller, O'Reilly, and others who have a PQ near 25.

In this magical world—call it a Ben Stein-ocracy—there would be just as many politicians to the left of Stein, O'Reilly, and Miller as there were to their right. The same thing would be true of policies—that is, Stein, O'Reilly, and Miller would complain just as often that U.S. policies were too conservative as they would complain that they were too liberal.

In such a world, American political values would mirror those of present-day regions where the average voter has a 25 PQ. Such regions include the states of Kansas, Texas, and South Dakota. They also include Orange County, California, and Salt Lake County, Utah.

To the liberal elite, such places are a nightmare. They are family-friendly, largely suburban, and a large fraction of their residents go to church on Sundays. "Ah, don't cross the Orange Curtain," I once heard a Hollywood acquaintance say to another Hollywood acquaintance, referring to a visit to Orange County.

In an episode of *The Sopranos*, Tony goes into a coma after being shot. He dreams that he is stuck in a hotel in Costa Mesa (a town in Orange

County). He and the other guests of the hotel slowly realize that they are not free to leave. The hotel, many believe, was intended by *The Sopranos* writers to represent Purgatory.

To the liberal elite, that's the way the world would be if media bias were to disappear—like Orange County, not quite hell, but a step in that direction.

Construction of the Book's Argument

To some people, these conclusions will sound shocking. However, they are supported by: (i) eight years of research; (ii) some state-of-the-art statistical and social-scientific methods; and (iii) recent, little-noticed, yet brilliant, research by some rising-star professors of economics and political science.

In addition, once you learn some not-so-shocking intermediate conclusions that I construct, the main conclusion might not seem so shocking. The following are some of those intermediate conclusions:

- The PQ is based upon issues chosen by the Americans for Democratic Action, a liberal interest group. Thus, to demonstrate liberal media bias, I use a measuring rod, that is based on criteria selected by liberals.
- Through the notion of a slant quotient, I show that media bias, like political views, can be measured objectively and quantitatively.
- According to these slant quotients, *every* mainstream national news outlet in the United States has a liberal bias.
- Of the one hundred or so news outlets I examine, only a handful lean to the right. These include: *The Washington Times, The Daily Oklahoman,* the *Arizona Daily Star* (Tucson), and Fox News *Special Report.*
- But even these supposedly conservative news outlets are not *far right.* For instance, the conservative bias of *Special Report* is significantly less than the liberal bias of *CBS Evening News,* and it is approximately equal to the liberal bias of *ABC World News Tonight* or *NBC Nightly News.*
- The *effects* of media bias are real and significant. My results suggest that media bias aids Democratic candidates by about 8 to 10 percentage points in a typical election. I find, for instance, that if media bias didn't exist, then John McCain would have defeated Barack Obama 56–42, instead of losing 53–46.

- In our current world, where views are distorted by media bias, the PQ of the average voter is approximately 50. This is about the score of Sen. Ben Nelson (D-Neb.) or Sen. Olympia Snowe (R-Me.).
- However, if we could magically eliminate media bias, then the PQ of the average voter would decrease to approximately 25 or 30.
- In our current world, where views have been distorted toward the left, news outlets such as *The Washington Times* and Fox News *Special Report* seem conservative. However, if we could remove the left-wing bias of the media as a whole—and thus change the average voter's PQ to 25 or 30—then *The Washington Times* and *Special Report* would seem slightly left-leaning.

Left Turn

Introduction

DISCUSSIONS ABOUT MEDIA bias can really inflame people's passions.

In the spring of 2002, I began a research project with Jeff Milyo, who at the time was a public policy professor at the University of Chicago. Our goal was to create a method that would objectively measure the bias of the media.

The motivation was simple. In social science we have lots of precise numerical devices that measure how liberal or conservative politicians are. There ought to be something similar for the media.

Three and half years later, after thousands of hours of gathering and analyzing data, we achieved that goal. For twenty major news outlets, we estimated a score, between 0 and 100, that described how liberal each outlet was. The beauty of the scores, which I now call slant quotients, is that they are directly comparable to political quotients. This means that they can answer questions such as: (i) "Is *The New York Times* to the left or right of Hillary Clinton?" or (ii) "Is Fox News to the left or right of John McCain?"

The results generally agreed with the claims of conservatives. For instance, our method found that eighteen of the twenty outlets were left of center. The only two that were not were *The Washington Times* and Fox News *Special Report with Brit Hume.*

Our findings, however, contradicted a few claims of conservatives. For instance, they showed that some mainstream news outlets are nearly perfectly centrist, albeit still left-leaning. Two were ABC's *Good Morning*

America and *The NewsHour with Jim Lehrer.* Also, we found that many supposedly far-left news outlets were not *that* far left. For instance, we found that National Public Radio was no more liberal than *The Washington Post, Time,* or *Newsweek.* And we found that it was *less* liberal than the average speech by Sen. Joe Lieberman.

We thought that maybe people on both sides of the political spectrum would appreciate the study, that each side would say something such as "Finally, an answer to the age-old debate."

We now realize how naïve that thought was.

We posted the results on my Web site. The public relations office at UCLA, where I work as a professor of political science and economics, wrote a press release that summarized the results.

Then came the firestorm. Our study was denounced by hundreds, and maybe thousands, of left-wing blogs, including Media Matters, the Daily Kos, and the Huffington Post. At one point if you Googled "crap UCLA study," most of the first ten listings would refer to our study.

On January 5, 2006, I appeared on C-SPAN's *Washington Journal* to discuss the study. That morning, the Daily Kos made me the focus of an "action alert," which encouraged readers to call C-SPAN and force me to "answer some tough questions" about my "highly flawed study."

Many blogs attacked Milyo and me personally and tried to insinuate that right-wing groups had paid us to fudge our results. The emails were even more vicious. "I've been in media relations for twelve years, and I've never seen anything like this," said Meg Sullivan, the UCLA publicist who wrote the press release and who was listed as the contact person. "Every other study that I've been involved with will get maybe a few emails. This one has gotten hundreds. And some are scary. I hope your home address is not public."

A few people emailed the UCLA chancellor, insisting that I be fired. One noted on the subject line "Groseclose must be fired IMMEDIATELY," as if simply firing me next week would be a grave injustice.

Of the many emails that left-wing strangers sent me, the first one was representative of the anger and viciousness:

> Dear Tim,
>
> Sounds like that cockamamie load of bulls**t study of yours started with the results you wanted (i.e., that Fox News is "fair and balanced") and then concocted the most ridiculous, asinine set of parameters you could think of to ensure the results you were after.

> You've obviously never watched Fox News, [otherwise you'd realize how many people] will be laughing at your "study" . . .
> Sorry man, sounds like a bunch of BS to me, and that's from an independent. . . .
> Xxxx Xxxx

One of my colleagues at UCLA, whom I'll call Byron B. Bright, may be the smartest political scientist on the planet. He knows seemingly everything about politics, economics, math, and computers. And he's the best person to ask if you need your car, refrigerator, or anything else fixed. Once, a statistical software package wouldn't do what he wanted, so, to solve his problem, he wrote a computer program that would write a series of other computer programs, which would successively execute the statistical package—that's right, he wrote a computer program that would write other computer programs.

At the same time, he's a staunch liberal, approximately as staunch, maybe stauncher, than I am a conservative. Our first debate occurred only a few weeks after we first met, almost twenty years ago. He casually mentioned how the only people who listened to Rush Limbaugh were ignorant extremists. I quickly explained why he was wrong, and told him, in fact, that I had been listening to Limbaugh that day.

In a more recent debate, I told him, "No, it's not true that liberals and conservatives are equally decent. Liberals have worse manners; they go to church less; they more often live in aggressive, urban environments; they shout people down at public speeches; and they use more vulgarity when they talk." At first he didn't respond. I think he decided that the best response was just to give me a look as if I had claimed that the earth was flat. But then, just for good measure, he said, "Funny how all of those well-mannered conservatives favor preemptive strikes against innocent Iraqis."

So after I received the above email, I gleefully showed it to Byron. I responded to the email even more gleefully:

Dear Mr. Xxxx,

> Thank you for your thoughtful comments.
> Please keep in mind, however, that in creating the statistical estimation method and in designing the set of parameters for it, I have benefited greatly from the help and comments of Byron Bright, a colleague at UCLA. An argument could be made that he deserves to be a coauthor. His email address is byronbbright@ucla.edu.
> Tim

At the University of Missouri, where my coauthor, Jeff Milyo, had just taken a job, the press office described our study in favorable terms and posted it on a prominent university Web site.

Soon after the posting, the chairs of the humanities and social-science departments held a regular meeting with the dean. Although it was not supposed to be a topic for the meeting, our study soon became the focus of a heated discussion. The chairs of the departments of sociology, religion, and German and Russian languages were especially angry, calling the study "offensive" and "scandalous." One said, "The study isn't research. It's agitprop for the conservative blogosphere."

After the meeting, one of the professors sent Milyo an email to reprimand him:

> . . . In that lay part of my objection, and here I have to say that it's not to your work qua research at all. . . . [Y]our study is complex and sophisticated enough to treat many of [the issues discussed on the university's Web site]; far more subtle and nuanced than the journalistic reductio. There are of course issues outstanding or open to discussion (what's included by way of news sources, whether conceptual categories like liberal and conservative have veridical legitimacy as identity markers, where and how one designates boundaries of same . . . how one categorizes constellations of dispositions, how one treats what Bakhtin called dialogism in discourse analysis, and so forth. . . .

Milyo and I couldn't understand him, either. But the fact that he would take the time to write such an email is yet another example of the passions that the study inflamed. It wasn't Milyo's idea to post a description of the study on the university Web site. Also remember, Milyo had just moved to the University of Missouri. That was his welcome.

The most vicious response was by Eric Alterman, a writer at Media Matters. He insinuated that we had been paid by right-wing think tanks to fudge our results. "Rigging the Numbers" was the title of his essay. The following were his concluding paragraphs:[1]

> Check the fine print and one finds this study—naïvely touted as both objective and significant by the UCLA public affairs office and published, inexplicably, by the previously respected *Quarterly Journal of Economics,* edited at Harvard University's Department of Economics, was the product of a significant investment by right-wing think tanks. In 2000–2001, Groseclose was a Hoover Institution

national fellow, while Milyo has been granted $40,500 from the American Enterprise Institute; both were Heritage Foundation Salvatori fellows in 1997.

And yet despite its shockingly desultory intellectual underpinnings and almost comically obvious ideological imperatives, we can be certain we will hear about this study over and over for the next decade—from the very people who have written off normative knowledge and scientific research as some sort of liberal plot to subvert the values of Heartland America.

Really, you just can't make these people up.

At one level I can understand why so many left-wing strangers sent me angry emails, and why writers, like Eric Alterman at Media Matters, would say such false and vicious things about Milyo and me.

If people believe the results of our study, then they will begin to believe that they are not getting the whole truth from the media. They might begin to think, "Maybe lower taxes are a better idea than I thought." "Maybe government should scale back its involvement in the economy." "Maybe affirmative action is not such a great idea."

Larry Greenfield, a fellow at the Claremont Institute, has made a profound observation about the psyche of the far left: "They worship the god of Equality." A corollary of his observation is the following: While other virtues, such as kindness and honesty, are important, they are secondary when they clash with Equality.

Our study, at least in small ways, harms the goal of Equality. In at least small ways, it works to make U.S. public policy less "progressive" and less consistent with "social justice." If you are an advocate of "social justice" and "progressive" values, then, even if you believe that our study is true, you *should* hate it. Further, if you value Equality more than other virtues, then it would be appropriate for you to conclude that "Smearing Groseclose and Milyo's study is justified, even if the smears are false." You would also be justified in attacking Milyo and me personally, even saying false and vicious things about our character. As the left-wing icon Saul Alinsky advised, "Pick the target, freeze it, *personalize it* [my emphasis], and polarize it."[2]

At this point, let me warn you, if you are such an advocate of "social justice" and "progressive" values, then you will hate this book even more than the original study by Milyo and me. I provide additional objective, precise measures that show that the media are at least as liberal as the original study concluded.

Plus, I provide evidence that *the bias really does affect people's views*. As I explain, the left does not yet understand that they should disagree with the latter fact. It implies that the present views of the average voter are distorted—that is, if it weren't for media bias, then those views would be more conservative. While my original study found that the media are to the left of the (distorted) position of the average voter, the above fact means that the media are even further away from the natural, non-distorted position of the average voter. That is, not only are the media biased, they're even more biased than people realize.

But before I describe that research, let me describe the most surprising response to our study—that of professors at elite universities.

First, before the study was published, several professors invited me to present the research at their universities. I gave presentations at Harvard, Yale, Princeton, Duke, and two presentations at Stanford. Although the audiences at those universities were overwhelmingly liberal, and often they raised methodological objections, not once did anyone attack me personally; nor did anyone ever suggest that I was anything but honest while conducting the research.

Next was the response at the University of Missouri. At the heated meeting of the department chairs, the chair of the economics department suggested, "Hey, we're all scholars here. Maybe we should settle this like scholars—with a debate. Let's allow Milyo to present his findings at a public forum, and we'll allow others to have a chance to criticize it." The dean agreed, and he set up such a forum. Not one of the professors who criticized the study showed up at the debate.

We submitted our paper to the *Quarterly Journal of Economics*. This is the oldest scholarly economics journal. It is based at Harvard University, and the three editors of the journal, all professors in the Harvard economics department, are almost sure to win Nobel prizes someday. All professional economists consider the *QJE* one of the top four economics journals, and some consider it *the* top journal.

One of the most wonderful aspects of the response to our paper is something that Milyo and I, and most other scholars, usually take for granted. This is that at no point in the review process did anyone at the *QJE* ask, "Are you currently, or have you ever been, associated with any conservative organization?" Many left-wing blogs, including Media Matters, denounced our paper because of our prior affiliation with conservative groups. Some blogs, for the same reason, even denounced the *QJE* for accepting our paper. The writers at these blogs should consider how much they sound like Joe McCarthy—once you substitute "conservative" for "Communist." The beauty of the review process at the *QJE*—and all other scientific journals of which I am aware—is that they don't care about the political views and associations of the authors who submit papers. They judge the papers strictly on their merits.

It may surprise some people that a group of Harvard professors approved of a paper that concludes that the media have a liberal bias. But if you think that's strange, just wait.

A few months after the *QJE* accepted our paper, instead of firing me, UCLA promoted me, from associate professor of political science to "full" professor of political science. That one surprised me. Out of the many hundreds of professors at UCLA, I'm aware of only nine who voted for John McCain in 2008, and one of those nine asked me never to reveal that fact to anyone at the school. I am almost certain that *not one* dean, chancellor, or vice-chancellor at UCLA voted for McCain in 2008 or for Bush in 2000 or 2004.

A few months later, the professors in the economics department at UCLA voted to give me a "joint" professorship in their department. Around the same time, Caltech invited me to be a visiting professor for a quarter. Shortly after, the University of Missouri promoted Milyo, from associate professor of economics to "full" professor of economics.

Then things got really strange. Yale University offered me a job . . . as a full professor. The average professor at Yale, I am certain, is even more liberal than the average professor at UCLA. Although I believe that Yale offered me the job *in spite of,* not because of, my media bias research, Yale did not consider that research a reason to blackball me.

Soon after that, the University of Chicago offered me a job as a full professor with an "endowed chair." UCLA responded with an endowed chair, plus a significant increase in salary.

But from a personal standpoint, the most wonderful response came from an email that was cc'd to me one day. "Dear Mr. Alterman," it began. (Alterman, you may recall, was the writer at Media Matters who said that Milyo and I had "rigged" our numbers and insinuated that we did it because right-wing think tanks had "invested" in us):

> I was very disappointed to read your review of my colleague Timothy Groseclose's paper on media bias. The lack of civility and the personal nature of your review struck a tone that I had not expected from you. . . .
>
> As much as you and, indeed, I want to believe that the results of Tim's study are false, they are not the result of cooking the books. Tim is nothing if not careful. Yes, he is a conservative and, yes, I am sure he is pleased with the way the results turned out. But, the

> method was laid out before the data were collected and I am confident that the paper would have been published regardless of the outcome.
>
> For what it is worth, here is the truth about the paper from someone who does not share Tim's politics. . . . It is academically honest research by careful and serious scholars who do not pursue a research agenda at the behest of any conservative patron.

Once I realized that the email was written by one of my UCLA colleagues, I quit reading and bolted down the hall. This deserved an immediate thank-you.

But as I approached his door, it occurred to me that I might not be able to express my thanks without my voice breaking or my eyes watering. So I slowed my walk, cleared my throat, and blinked my eyes. The reason the email was so touching was not so much its words but who wrote them: Byron B. Bright.

PART I

Political Quotients and the Science of Politics

1. What Are PQs and How Do They Reveal Media Bias?

"COME ON. POLITICAL science isn't *really* a science," said my friend Dawson Engler one day, trying to goad me.

Engler, one of the country's premier computer scientists, is currently a professor at Stanford, where his specialty is operating systems. He has constructed his own operating system . . . twice.

He is the type of person who succeeds at nearly anything he tries. Born in Yuma, Arizona, during high school he placed second in the "Teenage Mr. Arizona" bodybuilding contest. After graduating from Arizona State University, he enrolled in the highly prestigious computer-science PhD program at MIT. It is unusual for a PhD student to publish a paper in a peer-reviewed scientific journal. Yet Engler published *eight* while a doctoral student. Shortly after Stanford hired him, for a brief period he dated one of the actresses from *Baywatch*.

When Engler goaded me, both of us held positions at MIT, and he knew that my position was in the political-science department. At MIT, which is filled with "real" scientists and engineers, you often hear quips like Engler's. So when he made it, I was prepared.

"Look," I said. "We can both agree that if you can graph something, then you can describe it mathematically."

"Yeah," said Engler.

"And people, all the time, talk about politicians being left wing or right wing."

"Okay," said Engler.

"And so if a position is left wing or right wing, then you can graph it. . . . Which means you can describe it mathematically. . . . Which means it's science."

Engler smiled. I don't think I really convinced him, but he didn't goad me any further. At least in my mind, I'd won the day's debate.

WITHIN POLITICAL SCIENCE a small industry exists to do the "science" that I described to Engler: to calculate precise, numerical measurements that describe the liberalness or conservativeness of politicians. In fact, at the time Engler made his quip, I was working on such a project. Indeed, the political quotients that I describe in this book are based on that research.

A person's PQ is a number, generally between 0 and 100, that describes how liberal he or she is. I have created a Web site, www.timgroseclose.com/calculate-your-pq, which allows you to compute your own PQ. I have computed PQs for members of Congress by observing their record on roll call votes.

By answering the following ten questions,[1] you can get a rough approximation of your PQ. When you answer the questions, try to put yourself in the shoes of the members of Congress and decide how you would have voted *at the time that the politicians considered the measure.* For instance, some people feel that the "Cash for Clunkers" program was not as successful as they hoped or thought it would be. Accordingly, when you answer the question related to this program—as well as when you answer the other questions—think about your opinion of the issue *when it was considered in Congress,* not necessarily about how you feel about it now.

1. On January 29, 2009, the Senate passed the SCHIP bill (State Children's Health Insurance Program). The bill would provide matching funds to states for health insurance to families with children. The funds would be limited to families with incomes less than three times the federal poverty level. The cost would be offset by increasing the federal tax on cigarettes from $0.61 to $1.00 a pack. Democrats voted 58–0 in favor of the bill; Republicans voted 8–32 against the bill.[2]
    a. **I would have favored the bill.**
    b. **I can't decide.**
    c. **I would have opposed the bill.**
2. On February 26, 2009, the Senate passed the District of Columbia House Voting Rights Act. The act would create a House district for

D.C., and simultaneously create an additional House district in Utah. The Utah district would be subject to change or elimination by future censuses. The act would give D.C. one vote in the Electoral College, however it would not give D.C. representation in the Senate. Democrats favored the bill 56–2; Republicans opposed it 5–35.

  a. **I would have favored the bill.**
  b. **I can't decide.**
  c. **I would have opposed the bill.**

3. On April 1, 2009, the House passed a bill that would limit the bonuses of executives if their company received TARP (Troubled Asset Relief Program) funds. It granted authority to the secretary of the treasury to set standards for such executive compensation, including determining what is "excessive compensation." Democrats favored the bill 236–8; Republicans opposed it 11–163.
   a. **I would have favored the bill.**
   b. **I can't decide.**
   c. **I would have opposed the bill.**

4. On April 30, 2009, Senator Richard Durbin proposed an amendment to the Helping Families Save Their Homes Act. His amendment, titled "Prevention of Mortgage Foreclosures," was sometimes called the "cramdown" provision. According to the provision, if a homeowner's income was low enough (less than 80 percent of the median income), then a bankruptcy judge could reduce the level of the interest and principle that the home owner owed on a mortgage. Democrats favored the amendment 45–12; Republicans opposed it 0–39.
   a. **I would have favored the amendment.**
   b. **I can't decide.**
   c. **I would have opposed the amendment.**

5. On June 18, 2009, the House considered a major appropriations bill. Jerry Lewis, a Republican from California, introduced an amendment to the bill that would bar funds from being used to shut down the Guantánamo Bay prison. The amendment would have acted against an executive order that President Obama had issued to close the facility. Democrats opposed the amendment 39–213; Republicans favored the amendment 173–3.
   a. **I would have *opposed* the amendment (that is, I would have favored shutting down Guantánamo).**
   b. **I can't decide.**
   c. **I would have *favored* the amendment.**

6. On June 26, 2009, the House passed the American Clean Energy and Security Act, the main provision of which was to create a "cap and trade system." Under the system, energy producers would be allotted a cap on the pollutants they could emit, but they could buy credits from other energy producers if they wanted to emit more pollutants. Or, if they emitted less pollutants than their cap, they could sell some of their credits to other producers. The bill set a target of reducing emissions to 83 percent of the 2005 level by the year 2050. The act also included several billions of dollars for incentives for businesses to invest in green technologies. Democrats favored the bill 210–43; Republicans opposed it 8–169.
   a. I would have favored the bill.
   b. I can't decide.
   c. I would have opposed the bill.

7. On July 31, 2009, the House passed the "Cash for Clunkers" bill (officially named "The Consumer Assistance to Recycle and Save Program). It provided $2 billion in vouchers to people who traded in an older, less fuel-efficient car and bought a newer, more fuel-efficient car. Democrats favored the bill 238–14; Republicans opposed it 78–95.
   a. I would have favored the bill.
   b. I can't decide.
   c. I would have opposed the bill.

8. On August 26, 2009, the Senate voted on the confirmation of Sonia Sotomayor to be a justice on the Supreme Court. Democrats favored her confirmation 58–0; Republicans opposed it 9–31.
   a. I would have favored her confirmation.
   b. I can't decide.
   c. I would have opposed her confirmation.

9. On November 8, 2009, the Senate considered an amendment proposed by Senator Ben Nelson (D-Neb.) to the "Obamacare" health bill. His amendment would have barred federal money to be used to pay for an abortion. Further, federal money could not help pay for any health plan that covered abortions. The Democrats opposed the amendment 7–52; Republicans favored it 38–2. (Technically, the vote was on a motion by Barbara Boxer to table the Nelson amendment.)
   a. I would have opposed the amendment.
   b. I can't decide.
   c. I would have favored the amendment.

10. On December 15, 2009, the Senate voted on a provision to allow U.S. citizens to import prescription drugs. Most important, it would have allowed citizens to order prescription drugs from Canadian pharmacies, which often sold the drugs at lower prices than U.S. pharmacies did. (The provision was the Dorgan amendment to the Reid amendment to the Pharmaceutical Market Access and Drug Safety Act.) Democrats opposed the measure 28–31; Republicans favored it 23–17.
    a. **I would have favored the provision.**
    b. **I can't decide.**
    c. **I would have opposed the provision.**

Give yourself ten points for each time that you answered "a," five points for each "b," and zero points for each "c." Next, add up the points. That is approximately your PQ.

One feature of the PQ is that it is constructed from roll call votes in Congress. This means that simply by noting how members of Congress voted on those roll calls, I can calculate their PQs, and you can compare your PQ to theirs. The following are the PQs of some well-known politicians.

TABLE 1.1

PQs of Some Well-known Politicians[3]

Michele Bachmann (R-Minn., 2007–09)*	–4.1
Jim DeMint (R-S.C., 1999–2009)	4.8
Newt Gingrich (R-Ga., 1979–94)	11.4
Richard Nixon (R-Calif., 1947–52)	12.5
Lindsay Graham (R-S.C., 1995–2009)	14.9
John McCain (R-Ariz., 1983–2006, 2009)	15.8
Joe Scarborough (R-Fla., 1995–2000)	16.4
Jack Kemp (R.-N.Y., 1971–86)	20.4
Charlie Stenholm (D-Tex., 1979–2004)	28.5
Ron Paul (R-Tex., 1976–2009)	31.8
Rick Lazio (R-N.Y., 1993–2000)	34.4
Tom Ridge (R-Pa., 1983–94)	37.4
Sam Nunn (D-Ga., 1973–96)	39.5
Susan Collins (R-Me., 1997–2009)	44.2
Olympia Snowe (R-Me., 1979–2009)	47.9
Arlen Specter (R-Pa., 1981–2008)	50.6
Ben Nelson (D-Neb., 2001–09)	55.6
Christopher Shays (R-Conn., 1987–2008)	61.0

(continued)

TABLE 1.1 (continued)

John F. Kennedy (D-Mass., 1947–60)	63.7
Arlen Specter (D-Pa., 2009)[†]	67.4
Joe Lieberman (Ind.-Conn., 2005–09)[‡]	74.0
Joe Lieberman (D-Conn., 1989–2004)	74.7
Harry Reid (D-Nev., 1983–2009)	75.6
Joe Biden (D-Del., 1973–2008)	80.5
Hillary Clinton (D-N.Y., 2001–06)	87.6
Barack Obama (D-Ill., 2005–06)	87.7
Ted Kennedy (D-Mass., 1963–2007)	89.2
Robert Kennedy (D-N.Y., 1965–67)	96.5
Nancy Pelosi (D-Calif., 1987–2006)	100.7
Barney Frank (D-Mass., 1981–2009)	103.8
Ron Dellums (D-Calif., 1971–97)	107.4

* Years in parentheses are years I used to calculate the politician's PQ.
[†] Arlen Specter switched parties on April 29, 2009. His PQ as a Democrat, 67.4, is based on all the votes he cast in 2009.
[‡] Joe Lieberman has two different PQs, one based on his years as a Democrat and one based on his years as an Independent.

PQs and Media Bias

Perhaps the main contribution of the book is that it uses PQs to judge *media bias.* To do this, I conduct the following thought experiment. Suppose you were given a set of stories that a media outlet reported. But suppose, instead of knowing that they were news stories, you were told that they were speeches by a politician. After reading the would-be speeches, what would you guess to be the PQ of the would-be politician?

I define the slant quotient, or SQ, of an outlet as the solution to that thought experiment. In the article that Milyo and I wrote for the *Quarterly Journal of Economics,* we developed a statistical technique that calculates a precise, numerical SQ for the twenty news outlets that we examined. We found, for instance, that *The New York Times* has an SQ of 74, which is approximately the PQ of Sen. Joseph Lieberman.

The primary data that we used were citations to think tanks. This means that *The New York Times*'s citation patterns to left-wing, centrist, and right-wing think tanks were very similar to the patterns that Joe Lieberman adopted when he made speeches on the Senate floor.

The following figure illustrates the main results of that article. For now, the details behind the figure are unimportant. (But I will explain them in a later chapter). What *is* important is that, as the figure shows, we can describe numerically (i) the political views of politicians and (ii) the slants of various media outlets. Further, we can map these two sets of numbers to the same scale.

Despite what my hard-science friends might say, it *is* possible to analyze politics, including media bias, objectively, numerically, and, yes, scientifically.

FIGURE 1.1

PQs and SQs of Selected Politicans and Media Outlets

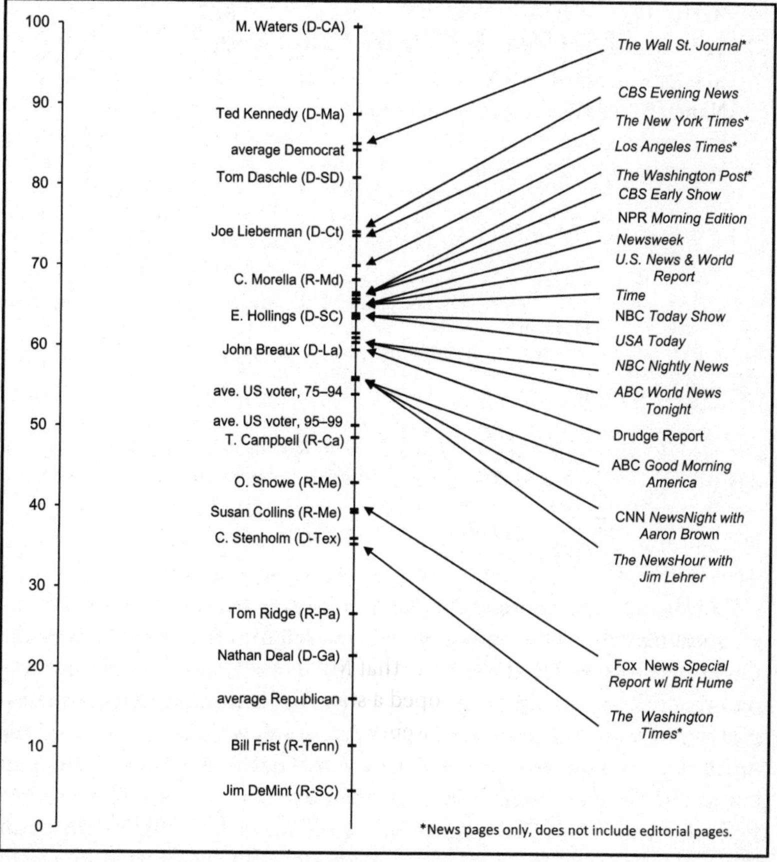

**News pages only, does not include editorial pages.*

2. Caught in a Trap

PROBLEMS IN JUDGING MEDIA BIAS

IN AN OLD joke a man tells his friend about the fine qualities of his girlfriend:

MAN: Not only that, she's a virgin.
FRIEND: How do you know she's a virgin?
MAN: She told me.
FRIEND: How do you know she's not lying?
MAN: Virgins don't lie.

This book makes a bold proposition: The joke not only reflects the way many people form their views on media bias, it also reflects the way many people form their political views in general. All of us base our political views, to a large degree, on information we learn from the media. Of course, we trust some media sources more than others. So we are careful to filter out the untrustworthy sources from the trustworthy ones. The problem is that our political views often determine which media outlets we consider trustworthy or untrustworthy. Thus, our thinking is circular: our political views influence where we go for news, which influences our political views, which further influences where we go for news, and so on.

The circularity makes our political views flimsy. That is, for instance, a little bit of liberal media bias can make us more liberal, which causes us to seek more liberal media outlets, which causes us to become more liberal, and so on.

The circularity also makes us bad at judging and detecting media bias, and often we don't realize how bad at it we are. As an example, consider the following hypothetical conversation, which is only a slight caricature of perhaps dozens that I have had with fellow political-science professors.

ME: The evidence is clear that the mainstream media cite left-wing think tanks more than they cite right-wing ones.

COLLEAGUE: Yes, but that's because experts at left-wing think tanks tend to be more respected and scholarly, while the experts at right-wing think tanks tend to be hired guns for corporations. The media are not showing a left-wing bias, only a bias for respected and scholarly experts.

ME: But how do you know that left-wing experts are more respected and scholarly than right-wing experts?

COLLEAGUE: Just read or watch any reputable news source. It's well documented.

If pressed, such a colleague would say that "reputable news source" means an outlet such as *The New York Times, The Washington Post,* National Public Radio, CNN, or possibly the evening news shows of ABC, CBS, or NBC.

Like the virgin-girlfriend joke, however, the argument is circular. To bolster his claim that the mainstream media is not biased, my colleague cites evidence from . . . the mainstream media.

It is not just liberal political-science professors who are guilty of such circular arguments. The following is a typical claim of a conservative: "The only place you can get the real truth is from sources like Fox or conservative talk radio. All the rest are a bunch of Godless, baby-killing America haters." "But, how do you know all the others are a bunch of Godless, baby-killing America haters?" a skeptic might ask. "Just watch Fox or listen to conservative talk radio, and you'll see."

The Fundamental Trap and Why It Makes Us Bad at Judging Media Bias

The circularities in such arguments are examples of what I call the *Fundamental Trap* of judging media bias. To determine if the media are biased, we need an accurate and unbiased source of information. But almost all of us, on almost any political topic, must rely on the media as our main source of information. We rarely have other sources.

As Walter Lippmann famously observed:

> Each of us lives and works on a small part of the earth's surface, moves in a small circle, and of these acquaintances knows only a few intimately. Of any public event that has wide effects we see at best only a phase and an aspect . . . Inevitably our opinions cover a bigger space, a longer reach of time, a greater number of things, than we can directly observe. They have, therefore, to be pieced together out of what others have reported and what we can imagine.[1]

As a concrete example, consider the question "To what extent do guns deter burglars from entering our homes?" Almost none of us has any direct knowledge about this question. That is, few of us have ever interviewed a burglar, much less peered inside his head to see if his burglary decisions were influenced by whether his next victim might own a gun. Instead, almost all our knowledge on this topic comes from what we read, watch, or hear from the media.

Now consider the question "How many stories should the media report about guns doing good, say, thwarting a burglary, versus stories about guns doing harm, say, causing an accidental death?"

First, we can all agree that the media cannot report *all* the stories where a gun has done harm or good. There are simply not enough minutes in a newscast, nor pages in a newspaper. We can also agree that the number of stories should reflect the truth—that is, the stories should reflect the proportion of the two types of cases that actually occur in the world. For example, if, in the universe of all cases, a gun does good 30 percent of the time and harm 70 percent of the time, then, in an ideal journalistic world, 30 percent of the media's gun stories would be about a gun doing good and 70 percent about a gun doing harm.

Of course, no one knows the actual percentage of cases in which guns do good or harm. The best we can do is form opinions and educated guesses about the true percentage. The problem is that our opinions and educated guesses are based almost entirely upon information we learn from the media. Accordingly, how can we know how accurate are our educated guesses and opinions? And if we cannot know this, how can we judge how biased or unbiased the media are?

To take the argument to the extreme, suppose that the media were your *only* source of knowledge. Then they could be extremely biased, and you would never know it. It would be as if your only information about the world came from watching professional basketball games. If so, then you would think that six foot eight was a normal height, and six-three was short. Further, you would have no idea that your primary source of information about the world, televised basketball games, was giving you a distorted picture of the true distribution of people's heights.

The analogy illustrates another point about judging the media: People often mistake bias, relative to other media outlets, as an absolute bias. That is, for instance, Fox News is clearly more conservative than ABC, CBS, CNN, NBC, and National Public Radio. Some will conclude that "therefore, this means that Fox News has a conservative bias." But this says nothing about its bias on any absolute scale. Instead, maybe it is centrist, and possibly even left-leaning, while all the others are far left. It is like concluding that six-three is short just because it is short compared to professional basketball players.

The point illustrates a common misconception about the Drudge Report. According to my analysis, the Drudge Report is approximately the most fair, balanced, and centrist news outlet in the United States. Yet, the overwhelming majority of media commentators claim that it has a conservative bias. The problem, I believe, is that such commentators mistake relative bias for absolute bias. Yes, the Drudge Report is more conservative than the average U.S. news outlet. But it is a logical mistake to use that to infer that it is biased on an absolute scale.

The same is true, I believe, with ABC News anchor Charles Gibson. He is nothing but fair and centrist in my judgment. In fact, one of the methods that I document finds that ABC's *Good Morning America*, during his tenure, was approximately the most unbiased of all U.S. media outlets. In my view, he was willing to ask tough questions, equally, to the two candidates during the 2008 election. However, because he directed more tough questions to Barack Obama than most of the other mainstream outlets did, he was charged with a conservative bias. Here again, such a claim mistakes relative bias with absolute bias.

Although most of us think we can accurately judge which media outlets are conservative, which are liberal, and so on, we should all ask ourselves, "Are we basing this upon any outside source of information—that is, on anything besides what we've learned from the media?" If not, we are no different from the person judging people's heights from watching basketball games.

Alpha Intellectuals and Why They Are Especially Vulnerable to the Fundamental Trap

Many people would respond to my argument as follows: "While plausible, the Fundamental Trap does not affect me, since I am better informed and more educated than most people." In some ways, however, the trap is even worse for these people, since, more than average people, they tend to base their worldviews on knowledge from the media, instead of outside sources such as personal experience and conversations with friends.

The extreme form of the latter-type person is what I call an *alpha intellectual.* Such a person is highly educated, or at least considers himself highly educated. He spends much time reading and watching the news, and he has convinced himself, to the point of near certainty, that his media sources are the most "highly respected" and "trustworthy" of all sources. As a consequence, he dismisses other sources, particularly media-independent sources of information, and especially media-independent sources who are not as highly educated or as well informed as he considers himself. Like an alpha male in an animal tribe, he is sometimes boorish if someone mentions a fact that contradicts his "highly respected" and "trustworthy" sources.

One of the best illustrations of this concept is the response by actor Richard Belzer to Congresswoman Ileana Ros-Lehtinen, when both appeared on HBO's *Real Time with Bill Maher*:

CONGRESSWOMAN ILEANA ROS-LEHTINEN: [When I visited the troops in Iraq and Afghanistan, they told me that they are proud of their mission, and it is going well.] And there is a great sense of determination that what they are doing is making a difference. . . .

RICHARD BELZER: Yeah, come on. Our soldiers now are at—

ROS-LEHTINEN: Are a volunteer force, a volunteer force.

BELZER: Okay, fine. No one questions the nobility and the honor that these men and woman who are serving and what they're doing. No one questions that. But now they're targets, they're not going out. Now they're just protecting each other and they're in the middle of a civil war. So it's really not fair to have these people who volunteered their lives to protect our nation under false pretenses to now be . . . targets—

ROS-LEHTINEN: Ask them. Ask them if it's fair! Wait a minute, wait a minute. My stepson, wait a minute, my stepson—

BELZER: That's bulls**t: ask them? They're not, they don't read twenty newspapers a day. They're under the threat of death every minute. They're not the best people to ask about the war because they're gonna die any second.

ROS-LEHTINEN: Wait a minute! You are talking about my stepson, my stepson who just finished last week eight months of duty—

BELZER: God bless your stepson. Doesn't mean he's a brilliant scholar about the war because he's there. And God bless him.

. . .

MAHER: I think the point he's trying to make is that a nineteen-year-old who is in that army because he probably couldn't find other employment—

(Ros-Lehtinen and Belzer continue their exchange. Belzer spiritedly argues that Ros-Lehtinen's stepson is the exception to the rule [in terms of being an educated soldier]. Ros-Lehtinen argues that he's not.)

BELZER: You think everyone over there is a college graduate? They're nineteen- and twenty-year-old kids who couldn't get a job . . .
ROS-LEHTINEN: Yeah, you know because you've been there and . . .
BELZER: What, I don't f**ing read!? Don't do that![2]

In defining the notion of alpha intellectual, let me make two clarifications: First, I don't believe that anyone, not even Richard Belzer, is a pure alpha intellectual. For example, I'm certain that some media-independent sources of information, including possibly soldiers, could, in theory, convince him that U.S. soldiers in Iraq are more than just targets. Second, all of us, at least to a small extent, are partial alpha intellectuals. That is, for instance, we all tend to trust our usual sources of political information more than other sources, and when we hear of contradictory information from other sources, even if we do not dismiss them entirely, we are at least skeptical of them.

Now, as a thought experiment, imagine a world where everyone is a pure form of alpha intellectual: we either never hear from media-independent sources of information, like Congresswoman Ros-Lehtinen's stepson, or we discount completely such sources when we do. How would this affect our beliefs about the world?

First, our political views would be highly susceptible to media bias. That is, for instance, if the media claimed that the typical U.S. soldier was a kid "who couldn't get another job," then that is exactly what we would believe. We would have no other source to tell us any differently.

Second, we'd be completely oblivious to any bias in the media. When the media reported such a claim, we'd think "I agree with that claim. Therefore, that must be a trustworthy source."

Third, the two factors feed upon themselves. That is, our obliviousness to media bias allows the media to get away with more bias, which distorts our views even more, which allows the media to become even more biased, and so on. The result is that our beliefs continue to wander further and further from the truth.

Of course, however, we're *not* pure alpha intellectuals; thus, the previous analysis is exaggerated. Nevertheless, we *are* all partial alpha intellectuals. Consequently, our political beliefs will be partially influenced by media bias, and we will be partially oblivious to that bias. Further, the two factors will still feed off of each other; however, instead of our beliefs wandering continually further and further from the truth, the wandering will be finite—albeit possibly a very far distance from the truth.

Let me be clear. I am not suggesting that this will generally be the case with all issues. After all, if on some issue the media are not biased, then the opposite will happen: the people who consume the most news, including the alpha intellectuals, will have the most accurate worldviews.

Further, I'm not suggesting that personal experiences and conversations with friends are necessarily more accurate than the media. On some issues I'm certain, for example, that Richard Belzer's proclivity to read many, many newspapers will make him more accurately informed than Congresswoman Ros-Lehtinen's stepson.

My point is that if the media are your only, or almost only, source of information, and if you rarely learn anything from personal experiences or any other media-independent sources of information, then you are stuck in the trap. You will trust the media simply because what they say is consistent with your beliefs, which are based upon what you have learned from the media. You might get lucky—the media might be truly unbiased—but if they are biased and presenting an inaccurate picture of the world, then you will never learn that.

How to Escape the Trap

The key to avoiding the Fundamental Trap is to find a source of information that is independent of the media and also independent of the personal beliefs of the analyst judging the media. This may seem difficult, but it can be done.

One excellent example is a study by John Lott and Kevin Hassett.[3] They analyze newspaper headlines that focus on economic news, specifically unemployment, GDP growth, durable goods production, and retail sales. They note whether a given headline describes the news in a positive or negative fashion, and they analyze whether the media outlet's choice was related to whether the president was Republican or Democrat.

One noteworthy aspect of the study is that it documents a well-kept secret in journalism: two media outlets covering the exact same story can use vastly different headlines to describe it. For instance, on January 31, 2004, the Commerce Department reported that GDP grew 4 percent (annualized) during the fourth quarter of 2004. "Economy Remained Strong in 4th

Quarter" was *The New York Times* headline. In contrast, "GDP Growth Disappoints" was the *Chicago Tribune*'s headline.

At this point, if you are a careful reader, you should sense that the Fundamental Trap potentially applies to the Lott-Hassett study. That is, there is no reason for journalists necessarily to describe economic conditions under Democrat and Republican presidents *equally*. That is, for instance, economies under Democratic administrations might in general perform better than economies under Republican administrations. If so, then a newspaper *should* describe them asymmetrically.

But if "unbiased" does not necessarily mean symmetric, then how should a journalist, or a researcher of media bias, decide upon the proper degree of asymmetry? After all, won't the judgments of Lott and Hassett regarding whether a headline should be positive or negative be colored by what they have read or heard in the news?

Yes, but here's the most brilliant aspect of their study . . . and the way they escape the Fundamental Trap. Lott and Hassett focus only on news stories that describe official statistics from the U.S. Commerce Department. Thus, the authors focus only on stories where the underlying news is an objective piece of data, which does not come from the media. They then construct a statistical technique that explicitly controls for these data. Most important, their assessment, whether the economy is good or bad, does not rely on their own judgment and intuition.

Lott and Hassett indeed find a liberal bias in the media. They find that for the same piece of news, major U.S. newspapers are 20 to 40 percent more likely to report a negative headline if the administration is Republican than if it is Democratic.

At least for now, however, the details of their conclusions are unimportant. What is important is that the Lott-Hassett study demonstrates that it really is possible to measure media bias while avoiding the Fundamental Trap.

In later chapters I describe three additional methods—two of which I helped to develop—that judge media bias while avoiding the Fundamental Trap.

3. But I've Been to Oklahoma

ON SEPTEMBER 22, 1964, Barry Goldwater made a campaign stop in Tulsa, Oklahoma. That morning, Tulsa residents awoke to read on the front page of their newspaper, "Tulsa World Endorses Goldwater."

I was born on that day in Tulsa. To this day, I consider Goldwater one of my political heroes. Four other political heroes are Ronald Reagan, Jack Kemp, Bob Dole, and New Jersey Governor Chris Christie. Four more heroes, in addition to being successful politicians, are genuine scholars: Newt Gingrich, Phil Gramm, Dick Armey, and Dick Cheney.[1]

My own PQ is approximately 13. This means that I usually side with conservatives on controversial issues. For instance, I favor lower taxes, less government regulation in the economy, a stronger military, and fewer restrictions on guns. I believe that *Roe v. Wade* was unconstitutional—namely, it violated the Tenth Amendment, which reserves abortion law decisions for the states. On some issues, however, I agree with liberals. These include: (i) allowing the government to pay for stem-cell research; (ii) giving partial amnesty to illegal immigrants (as would have been required by the 2007 Comprehensive Immigration bill, sponsored by John McCain and Ted Kennedy, and endorsed by President Bush); and (iii) increasing gasoline taxes. Although the judgment would be based on only casual observation, I believe that if you conducted a systematic study, you'd find that my views are to the right of Bill O'Reilly's but left of Sean Hannity's.

Six politicians who have PQs similar to mine are Gov. John Kasich (R-Ohio) (PQ = 14); former Congressman Joe Scarborough (R-Fla.) (PQ = 16); Sen. Lindsey Graham (R-S.C.) (PQ = 15); former Sen. Bob Dole (R-Kans.) (PQ = 12); former Speaker of the House Newt Gingrich (R-Ga.) (PQ = 11); and Sen. John McCain (R-Ariz.) (PQ = 16). Nearly everyone who has studied their voting records would agree that: (i) they are significantly more conservative than all Democrats currently serving in Congress; (ii) they are more conservative than moderate Republicans, such as Maine senators Olympia Snowe and Susan Collins; yet (iii) they are not as conservative as far-right Republicans such as Michele Bachmann or Jim DeMint.

Is This Book Biased?

There. I have now done something that almost no journalist will ever do. I've given you a detailed account of my political views, including some information about my political heroes and the birthplace that influenced those views.

Is this book biased? On one level it matters not a whit where I was born or what my political views are. The methods that I use to measure media bias are completely objective—indeed, a computer executes them.

But on another level my views and background do matter. As I will explain, the *topics* that journalists choose depend partly upon their political views and the views of the people who surround them. So let me admit, I don't think I would have written a book about media bias if I didn't have conservative views or if I hadn't received a Central Time Zone upbringing.

Later in the chapter, I'll explain why I think that conservatives are more interested than liberals in conducting objective studies of media bias. Before I do, however, let me take a detour to explain the difference between positive and normative questions in social science and why they are related to the questions that a researcher chooses to study.

Positive versus Normative Questions

Since John Neville Keynes (the father of John Maynard Keynes) first introduced the terms, economists have been careful to distinguish between *normative* and *positive* questions. Normative questions address what should be—that is, what is fair and appropriate. Positive questions address what is—that is, what logic or nature has determined is true or untrue.

The following are some examples of normative questions:

- Should the United States fight a war in Iraq?
- Should there be a death penalty?
- Should divorce laws be relaxed?
- Should the United States pass affirmative-action laws to combat racism?

The following are some examples of positive questions:

- Do people join the U.S. military mainly because they lack other career options?
- To what extent, if any, does the death penalty deter murder?
- To what extent, if any, do female suicide rates drop when laws make it easier for women to divorce their husbands?
- To what extent, if any, does racism still exist in the United States?

Positive questions can be answered with data and logical reasoning. In theory, if we had enough data and enough time to analyze and discuss the data, then we would all agree on the answer to any positive question.

That's not true with normative questions. Ultimately those answers depend, at least partially, on value judgments. For instance, if you're a pacifist, even if I could show you an overwhelming amount of data suggesting that the Iraq War is justified, you would still oppose the war.

That's not to say that the two types of questions aren't related. Indeed, there are times when the answer to a positive question influences a person's view on a normative question. For instance, suppose you're nearly indifferent between favoring and opposing the Iraq War. Now suppose that I give you some incontrovertible data showing that most U.S. soldiers join the military mainly because they can't find another job. Most likely, that would make you feel sorry for the soldiers, and it would tip you off the fence, toward opposing the war. On the other hand, suppose I showed you incontrovertible data demonstrating the opposite—that most soldiers have plenty of outside employment options and that they join the military mainly because of pride in serving their country. Then that would probably tip you the other way, toward favoring the war.

All of the positive questions in the above list are politically charged. I chose them that way on purpose. Although, as I've mentioned, with enough data we could all agree on their answers; currently, in our world of limited data, we don't all agree. Usually our disagreements divide along political lines—that is, liberals claim one answer, while conservatives claim the opposite. Part of the reason is that we're strategic: we understand that the answers will persuade some people, often political moderates, to change their normative views. Accordingly, we have an incentive to try to advocate certain answers to *positive* questions.

It'd be easy to think of hundreds of politically charged positive questions besides the four that I've listed. Let me suggest that, of those hundreds of questions, conservatives would be correct on some, and liberals would be correct on others. If you don't believe that, then I suggest you're a knee-jerk conservative or a knee-jerk liberal.

In fact, I chose the above list of positive questions because I'm near certain that conservatives are correct on the first question, while liberals are correct on the other three.

Why Conservatives Are Correct About Why Soldiers Join the Military, Why a Conservative Is More Likely to Know the Answer, and Why a Conservative Is More Likely to Conduct a Study on the Question

When I was six, my family moved to Hot Springs, Arkansas, where I lived until I left for college. Although the town is probably most famous for being the boyhood home of Bill Clinton, it and Tulsa are fairly conservative. In the 2008 elections, for instance, the counties that contain them respectively voted 61 percent and 62 percent for McCain.

Because of my conservative views and my conservative childhood environment, I understand, better than the average liberal, why people join the military. The main reason is that I've talked to more military people than the average liberal. Military people, after all, tend to be conservative, and so it's natural that *they* prefer to talk to conservatives. Also, military people tend to grow up in places like Hot Springs and Tulsa instead of East and West Coast cities. Among my liberal political-science colleagues, most have *no* friends from high school who served in the military.

Further, liberals sometimes have a disdain for members of the military. In 2006, a PhD student in my department became stranded in Lebanon when Israel began bombing Hezbollah-dominated areas. After the fighting began, the U.S. Navy docked a ship in Beirut and offered transport to U.S. civilians to Cyprus. The student refused the help. The reason, she told me, was because she despised the U.S. military and hated the idea of owing it gratitude. Instead, putting her own safety at risk, she found another way out of Lebanon.

At least nine of my relatives or high-school classmates have served in the military. Their first names, let's say, are Sid, Daniel, Alex, Larry, Steve, Clark, Carl, Charlie, and Anna.

Of the nine, two joined as officers. Carl entered the military's JAG program after he completed law school. Alex entered the U.S. Air Force Academy and, after graduation, trained fighter pilots. The other seven joined as enlisted men and woman.

Of the nine, only two, Sid and Charlie, could be accused of lacking outside career options. And even that would be a stretch. Both *chose* to join the military because they were not pleased with the way their lives were going. They *decided* that a drill sergeant barking at them would be good for them.

Charlie enlisted in the Air Force after he was fired from two jobs in a row. But once he joined, he quickly excelled. Eventually, the Air Force selected him for a special program to train him to be an officer. The training included money for college. He made a career out of the Air Force and eventually reached the rank of lieutenant colonel.

His primary work was as a communications officer. This meant running the various devices the Air Force uses to communicate, including satellite-to-ground, computer-to-computer, airplane-to-airplane, and the AWACS system. "If it weren't for us," Charlie explained, "commanders couldn't command anyone."

Just before the Iraq War, the Air Force sent Charlie to Saudi Arabia. His unit's main task was to help enforce the no-fly zone over Iraq, but the unit was also assigned to support operations in Afghanistan. Charlie suspected that the unit was sent for an additional reason: "I didn't know if or when the war with Iraq would start," he said, "although we all sensed that it might." As a consequence, he began to keep a journal, and he frequently emailed entries to friends back home.

Charlie is extremely proud of his military service. "After all," he said, "who goes to work every day with people who will *willingly* give their life for those they don't know and sometimes don't even like?"

Eight of the above nine military enlistees were not just good athletes, but star athletes. Six, including Charlie, were starters on their high school football or basketball teams. Larry, was the starting quarterback *and* safety of his football team. Alex, was one of the best golfers in the state.

Larry got married soon after he joined the Navy. He and his best man, Steve, wore their Navy uniforms during the ceremony.

According to his mother (who is my cousin), Daniel always had a love for military things. At age four he would march in the backyard while carrying a toy gun. On September 10, 2001, he ate dinner with his grandfather, who captivated him with stories about patriotic duty and his exploits during World War II. The next day, after bin Laden demolished the World Trade Center, Daniel wanted immediately to "defend my country" by joining the Marines. His mother successfully pleaded with him not to join. However, the pleading worked only temporarily. A few years later, he did join, taking a $10,000-per-year pay cut. A few weeks after joining, he got married. Like Larry and Steve, he wore his military uniform during the ceremony.

Now recall the comments of Richard Belzer and Bill Maher, mentioned in the previous chapter. Such comments are typical of liberals who did not grow up in places like Tulsa or Hot Springs, and I hear them frequently from my professor colleagues. In their view, the job of soldier is no more attractive or prestigious than the job of telemarketer, ditch digger, or fast-food worker. (I mean no disrespect to holders of the latter jobs; I chose them as examples because I have held each of them.)

But if you have views like Belzer, Maher, or my liberal colleagues, you should ask yourself: Do you know anyone who got married in his fast-food-worker uniform? Do you know anyone whose grandchildren ask him to tell stories about his days as a telemarketer? Do you know anyone who kept a journal about his work as a ditch digger?

Statements like Belzer's and Maher's are false, and conservatives understand this fact better than liberals do.

Now suppose a researcher was conducting a study that compared: (i) U.S. soldiers with (ii) telemarketers, ditch diggers, and fast-food workers. Suppose he was comparing the two groups along two dimensions: (a) the pride that each group had for their jobs, and (b) the aptitude and job skills of the two groups. If I learned of such a study, I'd immediately suspect that the researcher was conservative. I'd strongly suspect that he was a person, like me, with firsthand knowledge that soldiers have more aptitude and pride for their jobs than the latter group. I'd also suspect that he probably had a passion to reveal that fact to the world, and to expose how inaccurate are claims such as those by Belzer and Maher.

Why Liberals Are Correct on the Other Three Questions

Just before Justin Wolfers earned his PhD from Harvard in 2001, word had spread across the economics profession about his talent. Some were even saying that he'd be "the next Steve Levitt," the soon-to-be author of *Freakonomics* and the eventual winner of the award for the best American economist under the age of forty. Wolfers received job offers from many schools, including Harvard, Yale, Stanford, Columbia, Michigan, and the London School of Economics, but the one he accepted was from the Stanford

Business School, where I taught at the time. I soon discovered that the buzz surrounding him might, if anything, have understated his talent.

I was not the only person to think that. In January 2007, *The New York Times* published an article featuring him as one of thirteen young "economists to watch." The thirteen economists, the article explained, are "doing work that is both highly respected among experts and relevant to the rest of us."[2] The scholars, the article suggested, are the answer to the question "Who, in other words, is the future of economics?"

Once I began working with Wolfers, I also learned that he is as left-wing as he is smart and talented. He arrived at Stanford with a long blond ponytail. And even though promotions and tenure decisions depended on his impressing the business students, he didn't cut it. Shortly after he arrived, I offered him advice on housing in the Palo Alto area. I soon learned, however, that Palo Alto was too suburban and family-friendly for him. He and his partner (fellow economist Betsey Stevenson) chose instead to live in San Francisco. Each day, he commuted to Stanford on environmentally friendly public transportation. "Surely your views are closer to mine than Osama bin Laden's," I asked him once. "Oh, don't get me started on hegemonic American foreign policy," he replied.

A few pages ago, I mentioned that I believe that liberals are correct on the last three positive questions in the above list. The reason I believe this is because, with each question, *Wolfers* has conducted a study convincing me that liberals are right.

For instance, he conducted a few very careful and insightful studies that show that the death penalty likely has, at best, a very minimal effect on murder rates. He did a similarly extremely careful study that shows that women's suicide rates decrease when it becomes easier for them to divorce their husbands.

One of his most famous studies showed that white referees in the NBA, relative to black referees, are more likely to call fouls on black players than they are on white players (and the opposite is true with black referees).[3] You might remember the study. Several news outlets mentioned it, and it was publicly criticized by many people, including David Stern, the NBA commissioner; several conservative talk-radio hosts; and NBA legend Charles Barkley, who called the study "asinine." However, I've read the study, and I am personally familiar with Wolfers's research skills and honesty. I'm certain that he's right and that Stern, Barkley, and the radio hosts are wrong.

I'm also certain that Wolfers's political views had no influence whatsoever on the way he collected his data or conducted his analysis. However, I believe his political views did influence the *topics* he chose for his research. For instance, it'd be natural for a strong proponent of affirmative action, which Wolfers is, to think to himself, "Lots of opponents of affirmative action think racism hardly exists. What if I could show that it exists even in a profession where people least expect it?" I'm sure that similar thoughts occurred to him when he considered studies on the death penalty and female suicide rates.

Why a Conservative Is More Motivated Than a Liberal to Construct an Objective, Precise Measure of Media Bias

Now, back to media bias. The first thing to recognize is that media bias is a positive, not a normative, question. It is *not* the case, for example, "that ultimately, the answer depends upon each individual's values." The debate *can* be settled with data and statistical analysis. And that effort is to what I have devoted my working life for the last eight years.

Now, why would a conservative have more interest than a liberal in studying media bias? Often, before a researcher begins a study, he knows of theoretical reasons or strong anecdotal evidence that tip him off as to what the results likely will be. For instance, I bet that it crossed Wolfers's mind that "Most murders are conducted in the heat of passion. And of those that are not, the murderer is usually convinced that he won't be caught. How could the death penalty deter such cases?"

Similar thoughts cross the minds of researchers thinking about studying media bias. There are thousands of anecdotes about liberal bias in the media. And just about anyone with the faintest knowledge of the media knows that journalists, overwhelmingly, have left-of-center political views.

Of course, there are counterarguments, such as "a journalist slants the news exactly the way her conservative corporate boss tells her to." But if that really is the job of a journalist, simply to be a mouthpiece of her conservative boss, then why do liberals seek such jobs? And if conservative media bosses are really so powerful, why do they hire so many liberals?

Deep down, even liberals, I believe, understand that such counterarguments are flimsy. And, deep down, they understand that the media really are biased left, at least to a small degree.

Occasionally, liberals will even admit it. For instance, on July 25, 2004, Daniel Okrent, the public editor of *The New York Times*, wrote an article entitled "Is the *New York Times* a Liberal Newspaper?" It began:

> Of course it is.
>
> The fattest file on my hard drive is jammed with letters from the disappointed, the dismayed and the irate who find in this newspaper a liberal bias that infects not just political coverage but a range of

> issues from abortion to zoology to the appointment of an admitted Democrat to be its watchdog. (That would be me.) . . .
>
> I'll get to the politics-and-policy issues this fall (I want to watch the campaign coverage before I conclude anything), but for now my concern is the flammable stuff that ignites the right. These are the social issues; gay rights, gun control, abortion and environmental regulation, among others. And if you think *The Times* plays it down the middle on any of them, you've been reading the paper with your eyes closed.[4]

Andrew Heyward, the former president of CBS News, made a similar admission to then CBS reporter Bernard Goldberg:

> Look Bernie, of course there's a liberal bias in the news. All the networks tilt left. Come on, we all know it—*the whole damn world knows it*—but that doesn't mean we have to put it on the air![5]

Given such facts, once a liberal scholar considers conducting an objective study of media bias, it would be natural for him to think, "Do I really want to spend several months of my life collecting and analyzing data just so, at the end, if I'm honest, I have to write a conclusion that allows conservatives to say, 'See, I told you so'?"

In fact, objective studies of media bias *are* disproportionately conducted by conservative scholars. I know of only six scholars who (i) are trained in statistical methods at least at the level taught at a top-twenty economics PhD program, and (ii) have constructed objective, numerical measures of the biases of media outlets. Five out of the six call themselves conservative or libertarian. This fact is especially remarkable, given that of the professors who satisfy (i)—i.e. have the statistics training—approximately 75 percent are liberal.

Many liberal journalists and scholars are opposed to the very idea of objective studies of media bias. That is, not only do they not want to conduct such studies themselves, they do not want *anyone* to conduct them.

Such people, I believe, do not want the media bias debate to be settled by data and objective measures. Instead, they want it to remain one that is settled by who has the smoothest rhetoric and who can shout the loudest.

That is a harsh accusation, but occasionally I see evidence of it.

One instance occurred on December 20, 2005, in an issue of the *Columbia Journalism Review.* Among journalists and journalism professors, the *CJR* is considered one of the most erudite, high-brow, and highly respected journals. On its Web page, it notes that its mission is to foster a "conversation with a community of people who share a commitment to high journalistic standards in the U.S. and the world."

The issue contained a highly sarcastic critique of the study that Milyo and I published in the *Quarterly Journal of Economics.* "Bias Study Falls 43.7 Percent Short" was its title. In truth, however, the article was less a criticism of our particular study, and more a criticism of the very idea of trying to measure media bias precisely and numerically. The following, for instance, were some of its passages:

> For years, sizing up the media's shortcomings has been a popular if fuzzy sport, full of subjective observations, grand generalizations, and polemical abstractions. Al Franken, for example, is happy to tell us that "Rush Limbaugh is a Big Fat Idiot," but he never tells us precisely how big, or how idiotic.
>
> * * * *
>
> That's why we were excited this week to get a press release from UCLA touting a soon-to-be published study by a team of social scientists who have finally managed to size up the bias of various American news outlets . . . *with numbers.*
>
> * * * *
>
> [T]he study is chock full of memorable quantitative observations that could come in handy this holiday season if you're tossing back a few cups of eggnog.
>
> * * * *
>
> Thanks to the scientific underpinnings of this bias-detection method, it's probably only a matter of time now before the authors come up with some valuable spin-off technologies. We're thinking of, say, a News Pyramid (similar to the USDA's Food Pyramid) that could explain exactly how to plan your news consumption for an optimally nutritive media diet (or, for that matter, tell you which junk media to cut back on).

If liberals, in contrast, really believed that the media were unbiased, then, I believe, they wouldn't write passages such as the above. Instead, they'd *welcome* objective, numerical studies of media bias.

4. *P*s and *Q*s of PQs

Loucas George, Comma, Producer

While you've probably heard of Hollywood producer George Lucas, you probably haven't heard of Hollywood producer Loucas George. But you've probably seen some of his work, which includes the television shows *The O.C., Life, Commander in Chief* (starring Geena Davis), *Ed,* and *Early Edition.* He has also produced a few movies and "a ton of music videos," including Billy Joel's "Uptown Girl" and "Tell Her About It."

People who don't live near Hollywood are usually unaware that there exist such things as middle-class actors, producers, and directors. But there are several, and George is one of them. Some of his friends, in fact, have tried to convince him to create a reality show about the life of a middle-class producer. The title would be *Loucas George, Comma, Producer.*

George's economic lifestyle is very similar to that of a full professor at a very good public university—that is, very similar to mine. In fact, George and I live near each other, and we met through our children, who attended the same preschool. Several months after our children met, our wives became partners in a small start-up business.

It was one Saturday afternoon, while our wives worked and our children played at the Georges' house, that George and I decided to watch a football game at my house. To this day, however, neither of us can remember a single detail about the game—not even the teams who played. Instead, we bickered about politics.

Although George hasn't yet won an Oscar, to my ears at least, his political views sound no different from a speech by Sean Penn, Tim Robbins, Barbra Streisand, or any of the other celebrities you might hear on Oscar night.

"George Bush lied about weapons of mass destruction" and "Karl Rove belongs in jail," for example, were two of the points he explained to me that Saturday afternoon.

At one point, one of us—I think it was me—called the other an extremist, which led to a side argument about what the words *liberal, conservative,* and *moderate* mean. Although I didn't admit it at the time, George raised some profound points—at least as profound as some that I've heard from the most distinguished professors of political science. They included:

- "I thought conservatism was all about keeping the government out of our lives. Why not with abortion?"
- "What about gay issues? I don't want government regulating what happens in the bedroom. Why isn't that conservative?"
- "And what about the Patriot Act? That's more government into our lives than ever before."
- "I oppose NAFTA. Why isn't protecting American workers 'conservative' "?
- "Conservatives always talk about reining in the budget. Why not with the military?"
- "I opposed the Bush tax cuts because I want a balanced budget. Isn't that 'fiscal conservatism' "?

George's point was that, although he generally agrees with Democrats, on many issues you could call his stance conservative, depending upon how you define *conservative.* If, therefore, his political views are a mix of liberal and conservative positions, shouldn't you call him a moderate?

Why Does That Mean "Liberal"?

His point is not just profound. It also has important consequences. A significant fraction of Americans have views similar to his. Such people include Sean Penn, Tim Robbins, Nancy Pelosi, Barney Frank, Keith Olbermann, Rachel Maddow, and probably most readers of the Daily Kos, the Huffington Post, and Media Matters.

Such people often call themselves "progressives" instead of liberals. One reason is that they do not consider their views as falling along the traditional left-right spectrum. Instead, they consider much of politics as an up-down spectrum, where their views are up. That is, their views are more modern and reasonable, and it's only a matter of time before the rest of society catches up.

Indeed, many "progressives" have left the Democratic Party, declaring themselves "Independents." They consider the Democratic Party too "corporatist" and too similar to the Republican Party. Because they are "independent," and because they criticize the Democratic Party as much as they praise it, they naturally consider themselves centrists.

Understandably, such people will object when my PQ scores declare them extremists. Indeed, on all six of the previous bullet points, PQ scores define George's position as "liberal."

Similar disagreements about the proper definitions of *conservative* and *liberal* occur on the right. For instance, conservative radio host Michael Savage insists that Rush Limbaugh, Sean Hannity, and many other self-declared "conservative" radio hosts are not true conservatives because they often support free-trade agreements, which he claims are counter to true conservatism.

A similar dispute occurred during the 1996 Republican presidential primary. *The Wall Street Journal* asked Pat Buchanan, one of the leading candidates at the time, to name his favorite liberal. "Bob Dole," he answered. Of course, Bob Dole would have objected. And his low PQ, 12, would have justified the objection.

Some, however, would counter that Bob Dole really is a liberal, and would respond, "Well, if PQ scores deem Bob Dole conservative, then that just shows how faulty PQ scores are."

For that reason it is important for me to explain and defend some of the details behind PQ scores—most important, how they define "liberal" and "conservative." As the rest of this chapter illustrates, the definition of "liberal" that I use and the issues that I choose to construct PQs are not arbitrary. Many authorities, including almost all political scientists, adopt similar definitions. Further, my choices are meaningful—that is, the definition and the issues that I choose indeed reflect the main dimension of political conflict in the United States.

How PQ Scores Define *Liberal*

Reasonable people, including my friend Loucas George, may ask, (i) "What gives you the authority to decide what 'liberal' and 'conservative' mean?"

and, related, (ii) "What gives you the authority to decide the issues that measure a person's liberalness or conservativeness?"

The answer to both questions is that I don't decide. Instead, I let the Americans for Democratic Action decide for me.

Founded in 1947, the ADA is a self-described liberal interest group. According to its Web site, it is "the nation's most experienced organization committed to liberal politics, liberal policies, and a liberal future." Its honorary presidents include Barney Frank (D-Mass.), John Lewis (D-Ga.), George McGovern, and Charles Rangel (D-N.Y.).

Each year it picks twenty or so roll call votes in the U.S. House and Senate, and for each it decides whether the yea or nay position is "correct" from the liberal standpoint. I use those roll calls to construct PQ scores.

According to the roll calls, "liberal"—as the ADA defines it means agreeing with the following stances:

- relaxing anti-abortion laws
- raising taxes on the rich
- withdrawing militarily from Iraq
- strengthening environmental regulations
- increasing the power of unions
- increasing the minimum wage
- increasing affirmative action for racial minorities
- preserving the right to burn the flag
- increasing restrictions on foreign trade
- relaxing restrictions on immigration
- decreasing military spending

My decision to let the ADA define "liberal" and choose issues for me, however, does not necessarily answer the criticism that Loucas George and others might raise; it only shifts it. Namely, why does the ADA get to choose the issues and define "liberal"?

The short answer to that question is "It doesn't really matter." There are approximately a dozen measures that political scientists occasionally use to measure the liberalness or conservativeness of politicians. For instance, one is constructed by the American Conservative Union, which, like the ADA, rates politicians by how they vote on a set of roll calls. All of the measures place noted liberals, such as Barney Frank, Maxine Waters, and Ted

Kennedy, at one end of the spectrum, and they place noted conservatives, such as Jim DeMint, Jesse Helms, and Michele Bachmann, at the other end.

In 1995, I conducted a study with Barry Burden and Greg Caldeira, two political scientists at, respectively, the University of Wisconsin and the Ohio State University. We examined every measure, of which we were aware, that political scientists use to express the liberalness or conservativeness of politicians. We then computed the *correlation coefficient* between every pair of such measures. The correlation coefficient is a number between -1.0 and 1.0 that expresses the degree to which any two measures are related to each other. (If the coefficient is 1.0, then the two measures agree perfectly. If the coeficient is -1.0, then the two measures disagree perfectly. And if the coefficient is 0.0, then the two measures are completely unrelated.) We found that between any two measures the correlation coefficient was always greater that 0.7, and it was usually greater than 0.9.[1] That is, all the measures were very highly correlated with each other.

Thus, although some people may be skeptical of my decision to use the ADA to define issues, I would have obtained approximately the same results if I had used any other group or method to define issues or what "liberal" and "conservative" mean.

So why use ADA scores instead of some other measure? One reason is simply that the ADA has been around the longest. Related, I am not aware of any political scientist, or anyone else, who questions the liberal credentials of the ADA.

Another reason is that since the main conclusions of the book are ones that conservatives often assert, it is important to show that the conclusions hold even when I use a measuring device based on issues chosen by liberals.

The Primary Dimension of Political Conflict in the United States, and Why PQ Scores Reflect It

If you ask friends of Keith Poole which celebrity he most looks like, they will all tell you the same thing: Santa Claus. Although he doesn't literally say "Ho ho ho," he has a strong, distinct, and infectious laugh.

Poole, who currently teaches at the University of Georgia, is one of the most esteemed and prolific political scientists in the country. He has written more than fifty scholarly articles. Plus, he's written six monographs or books, including *Congress: A Political-Economic History of Roll Call Voting*, one of the most widely read and cited books in all political science.

Along with Howard Rosenthal, an emeritus professor at Princeton and an adjunct professor at New York University, Poole developed NOMI-

NATE, which stands for NOMINAl Three-step Estimation program. Some people, and I am one of them, believe that NOMINATE is the most impressive research achievement ever in political science.

The program—which originally was a several-page set of Fortran computer instructions—estimates politicians' "ideological positions in a spatial framework." To do this, the program uses the votes that politicians cast on roll calls in the House and Senate.

NOMINATE has estimated a position for every legislator who has ever served in the House or Senate. This means that it can do things such as predict how James Madison or Henry Clay or Daniel Webster would have voted on, say, NAFTA, the Iraq War resolution, or President Obama's health care package.

One of NOMINATE's most noteworthy accolades occurred in 1994, when the Smithsonian Institution, as part of an exhibit on applications of supercomputers, demonstrated some of its results.

Although Poole is universally recognized as one of the brightest and most acclaimed political scientists, you would not have predicted that if you'd known him in his youth. He spent most of his formative years in Ontario, Oregon. "Ontario," said Poole, "is not in the glamorous part of the state, like Portland or Eugene. It's in the rural, eastern part—like almost Idaho."

He did not excel at school. However, after he finished high school, he enrolled at Portland State University, partly so he could obtain a draft deferment from the Vietnam War. "But during fall and winter quarter of my second year," said Poole, "I basically flunked every class."

"No, it was none of that 'I was depressed' pop-psychology bulls**t. I just had fun. It's like that song, 'You gotta fight. For your right. To paaaarty.' That was me."

After flunking his classes, he received a letter from his local draft board notifying him that his draft status had changed to "1A." To avoid the draft, he decided to enlist. He chose the signal corps and enrolled for a three-year stint, which included one year in Vietnam. "We were mainly doing things like operating the radio towers," said Poole. "The radio men in the bush would send their signals; then our tower would relay them to headquarters." Poole was technically never in combat. However, during the second wave of the Tet Offensive, at least one Viet Cong guerilla fired eight to ten 122-millimeter rockets at his unit. "One landed by the fence and never exploded," said Poole. "The others exploded in the compound, but none hit a building or even injured anybody. To this day, I think about what might have happened if that guy had had better aim. A shell could have landed in the barracks and killed us all. Sometimes I think about the forty years of life I would have missed. When I get those notices in the mail for things like wounded veterans, I drop some money in the envelope and send it in. That could have been me."

Vietnam changed his attitude toward school. "After I came back," said Poole, "I re-enrolled at Portland State, and I nearly made all As. And after I retook the courses I flunked, I finished with something like a 3.5 [grade-point average]."

Poole applied to and was accepted to the highly prestigious political science PhD program at the University of Rochester. In early 1978 he graduated and took a visiting teaching position at the University of Oregon. Rochester had impressed upon him the importance of using mathematics to study politics. At Oregon, while holding a full-time teaching job, he began to take upper-level courses in calculus, topology, real analysis, and statistics. He found that he had a special talent for topology—a branch of mathematics that analyzes shapes and mappings from one space to another. "Some of those problems were a bear," he said. "Things like 'Suppose two planes intersect a sphere. Compute the volume between the two planes.'"

Poole thinks in spatial terms. His language is peppered with phrases such as "once you project the vector onto the hyperplane" and "if you rotate the entire space." Believe it or not, when he says things like that, he's usually talking about politics.

His political views are conservative, yet, unlike some academic conservatives, he is not bashful about revealing them. "I read it in *The New York* 'Communist' *Times* this morning," he will occasionally say. "Slick" was his favorite moniker for Bill Clinton during his presidency.

Poole may be the most well read person in America. If you know him, you will often learn information that the rest of the world won't learn for several days or weeks, sometimes months. During the 2004 elections, for instance, he explained why John Kerry would *not* withdraw troops from Afghanistan or Iraq if he won the election. "Even the Democrats understand that we *have* to win these wars," he said. "Otherwise it could be *real* bad—like the end of Western civilization. Just read Bernard Lewis. You'll realize what's at stake." Poole's insight, I believe, presaged President Obama's Afghan and Iraq policy. Although, during his campaign, Obama fooled his left-wing base into believing that he'd withdraw nearly immediately from the wars, those of us who've benefitted from Poole's insight doubted that he'd actually do that.

It was Poole who first informed me about Bill Clinton's affair with Monica Lewinsky. I vividly remember when he told me, and I also remember the clairvoyant feeling that I had over the next couple days. I knew some information that few people knew. I also knew that in a few days, most of America would learn that information and consider it explosive.

"Oh, man, this is good," he said on the phone one day. "Are you by your computer?"

"Yeah," I said.

"Okay, you gotta type this URL: w-w-w-dot-d-r-u-d-g-e-r-e-p-o-r-t, yeah all one word. . . . Okay are you reading it?"

"Amazing," I said. "Could this be true?"

"I don't know, but her co-worker's cooperating with the special prosecutor," said Poole, whose excitement was about to overwhelm him. "And she waaar a WAAAR!" he bellowed.

"She what?" I asked.

"She wore a WIRE!" he exclaimed.

ALTHOUGH POOLE IS conservative, there is nothing conservative, or liberal, about NOMINATE. It uses standard mathematical tools, albeit applied in some brilliant ways, to measure the ideology of politicians. Indeed, its co-creator, Howard Rosenthal, is liberal.

With the NOMINATE procedure, Poole and Rosenthal record the yea and nay votes of legislators. Their computer program then estimates a number for each legislator. That number indicates the position of the legislator on the *dimension that best describes the main conflict between legislators* on the roll call votes.

In theory that dimension could represent any sort of conflict—e.g., rural versus urban, South versus North, libertarian versus antilibertarian, pro–civil rights versus anti–civil rights, etc. In practice, however, the numbers indicate a very particular type of conflict: liberal versus conservative.

That is, once the NOMINATE computer program spits out its estimates, the legislators with the lowest scores are people—such as Nancy Pelosi and Barney Frank—who are commonly called liberals. And the politicians with the highest scores are people—such as Michele Bachmann and Jim DeMint—who are commonly called conservatives.

There is nothing in NOMINATE that forces this result. For instance, if issues and votes in Congress had been different, then the program might instead have generated numbers with, say, (i) southerners at one end and northerners at the other, or (ii) libertarians at one end and antilibertarians at the other end. The fact that the latter-type results did not occur means that we can infer the following about American politics: The conflict that we commonly call "liberal versus conservative" is indeed the main conflict within Congress.

At least two other sets of scholars have examined the same research question, to estimate legislators' preferences on "the dimension of maximal conflict," using roll call votes as data. The scores they have produced are:

- Heckman-Snyder scores, named after James Heckman, the Nobel-winning economist at the University of Chicago, and James Snyder, my occasional coauthor, who is now a professor of government at Harvard University.
- CJR scores, created by Josh Clinton, a political scientist at Vanderbilt University, and by Simon Jackman and Doug Rivers, both political scientists at Stanford University.

These scores make technical assumptions that are slightly different from NOMINATE's. However, their main results are nearly identical to those of NOMINATE. Most important, they find that the dimension of maximal conflict is what people commonly call liberal/conservative.

NOW BACK TO PQ scores. It happens that PQ scores are very highly correlated with NOMINATE and with Heckman-Snyder and CJR scores. Thus, while the previous section argued that PQs capture the conflict commonly called liberal versus conservative, this section shows that PQs are also meaningful—that is, they indeed reflect the main conflict in American politics.

Measuring Political Ideology Over Time

Recall Dawson Engler's quip in chapter 1: "Come on. Political science isn't really a science." When he said that, I was working at MIT on a project that analyzed vote scores from the Americans for Democratic Action and how the scores changed over time. One of my coauthors was James Snyder, then a professor at MIT. The other was Steve Levitt. At the time, Levitt was an unknown PhD student at MIT; however, a few years later he would write *Freakonomics* and win the John Bates Clark Medal, given to the best American economist under the age of forty.

When we began our project, political scientists would often use ADA scores to discuss how a politician's ideology changed over time. For instance, in 1986, John McCain received a 10 from the ADA. (That is, on the twenty Senate roll call votes that the ADA chose, he voted with the ADA 10 percent of the time.) In the next year, he received a 15. Many people would conclude that—since 15 is greater than 10—McCain became more liberal between the two years.

One purpose of my project with Levitt and Snyder was to explain why the latter conclusion is *not* necessarily true. The reason is that the ADA chooses a different set of issues (i.e., roll call votes) each year. This means that its "scale" for measuring liberalness changes from year to year.

It is similar to the situation in which a student takes two different tests, one early in the term and one late in the term. If he scores higher on the later test, it is tempting to conclude that he became smarter. However, another possibility is simply that the later test was easier than the earlier test.

Teachers understand this well. This is why they often grade "on the curve." That is, they add points to each student's grade if the test was especially difficult or subtract points if it was especially easy. Often the goal of the teacher is to "set the curve" so that the average "curved" score of the students who took both tests is the same on both tests.

Although it involves slightly more complicated math, what Levitt, Snyder, and I did with ADA scores is similar. We derived a mathematical formula that allowed us to convert a "nominal" ADA score (the actual score the ADA reports) to an "adjusted" ADA score. As we explained, while it is not appropriate to use nominal scores to measure ideology over time, it is appropriate to use adjusted scores for that task.

PQs are based on the "adjusted ADA scores" that I created with Levitt and Snyder. Therefore, they can be used to make comparisons over time. For instance, Richard Nixon's average PQ, based on his 1947–52 congressional service, was 12.5. Meanwhile, Jim DeMint's PQ, based on his 1999–2009 congressional service, was 4.8. Since Nixon's PQ was greater than DeMint's, we can legitimately conclude that Nixon was more liberal than DeMint.

Using similar calculations we can make similar over-time comparisons, such as:

- After Joe Lieberman switched from Democrat to Independent, he moved only the tiniest bit rightward—specifically from 74.7 to 74.
- After Arlen Specter switched from Republican to Democrat, he became more liberal—from 50.6 to 67.4.
- John F. Kennedy (PQ 63.7) was more *conservative* than Joe Lieberman (regardless of whether we judge Lieberman from his tenure as a Democrat or as an Independent).
- John F. Kennedy was more conservative than his brother Ted (PQ 89.2), who was more conservative than his brother Robert (PQ 96.5).

Why PQ Scores Are Like Inflation Indexes for Prices

PQ scores, in fact, are identical to the "adjusted ADA scores" that Levitt, Snyder, and I created, except for one minor modification. This involves the "base year" for the two sets of scores.

When economists compare prices over time, they often convert "nominal" prices to "real" prices. This is done by creating a price index for a basket of goods and choosing one year as the "base year." For instance, for many years the Bureau of Labor Statistics used 1967 as its base year. From this it calculated "price deflators" for other years. For instance, the price deflator for 1997 was 4.693. This means that in 1997 the cost of a basket of consumer goods was 4.693 times the basket's cost in 1967. It also means that to calculate the "real" price of an item listed in 1997, you take its nominal (listed) price and divide it by 4.693. Meanwhile, the deflator for the base year is 1. That is, in the base year real prices are the same as nominal prices.

When Levitt, Snyder, and I created our "adjusted ADA scores," we chose 1980 as the base year. Because the ADA chooses different roll calls for the two different chambers, we also selected a "base chamber." We chose the House. This means that for any House member serving in 1980, his or her nominal score is the same as his or her "adjusted" score. However, for any other year and chamber, you need to use the formulas that we published to convert nominal scores into adjusted scores.

When I created PQ scores, my original plan was to stick with 1980 as the base year. However, due to a conversation I had with Levitt, I switched the base year to 1999. This conversation occurred shortly after Milyo and I had derived some preliminary results for the article that was eventually published in the *Quarterly Journal of Economics.*

"We're finding," I told Levitt one day, "that Peter Jennings and Tom Brokaw basically get scores of about 52 or 53. Meanwhile, the average adjusted score for Congress is something like 40. Thus, Brokaw and Jennings have a liberal bias of about 12 or 13 points."

"If I were you," said Levitt, "I'd normalize the scale so that 50 is the average for Congress. Otherwise, you're going to get some idiot saying, 'What do you mean 40 is the center? Everyone knows that 50 is the center.' "

"But, surely, everyone can understand that there's nothing magic about fifty," I replied. "The scale is arbitrary. Anyone who can convert Celsius to Fahrenheit can understand that."

"I don't know," said Levitt. "I'd normalize it."

I should have listened to Levitt. I presented an early version of the paper, which defined "center" as the ADA score of the median member of

Congress. That turned out to be about 38 (using 1980 as the base year). Sure enough, several bloggers criticized Milyo and me for not understanding that 50 must be the center.

Rather than try to explain the scaling issue, I punted. That is, I followed Levitt's advice and renormalized the scale so that 50 would be the center. However, rather than following his exact advice, that is, to add the same number to all the SQs and PQs in my data set, I found that if I simply switched base years (from 1980 to 1999) this made the score of the average member of Congress 50.06—close enough to 50, I surmised, to thwart the criticism.

Milyo, however, was not as sanguine. "I still think we need to add a few sentences that explain the change in base years," he told me. "Lots of people will be looking for something to criticize. I'd like the paper to explain things so well that if a person does criticize the base-year issue, then it at least reveals that he doesn't understand Celsius-to-Fahrenheit conversions." Consequently, we added the following footnote to the paper:

> Importantly, we apply this conversion [i.e., from the 1980 House scale to the 1999 House scale] to congressional scores as well as to media scores. Since our method can only make relative assessments of the ideology of media outlets (e.g., how they compare with members of Congress or the average American voter), this transformation is benign. Just as the average temperature in Boston is colder than the average temperature in Baltimore, regardless if one uses a Celsius scale or a Fahrenheit scale, all conclusions we draw in this paper [and that I draw in this book] are unaffected by the choice to use the 1999 House scale or the 1980 House scale.

To their credit, no left-wing blogger, at least so far, has criticized us on this issue.

5. Defining the "Center"

BY NOW, YOU should have a working understanding of PQ scores and how I construct them. Also, you should have at least a vague idea about how I estimate slant quotients for media outlets.

Soon I will use SQs and PQs to calculate the bias of the media. By *bias,* I mean the degree to which a media outlet's slant differs from *the center of American political views.* Thus, to calculate bias, I need to be precise about the concept "the center of American political views."

The simplest way to define the "center" is to calculate, for a given year, the average PQ of all legislators who served that year in Congress. Under the assumption that Congress is approximately representative of voters—that is, on average, each legislator is no more conservative or liberal than the average voter in his district—then this calculation would give a good estimate of the PQ of the average voter. Figure 5.1 shows how the average PQ of the House and Senate has varied between 1947 and 2009.

One problem, however, with using the averages of the House and Senate is that not all American voters receive equal representation in Congress. For example, if you're a voter in Washington, D.C., then you get *no* representation in Congress (except for a "delegate" to the House, whose participation is mostly symbolic). And since voters in Washington, D.C., tend to be more liberal than the rest of the country, we should expect the average American voter to be slightly more liberal than the average member of Congress.

FIGURE 5.1

Average PQ of the House and Senate

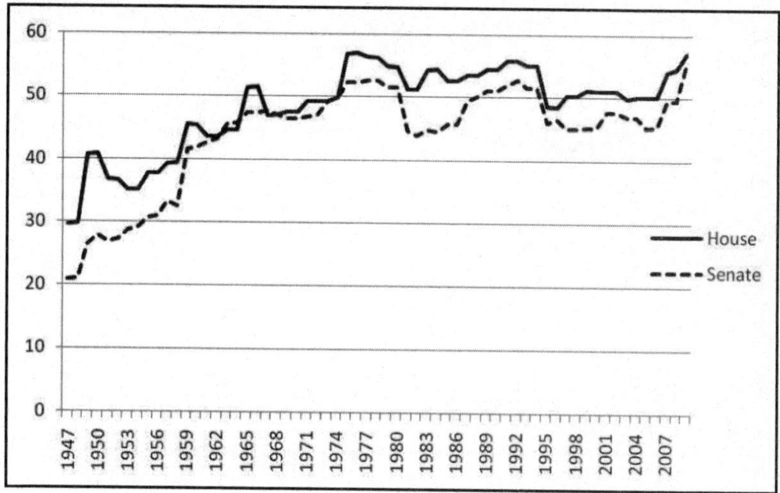

Another problem is the "small state bias" of the Senate—that is, each state gets two senators, regardless of the state's population. This means, for example, that the average Californian receives about one sixtieth the representation of the average North Dakotan in the Senate. This is especially problematic if small states tend to be more conservative than large states (or vice versa).

To overcome the first problem (lack of representation for Washington, D.C.) to compute "the center," I added a phantom D.C. House member and two phantom D.C. senators. I assumed that if such legislators actually existed, then their PQ would equal the highest PQ of the other members serving that year in their respective chamber.

To overcome the second problem (the small-state bias in the Senate), I calculated a *weighted* average of Senate PQs, where the weights were proportional to the population of the state. (That is, for instance, California's weight is approximately sixty times that of North Dakota.)

After calculating these averages, I calculated the average of the two averages (i.e., the House average and the Senate average). I call this the center of American political views. Figure 5.2 illustrates how this center has evolved since 1947.

Note, as the figure illustrates, a different "center" exists for each different year. This reflects the simple fact that voters' views change over time.

FIGURE 5.2

PQ of the Average U.S. Voter

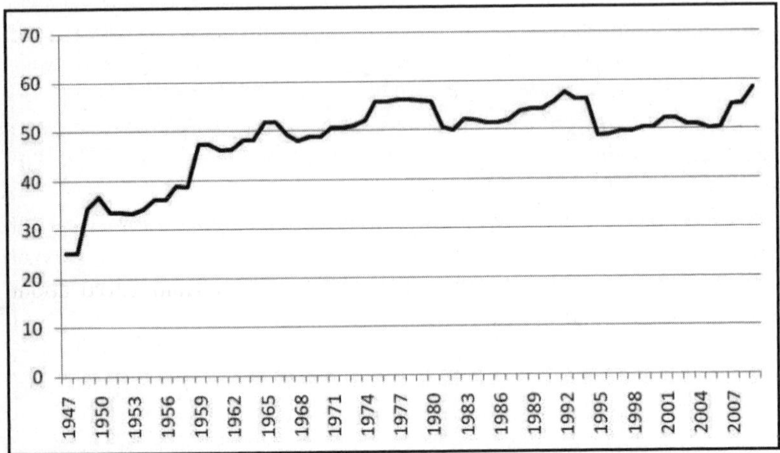

My data on media slants come primarily from stories reported in the late 1990s and early 2000s. Accordingly, to define the "center" for this period I calculated the average of the ten "centers" over the period 1995–2004. The average of those ten averages was 50.4. (The number differs slightly from the estimate, 50.06, that Milyo and I derived for our *QJE* article. The main reason is that the earlier work used only scores from the 1995–99 period.) Thus, for the remainder of the book, when I say "centrist" or "moderate," I mean someone whose PQ is near 50.4.

Some people may criticize my choice of time period, 1995–2004. One reason is that in 1995 the House and Senate moved significantly rightward. Further, unlike other periods, for each year during 1995–2004, Republicans held a majority in the House. Accordingly, so goes the criticism, this causes the "center" to be artificially conservative, or at least more conservative than if I had chosen various other time periods.

For at least two reasons, however, my choice is defensible. First, 1995–2004 is the period for which I obtained *media* data. To use a different period would be to compare "apples with oranges."

That is, for instance, in the *QJE* article that I wrote with Milyo, we found that PBS's *NewsHour*, during the 1999–2003 period we examined, had a slant quotient of 55.8. Thus, the slant is slightly liberal if you compare it to the 1995–2004 definition of "center," 50.4. However, if you compare it to, say, the 1977 definition of "center," which is 56.2, then the slant is slightly conservative.

The latter comparison, however, does not make sense. The main reason is the simple fact that it was impossible for people in 1977 to watch the 1999–2003 *NewsHour* shows—that is, unless they had a time machine. One goal of this book is to examine the *influence* of media bias—that is, for instance, the extent to which *NewsHour* can change the political views of voters. It would be silly to posit that the 1999–2003 shows had any influence upon 1977 voters.

Another goal is to examine the extent to which media outlets try to cater to the wishes of their viewers. Once again, it would be silly to posit that the 1999–2003 producers and reporters at *NewsHour* cared about what 1977 viewers would think of their shows.

A second reason why my choice is defensible is that even if I had chosen a different set of years to calculate the "center," the choice would hardly matter. For instance, suppose instead I had chosen the prior ten years, 1985–94. Then this would have changed the estimate of "center" only by 3.8 points, from 50.4 to 54.2. Even if we judge media by the latter definition of "center," then my and Milyo's original *QJE* paper would still have concluded that eighteen out of the twenty outlets were left of center.

Moreover, even if I had cherry-picked the data so that "center" was defined by the ten most liberal years over the entire 1947–2009 sample, then this would have caused the estimate of the "center" to move only to 56.4. Even by this definition, the original paper by Milyo and me would still have concluded that sixteen out of twenty outlets were left of center.

"But Those Calculations Ignore 'Disenfranchised' People Who Do Not Vote"

In a typical presidential election, only about half of the people who are eligible to vote actually cast a ballot. Further, there are many other people residing in the United States who, because they are not citizens, are not *eligible* to vote. There is a school of thought, primarily among the left, that asserts that these nonvoters are much more liberal than actual voters, and thus if the United States could persuade—or, as the left sometimes prescribes, force—these people to vote, then Democrats would fare much better in elections.

For at least three reasons, however, I'm skeptical of the claim. One is a theoretical reason that involves the way people decide how to vote. If you vote, usually it is because you feel strongly about at least one of the candidates you are voting for or against.

However, if you are approximately indifferent between two candidates, then there's not much reason to vote—especially if your time is valuable and it takes you more than a few minutes to travel to the polls. As a consequence, many nonvoters—and maybe the vast majority of them—do not have strong preferences for the Republican or Democratic candidate. That is, they are moderates. Consequently, even if we could force all of these people to vote, then it is doubtful that they would overwhelmingly vote for the Democrat. More likely, since they are approximately indifferent, they would approximately split their votes between the Republican and the Democrat.

Another reason why I am skeptical of the claim involves evidence from polling. Whenever you hear the results of a political poll, the pollster often splits his sample into two categories: (i) likely voters and (ii) all respondents. For instance, the typical report may say something like, "Among likely voters, 53 percent say they intend to vote for Obama; whereas, among all respondents, 54 percent say they intend to vote for Obama." If nonvoters really were much more liberal than voters, then the second number would tend to be much larger than the first. Instead, in such polls the two numbers rarely differ by more than one or two percentage points. In fact, often the likely-voter number favors the Democrat *more* than the all-respondents number, which suggests that the vast army of nonvoters are more *conservative* than voters.

A third reason involves evidence from the 1993 "Motor Voter" act. The intention of the law was to make it easier for people to register to vote. For instance, one of its provisions required state governments to allow people to register to vote when they visited one of the state's motor vehicle offices or when they received social services from the state government. Many liberals believed that the law would tap the vast army of "disenfranchised" liberals who were not voting, which in turn would aid Democrats. Indeed, when the U.S. Senate voted on the law, all Democratic senators voted for it, and all but six Republican senators voted against it.

In one way the law was very successful: many additional people registered to vote. One researcher found that voter rolls increased by 20 percent between 1994 and 1998.[1] There was little evidence to suggest, however, that the newly "enfranchised" voters were any more liberal than the old voters. In fact, if anything, results from the next election, in 1994, suggested that they were more conservative. In that election Republicans made record gains in the House and Senate. Their success, in fact, allowed Newt Gingrich to become the first Republican speaker of the House since 1955.

"But This Means That 'Unbiased,' as You Define It, Is a Moving Target"

Shortly after Milyo and I published our *QJE* article, a number of television shows invited us to discuss our results on air. We were both novices at television and therefore very nervous about appearing on television.

The first show on which either of us appeared was MSNBC's Tucker Carlson show, on which Milyo appeared. I missed seeing the show because I was out of the country, but soon after I called him.

"I guess it went okay," said Milyo. "But once you watch the tape, you'll see that my eyes keep darting back and forth. I looked like I was some kind of serial killer."

Eventually, I saw the tape. Milyo did a fantastic job, and he looked nothing like a serial killer. But as I sat in a Los Angeles studio awaiting my first television interview—on C-SPAN's *Washington Journal*—all I could think about was "Keep looking at the camera. Don't look like a serial killer."

The interview was live, and most of it consisted of call-in questions from viewers.

"Austin, Texas. Go ahead, please," said Susan Swain, the C-SPAN host, about midway through the interview.

The Austin caller then responded:

> Uh, yeah. It's kind of absurd to think that you can define the collective media ideology [from] think-tank citations. Sometimes conservatives cite liberal think tanks. Sometimes liberals cite conservative think tanks . . . because it might fit the argument they want. But just to say that—that's how we can prove it—is absurd, and it doesn't take into account the content. . . . It's like what happens if Congress is all 100 percent Democrat or 100 percent Republican. Then—then doesn't somehow a liberal become, or, the media become more liberal or more conservative somehow? It just doesn't make any sense. . . .
>
> And what I want to know is . . . uhh, I read something about this gentleman and his partner actually accepted money from conservative think tanks. Does that make their study biased . . . ?[2]

If you watch me during his questioning, at one point I look down nervously and start to reach for something, but then I stop and look up again. On my lap was a copy of my research paper, and nearby was a pen. I was about to try to write some notes about the caller's many questions, but then the thought jumped into my head: "Don't look like a serial killer. Keep looking at the camera."

As a consequence, when I responded, I couldn't remember all of his critiques. And I completely ignored one of them, which happened to be, I believe, his most astute. This was his question: If Congress becomes 100 percent Republican, then doesn't "the media become more liberal or more conservative somehow?"

Strictly speaking, the answer is no. That is, for instance, our method calculates 74 as the SQ of *The New York Times* (for the 2003 time period that we examined the newspaper). Our estimate remains at 74 no matter how liberal or conservative Congress was or becomes.

However, what I think the caller meant to ask was, "If Congress were more Republican, wouldn't this change the *bias* of the media, by your method?"

The answer to that question, at least by one interpretation, is yes. Our notion of bias is a relative one—specifically, it is the media outlet's SQ relative to the PQ of the "center." Thus, if our estimate of the center were, say, ten points less (because Congress was much more conservative), then of course this would change our estimates of the bias of various media outlets.

Some have criticized this notion and responded with statements such as, "'Unbiased' should be defined by truth and accuracy, not by how well a journalist imitates the average voter or politician."

In a moment, I'll explain why my notion of bias *is* related to truth and accuracy, but for the moment, suppose it's not. Suppose, as critics might say, "unbiased," as I defined it, means nothing more than appealing to the whims and beliefs of the average voter—who may be much less intelligent, educated, and enlightened than, say, voters at the liberal end of the PQ scale.

Even if that's true, let me suggest that our findings are still interesting. Before Milyo and I published our paper, left-wing media analysts often claimed the opposite—specifically, that although, yes, the personal views of journalists might be liberal, when they make political judgments, they make those judgments as if they were political centrists. Our results, however, clearly show that that was not the case.

Instead, media critics began to echo the comments of the Austin caller: "Okay, maybe the mainstream media don't act like political centrists. But who says they should? Who says that centrists are any more truthful or accurate than liberals and progressives?"

Why Centrists Have More Incentive to Be Truthful Than Extremists

Now, let me explain why *unbiased,* as Milyo and I defined it, *can* be interpreted as more truthful and accurate.

First, a disclosure. In our article, we included the following passage:

> [Our definition of *bias*] has nothing to do with the honesty or accuracy of the news outlet. Instead, our notion is more like a taste or preference. For instance, we estimate that the centrist United States voter during the late 1990s had a left-right ideology approximately equal to that of Arlen Specter (R-Pa.) or Sam Nunn (D-Ga.). Meanwhile, we estimate that the average *New York Times* article is ideologically very similar to the average speech by Joe Lieberman (D-Conn.). Next, since vote scores show Lieberman to be more liberal than Specter or Nunn, our method concludes that *The New York Times* has a liberal bias. However, in no way does this imply that *The New York* Times is inaccurate or dishonest—just as the vote scores do not imply that Joe Lieberman is any less honest than Sam Nunn or Arlen Specter.

My thinking has evolved since then. Biased news outlets, I now believe, are less accurate than unbiased ones. At a minimum, they have less incentive to tell the truth—or at least the whole truth—than unbiased ones. Similarly, noncentrist politicians, I believe, are less likely to tell the whole truth than centrist politicians.

What changed my view? It was two very important theoretical results in social science: (i) Duncan Black's Median Voter Theorem, and (ii) Vincent Crawford and Joel Sobel's model of "Strategic Information Transmission."

In the next two sections, I'll explain the results and why they imply that centrist news outlets should be more honest and accurate than noncentrist ones. However, for now, the basic reasoning is the following: Extremists, more than moderates, want to sell you a bill of ideological goods. They, accordingly, have an incentive to lie or exaggerate—or at least to withhold relevant facts that do not support their position. Centrists, as I'll explain, do not have the same incentive.

The Crawford-Sobel Model of "Strategic Information Transmission"

Many readers are familiar with John Nash, the subject of the award-winning movie *A Beautiful Mind*. As the movie chronicles, he is one of the pioneers of game theory.

In the earliest models of game theory, researchers typically assumed that the players have *symmetric* information—that is, no player knows anything more than any other player. However, a decade or two after Nash's early work, scholars frequently began to construct models of *asymmetric* information.

One of the most famous and brilliant of such models is the Crawford-Sobel "signaling" game. Indeed, I believe that their model was the most important contribution to economic theory of the entire 1980s.

In the game, one player, the "Sender" (like a journalist), has some information, which the "Receiver" (like a news consumer) does not know. The Sender gives the Receiver a "message," which might or might not reveal the information. After seeing the message, the Receiver chooses a "policy," which affects the well-being of both players.

In 1982, Crawford and Sobel published their model in *Econometrica*, an economics journal known for its highly complex and mathematical results. In a moment I'll try to summarize the main results of their model in nontechnical terms. However, before I do that, let me say that such an exercise is futile. Some of the most important and brilliant insights of the model simply can't be explained if you don't work through the math.

Such an exercise is similar to a fable, often discussed by economists, where a king tells his advisors, "I want you to condense all of the world's economic knowledge into one short book that I can read in a weekend." After several months, the advisors complete the task and present the book to the king. The king, however, replies, "This is too long and difficult. I want you to summarize the knowledge further into a single page." After several weeks, the advisors do just that. However, the king replies, "This is still too long and difficult. Here is an index card. I want you to condense all economic knowledge into one sentence, and write it on the card." After huddling with each other, the advisors return with the index card. On it they've written, "There is no free lunch."

In that spirit, let me now summarize the Crawford-Sobel model in one sentence: "If you want truthful and accurate advice, ask someone who has tastes and values similar to your own."

More specific, here's a political example where that insight applies. Suppose you're a moderate voter completely uninformed about two candidates, a Republican and a Democrat. You want to learn who is the best candidate, so you decide to ask one of three people, each of whom has studiously researched the two candidates, and each of whom knows all there is to know about them. The three people are: (i) a far-right blogger, (ii) a far-left blogger, and (iii) your twin brother, who, like you, is a political moderate. Most people, without even knowing the Crawford-Sobel model, realize the answer is obvious: ask your brother.

However, here is another result of the Crawford-Sobel model that is not so obvious. Given that you fully trust your brother, yet are skeptical of the bloggers, consider how your brother and the bloggers will react. How does your trust, or lack of it, affect the messages that they tell you?

Consider, for instance, the thought process of the far-right blogger. He thinks, "You probably believe that I'll exaggerate the virtues of the Republican. Therefore you'll probably discount the positive things I say about him. Consequently, if I want you to be accurately informed, I need to exaggerate his virtues. But if you understand this, then you'll discount my message even more. Therefore, I need to exaggerate *even more* the virtues of the Republican. But this causes you to discount my message even more. And so on." A similar thought process occurs with the far-left blogger. The end result is that both bloggers—even if their motivations are pure and they only want you to be accurately informed—have an incentive to exaggerate, simply because you don't fully trust them.[3]

In contrast, the same logic doesn't apply to your brother. He understands that you fully trust him. Consequently, he has no incentive to lie or exaggerate.

In this example, note that there is no inborn character trait that makes the far-left or far-right blogger less honest than your brother. The key is that you—in this example, the sole audience of the three possible informants—have political values that differ from those of the bloggers.

Meanwhile, however, if your political values magically became far-left, then, according to the Crawford-Sobel model, this would cause the far-left blogger to become the most honest of the three. Your brother, assuming he remained a moderate, would become the second-most honest. And the far-right blogger would become the least honest. The opposite would happen if your political values magically became far right.

Thus, here is another lesson of the Crawford-Sobel model. For any political issue, note who is the main audience of journalists. The journalists who have political values most similar to that audience have the most incentive to report truthfully and accurately.

Black's Median Voter Theorem

Let me now argue that if a journalist wants to influence policy, then her primary audience is moderates, not conservatives or liberals. The reason involves the Median Voter Theorem.

First proposed by economist Duncan Black in 1958, the theorem says that if you take a body, say, the U.S. House of Representatives, and if you line up all its members from most left wing to most right wing, then the person in the middle, the median, gets his way in terms of policy.[4]

For example, in 2010 the Democrats held a majority of seats in the House, specifically 255. The *total* number of House seats (not counting two unfilled seats) was 433. This means that the median of the House was the 217th most liberal member. That member had an ideology somewhere in the middle of the 52 or so Blue Dog Democrats, a coalition of legislators who, although Democratic, felt that many positions of their party were too liberal.

Let's assume, for simplicity, that all Blue Dogs stick together when voting. If so, then the Median Voter Theorem implies that a policy would pass the House if and only if the Blue Dogs supported it.

To see why, note that there were approximately 203 mainline (i.e., non–Blue Dog) Democrats. If the Blue Dogs were to join them, then their coalition size would be 255, which is more than a majority. Meanwhile, there were 178 Republicans. If the Blue Dogs instead joined them, then the size of the coalition would be 230, which, again, is more than a majority. Thus, if the Blue Dogs favored a certain policy, then they could pass it by joining either the Republicans or the mainline Democrats.

Of course, the mainline Democrats could have joined the Republicans to form a coalition against the Blue Dogs. But if these two groups agreed on a policy, then it would be strange for the Blue Dogs to oppose it. (In fact, Duncan Black showed that such a two-ends-against-the-middle coalition is impossible if all actors have what he calls "single-peaked preferences.") All this means that, under some reasonable assumptions, a policy would receive majority support if and only if the Blue Dogs supported it. As Black phrased his theorem, a policy receives majority support if and only if the median member of the body supports it.

Now consider that, ultimately, voters decide policy. Of course, you might argue that voters actually decide policy only *indirectly*—that is, their influence is exerted only through their representatives. However, they can pressure those representatives. Further, even if their representatives resist the pressure, the voters can oust them at the next election.

As a consequence, at least approximately, the median voter in the United States should get his way with policy. As I've argued in earlier chapters, that voter is a moderate—with a PQ of approximately 50.4.

Consequently, this means that if you're a politically motivated journalist—i.e., you want to affect policy—then for any story you report, the key person you want to persuade is the median voter. That is, *your main audience is a moderate.*

Now let's combine the results of the two models. The latter result, coupled with the main result of the Crawford-Sobel model, implies that *moderate* journalists have the most incentive to report truthfully and accurately. Accordingly, this logic implies that the media outlets with slant quotients near 50.4 should tend to be the most truthful and accurate.

Some Caveats

Let me admit, that last statement probably seems like a bold and controversial one. However, it's actually not so bold and controversial once you know what I mean by "truthful and accurate." As I will discuss in later chapters, it's very rare for journalists, at least intentionally, to make false statements. Accordingly, if you're looking for lies, I don't believe that extremist media outlets are any worse than centrist ones.

However, the story is different if "truthful and accurate" means telling the *whole* truth. To see this consider the following thought experiment. Suppose Congress is considering whether to implement a "public option" for the nation's health care system. Suppose that moderate voters—those with a PQ near 50—can't decide whether they favor or oppose the public option. However, two very important facts are relevant to the debate. The first fact, call it Fact A—is a positive fact for the public option. That is, if moderate voters learned it, then this would tip them off the fence, toward favoring the policy. The second fact, Fact B, is a negative one. If moderate voters learned it, then this would cause them to oppose the public option.

If this thought experiment actually occurred in practice, then—consistent with the Crawford-Sobel model—I believe you'd see the following: News outlets with very liberal SQs—say, many of the shows on MSNBC—would report only Fact A. Meanwhile, the news outlets with very conservative SQs—say, many conservative talk-radio shows—would report only Fact B. Meanwhile, the news outlets with SQs near 50—such as ABC's *Good Morning America, NewsHour,* the Drudge Report, and Fox News *Special Report*—would report both facts.

Of course, that's only conjecture. Most important, however, even if my conjecture is false, it still illustrates, at least theoretically, what I mean when I suggest that centrist outlets are more "truthful and accurate" than extremist ones. The centrist ones have more incentive to tell *the whole truth.*

One final caveat is that the latter analysis makes a number of assumptions, including: (i) that there exist such things as positive and negative facts about a policy issue; (ii) that journalists, at least at times, are opportunistic about reporting such facts—that is, they might report facts that aid their political goals more frequently than those that don't aid those goals; and (iii) the choice of which facts to report and which not to report is consequential—that is, such choices, at least at times, change people's views on political issues.

Of course, while I'm convinced that these assumptions are true—indeed, I think they're almost self-evident—other people might not be so convinced. Consequently, the assumptions deserve a thorough examination. Such an examination is the focus of the next three chapters, where I explain my *distortion theory* of media bias.

PART II

A Distortion Theory of Media Bias

6. Lies, Damned Lies, and Omitted Statistics

A CASE STUDY IN DISTORTION THEORY

IN THE PREVIOUS chapter I applied an economic signaling model to the media. In particular, I suggested that the news reports of a journalist are similar to the "messages" that the Sender in such a model reports to the Receiver.

For such an application to be appropriate, however, a particular principle must be true: The journalist must be more informed about the particular news topic than her readers or viewers. Rarely, I suggest, will this principle not be true. Journalists, at least usually, read lots of background material and interview many key observers to make sure that it is true.

Sometimes, however, it *won't* be true. That is, if you are lucky, there will be a rare moment or two in your life where you read or watch a news story and you know at least as much about the story as the journalist knows. Usually, for this to happen, you must be one of the participants in the story or, due to special circumstances, a very close observer.

"A Startling Statistic at UCLA"

Such an occasion happened to me on June 3, 2006. "A Startling Statistic at UCLA" was the headline I read that morning on the front page of the *Los Angeles Times*. The article noted the low number of African Americans who would enroll as freshmen at UCLA that autumn; it implied that the applications process was stacked against them; and at times it hinted—mainly through quotes of some far-left students and other observers—that the problem was that UCLA faculty and administrators did not have sufficient desire for racial diversity.

At the time, I was a member of the faculty oversight committee for admissions at UCLA. Thus, I was intimately familiar with the admissions process and the facts and statistics that resulted from the process.

The author of the article, Rebecca Trounson, presented a very misleading picture of that process and its results, and I became outraged when I read her article. While the rest of the world would think one thing about UCLA admissions, I knew that if they were fully informed, they would think something vastly different.

Yet, while the article was misleading and outrageous, *it contained zero false statements.*

What to Report? What to Omit?

The article began as follows:[1]

> This fall 4,852 freshmen are expected to enroll at UCLA, but only 96, or 2%, are African American—the lowest figure in decades and a growing concern at the Westwood campus.
>
> For several years, students, professors and administrators at UCLA have watched with discouragement as the numbers of black students declined. [But the new numbers, university leaders feel, have imposed a crisis on campus.]
>
> UCLA—which . . . is in a county that is 9.8% African American—now has a lower percentage of black freshmen than either crosstown rival USC or UC Berkeley. . . .
>
> The 96 figure—down by 20 students from last year—is the lowest for incoming African American freshmen since at least 1973. And [of the 96 expected to enroll] 20 are recruited athletes.

Although the article did not explicitly say it, some of its facts, and many of its quotes, would make reasonable readers suspect that UCLA was practicing at least mild forms racism. The following are some passages that would bolster such a suspicion.

- [Karume James, the chairman of UCLA's Afrikan [sic] Student Union remembered his impressions of UCLA when he arrived in the summer of 2003.] "That was a real shock. I spent about 14 hours at the campus, and I counted only about 12 black people. I guess I'd had this feeling that UCLA was going to be this truly diverse place, and it just wasn't. Not for black students."

- [Darnell Hunt, a UCLA sociology professor, who heads UCLA's Bunche Center for African American Studies, helped write a report about admissions at UC Berkeley, UCLA, and UC San Diego. The report found that the admission rate of black students was highest at UC Berkeley and lowest at UC San Diego.] The report found that UC San Diego's admissions process relied most heavily on numbers, while UC Berkeley's was most "holistic," allowing a single reader to review all parts of an applicant's file. . . . At UCLA, in what admissions officials have described as an attempt to increase fairness and objectivity, applicants' files are divided by academic and personal areas, and read by separate reviewers.
- [Hunt] criticized the school for rejecting many black students based on what he described as factors of questionable validity.
- Some of those interviewed . . . said the campus could be doing more than it is [to enroll more black students].

Drive-by Media

"If you're so smart," so goes a common expression among economists, "then why aren't you rich?" If we judge media analysts by that standard, then the smartest analyst of all, by far, is Rush Limbaugh. According to *The New York Times Magazine*, he earns approximately $38 million a year.[2]

Before you dismiss completely the possibility that Limbaugh really is so astute at analyzing the media, consider that he has devised possibly the most brilliant concept ever to describe the usual method by which media bias is perpetrated. His concept, *the drive-by media*, is best described, in his own words, as follows:

> They [journalists] are exactly like drive-by shooters, they pull up to a congested area; they spray a hail of bullets into the crowd. It causes mass hysteria, confusion, mistakes, and misinterpretation. Sometimes people and their careers actually die, and then the drive-by media smirk and they ride away, unnoticed in the excitement. They're never blamed, they're never held accountable. In fact, they're lauded! They're held up as heroes (mostly by themselves) and then the rest of

> us have to engage in mopping up the mess that the drive-by media caused.[3]

Notice that Limbaugh doesn't call journalists liars. Nor does he suggest that the media *intend* to do harm. Nevertheless, the statements that they spray into the air, even if technically all true, can distort people's worldview away from the truth. The statements often, I believe, cause just as much damage as false statements.

If you knew the whole truth about UCLA admissions, and you wanted to mop up the mess, here are some of the facts you would report alongside the facts that actually were reported.

- At UCLA almost half of all entering undergraduate students are transfers, not freshmen. During the time in question, early summer of 2006, 108 black *transfer* students were expected to enroll—22 more than the year before.[4]
- Thus, on net, when you count freshmen *and* transfers, compared to the year before, the total expected black undergraduate enrollment *increased* by 2 students.
- Like many universities, UCLA has a separate admissions process for star athletes. Because the NCAA had imposed stricter standards in 2006, UCLA coaches requested that the admissions office hold athletes to a higher academic standard, which resulted in fewer black athletes admitted to UCLA. Specifically, in 2006 only 20 black athletes were expected to enroll, compared to 27 the prior year. Thus, if the NCAA had not changed its rules, UCLA would likely have enrolled approximately 7 more black students. Accordingly, its net increase, compared to the year before, in total undergraduate black enrollment would have been not 2, but approximately 7 more, or 9. (University officials told me that Trounson was given this information. However, the only part that she reported was that 20 of the 96 incoming black freshmen were athletes, not that this was a decrease from the year before, nor that this decrease was caused by new NCAA rules.)
- Attitudes among UCLA faculty and staff are extremely politically correct, and they strongly favor preferences for racial minorities. The best evidence of this came in 1996, when California voters passed Proposition 209, which disallowed public universities to consider race in admissions. After it was implemented, black admissions decreased by approximately 50 percent.[5] Thus, Proposi-

tion 209 revealed that when law did not constrain UCLA's ability to practice racial preferences, about half of all black students would not have been admitted had their skin color been different.

- Other evidence of the politically correct attitudes at UCLA was how the university changed its admissions rules in response to Proposition 209. Shortly after the new law and the resulting decrease in black admissions, UCLA created a *Life Challenge Index* to help judge applicants. This gave students additional points if, for example, their parents were poor, the quality of their high school was low, or if they faced a physical handicap. While most of the factors in the index were fairly uncontroversial, some were not. For instance, a student gained a point if he or she was a single parent. Also controversial was the motivation behind the Life Challenge Index. As no one denies, it was designed to be a proxy for race.
- Like many universities, UCLA rewards high school students who take difficult classes, especially Advanced Placement classes. Students who take these classes receive a grade from their own high school and a score from a national, standardized test. The test helps to eliminate idiosyncratic factors such as varying degrees of grade inflation at high schools. UCLA, however, ignores the scores from the national test; it considers only the grade that the student's high school reports. The reason, as one of my senior colleagues on the committee told me, is that if UCLA did consider scores from the standardized test, fewer minority students would be admitted.
- Many aspects of the UCLA admissions process violated the spirit of Proposition 209, if not its letter. Although sociologist Darnell Hunt said the campus was doing less than it could, an argument could be made that the campus was doing *more* than it could, at least legally.
- Students who apply to UCLA are aware of the politically correct, pro-racial-preference attitudes, and in order to exploit them, a large number of minority students reveal their race on the personal essays that they write in their applications.
- Although they would not say it, the pro-racial-preferences groups wanted a "holistic" system so that all readers could learn the race of applicants via the personal essays. In contrast, the old system allowed only some of the application readers to see the personal essays.

- Although the article noted that African Americans comprised 9.8 percent of the residents in Los Angeles County, it did not note that African Americans comprised only 4.6 percent of the applicants to UCLA.
- Only 31 percent of the students expected to enroll at UCLA in 2006 were white, just short of a record low. (Although Trounson did not mention this fact in the *text* of her article, a careful reader would learn this from a pie chart that accompanied the article.)

Omitted Statistics and Distortion Theory

"There are three kinds of lies. Lies, damned lies, and statistics." Although Benjamin Disraeli is sometimes given credit for that quote, usually the authorship is attributed to Mark Twain. Twain's point was a condemnation not so much of statistics, but rather of how humans can manipulate them.

If the *Times* article had just listed two or three of the above statistics and facts, then it would have conveyed a very different tenor.

A key point of this book is that dozens, and maybe hundreds, of facts and statistics are relevant to a given issue. Some of these facts and statistics are ones that a conservative would think important. Others are ones that a liberal would think important. It is impossible for a journalist to report all the facts—there are simply not enough pages in a newspaper or minutes in a newscast. He or she can only report a sample.

In general, journalists do not give us a representative sample. Instead—partly because of their own ideological views, and partly because of some institutional factors within the news industry—they give us a biased sample. That is, journalists are more likely to report facts and statistics that liberals want you to learn and less likely to report facts and statistics that conservatives want you to learn.

Stated differently, while the job of a journalist is to shine light on facts, in the current state of the U.S. media, journalists do not shine their light straight. Instead it is as if they use a prism, bending the light and causing it to make a left turn. The end result is that we, the readers and viewers of the news, are more likely to see facts from the left side of the spectrum. This is what I mean by a *distortion theory* of media bias. Such behavior of journalists also causes our political views to make a left turn—that is, to become more liberal.

Lies, Damned Lies, and Quotes from Experts

Let me now examine another biased aspect of the *Los Angeles Times* article: the sources whom the journalist chose to quote.

Like the facts and statistics of her article, the quotes that Trounson reported are also an illustration of distortion theory. The problem is not that the quotes were false, but that, except for a few cases, they offered the perspective of only one side of the political aisle. More specific, although the majority of the American public opposes racial preferences in college admissions, almost all the quotes were from strong supporters of affirmative action.

Specifically, the article contained quotes from six people:

1. Karume James, UCLA senior and chairman of the Afrikan Student Union;
2. Jenny Wood, president of the UCLA student government;
3. Darnell Hunt, UCLA sociology professor and director of UCLA's Ralph Bunche Center for African American Studies;
4. Janina Montero, vice-chancellor of student affairs at UCLA;
5. Albert Carnesale, chancellor of UCLA; and
6. Ward Connerly, a former regent of the University of California system and the author of Proposition 209.

Consistent with distortion theory, none of the quotations, in my judgment, were false. Most, in fact, were simply opinions.

For instance, "I think it's been really detrimental to see this decline in African American students, and, overall, in the number of students of color on our campus," said Jenny Wood in the article. The premise of Wood's statement—that the number of African American freshmen has declined since Proposition 209 passed—is doubted by no one. Slightly more controversial is her claim that this fact is detrimental. Earlier, I discussed how social scientists distinguish between normative and positive statements. Wood's statement is clearly a normative one. Thus, it does not make sense to call it true *or* false.

Another quote involved Carnesale describing the admission numbers as "a great disappointment." Once again, this is simply an opinion.

Some other quotes involved statements of fact that no one would claim as false. For instance, the article noted that "[Carnesale] and other officials at UCLA and elsewhere said that the problem of attracting, admitting, and enrolling qualified black students is found at competitive universities across the country and that its causes are complex."

The problem with the quotes is that, although they *appear* to come from a balance of perspectives, this is far from the case.

The first three people in the list are not just left wing; they are more left wing than the average Democrat. This is especially true of their views on affirmative action.

The first two, Karume James and Jenny Wood, were leaders of UCLA's Student Power, a coalition within UCLA's student government. The "mother groups" of Student Power, as its leaders call them, are racial minority groups—such as the Afrikan Student Union and MEChA—and other far-left groups, such as the Gay, Lesbian, and Transgender Association. The coalition was so left wing that the UCLA student Democratic association, the Bruin Democrats, broke with the coalition and joined the opposing student-government coalition, which happened to include the Bruin Republicans. That's right—Student Power was so far left that mainstream Democrats felt closer to Republicans than to it.

The third person on the list is Darnell Hunt, a professor of sociology at UCLA. He is also the director of the Bunche Center for African American Studies. According to several UCLA sources, he is at least as left wing as James and Wood, and he favors affirmative action at least as much as the two students. (He did not respond to my attempts to interview him.)

The fourth and fifth people on the list were senior administrators at UCLA. Albert Carnesale was the chancellor of UCLA. According to UCLA colleagues, his views are mainstream liberal. However, on foreign policy issues he will often take a centrist, at times even right-leaning stance. A "Hubert Humphrey Democrat" was how one colleague described him.

Janina Montero was the vice chancellor of student affairs. Her views are also mainstream liberal, perhaps slightly left of Carnesale's. "I find myself usually agreeing with Jimmy Carter and Bill Clinton," she said when I asked her to describe her political views. "It's hard to say, it's still so early. Maybe John Edwards," she said when I asked her in 2006 whom she most favored for the 2008 presidential election.

"Three of the people," I asked Montero, "whom the *L.A. Times* journalist interviewed were Karume James, Jenny Wood, and Darnell Hunt. According to everyone I've talked to, all three have extremely left-wing or progressive views. Would you say that you, Chancellor Carnesale, and Ward Connerly provide balance to their opinions?"

"Probably not," she said. "Just look at my quote. It's on the affirmative-action side. But I'd say my quote provided not so much political balance as institutional balance—balance in the sense of students on one side and the administration on the other."

The final person on the list is Ward Connerly. His political views are clearly right of center, and indeed he was appointed to the UC Regents by Republican governor Pete Wilson. Through him, Trounson's article provides some genuine conservative perspective.

The following are the two paragraphs of the article that refer to him or quote him:

> Ward Connerly, the conservative former UC regent who was an architect of Proposition 209, countered that the issue was not the law he helped to create.
>
> [Part of the problem, he said, is the small number of black students who are academically competitive. Another problem is that many black students choose to attend historically black colleges.] "But I don't think we solve this problem by tinkering with the admissions criteria to make it easier to get in."

Although the article gives *some* conservative perspective, it by no means gives equal treatment to the conservative perspective.

First, five out of six of the people quoted have left-of-center views, only one has right-of-center views.

Second, three of the six have *far*-left views. In contrast, none of the six has far-right views. Connerly, although right-leaning, is not as conservative, I believe, as the average Republican. For instance, he has a strong libertarian streak, and in fact, he once angered conservatives when he aided an effort to grant domestic-partner benefits to gay and lesbian couples at California universities.

Third, liberals and conservatives by no means received equal space in the article. Thirteen paragraphs were devoted to describing or quoting the three far-left individuals. Four paragraphs were devoted to describing or quoting the two mainstream liberals, Carnesale and Montero. Only two paragraphs were devoted to describing or quoting the lone conservative, Connerly.

A final asymmetry involves the way the article *described* the people who were quoted. Note how the article introduced Connerly, as "the conservative former UC regent." The article did not brand any of the five left-of-center individuals with an ideological label.

How the Article Illustrates Themes of This Book

The article illustrates many of the general themes that I will address in this book. First, the article has a clear liberal bias. That is, it reports the main facts that liberals would want you to learn, while it largely omits the main facts that conservatives would want you to learn. Further, it clearly offers more expert quotes from liberals than conservatives.

Second, although the article clearly has a liberal bias, the bias is not that strong. That is, the slant, although liberal, could have been much more liberal than it was. For instance, Trounson *does* quote a conservative, Ward Connerly. She also quotes Albert Carnesale, the chancellor of UCLA. Some of his remarks, it could be argued, were centrist, perhaps even right-leaning. Moreover, the article mentions a few key facts that conservatives would want you to learn. For instance, one is that Proposition 209 was the cause of much of the decline in freshmen black admissions at UCLA. Another, which a reader could glean from a graph that accompanies the article, is that white students comprised only about a third of recent freshmen classes.

As I note in chapter 1, my main methods to measure media bias revolve around a thought experiment—specifically, where I ask you to pretend that a news story was a congressional speech and I ask you to guess the PQ of the would-be politician.

Now suppose we perform the thought experiment on the *Los Angeles Times* article. By my judgment, the article indeed sounds like a speech by a Democrat—however, not one by a far-left Democrat, such as Al Franken or Barbara Boxer. In my view it sounds more like a speech by Joe Lieberman or Evan Bayh (D-Ind.). More precisely, if I had to guess, I would say that the article's Slant Quotient is approximately a 70 or 75. As I show in later chapters, this happens to be the score of the average news story from outlets such as the *Los Angeles Times*, *The New York Times*, the *CBS Evening News*, and many other mainstream news organizations.

A SECOND WAY the article illustrates themes of the book is its impact. It indeed changed peoples' views. People really began to believe, as the article insinuated, that UCLA was not concerned about admitting more African American students. In fact, as a conservative friend told me, "It made UCLA seem like it just didn't care about black students. I have to admit, when I read the article, I thought that that was true."

The article also changed policy. Shortly after it ran, Albert Carnesale, the UCLA chancellor, ended his term. He was replaced by Acting Chancellor Norman Abrams. Abrams soon began to feel pressure to alter UCLA's admissions process. The pressure came from many quarters, including donors and black alumni groups. Two months after the article appeared, the chair of the faculty oversight committee for admissions, on which I served, called a special meeting to discuss a possible new admissions policy. Almost unprecedented for the committee, the UCLA chancellor, Norman Abrams, asked to attend the meeting and address the committee.

"First, I want say how much I favor and respect faculty governance," he began. "I don't want to pressure you. But at the same time, we worry about many of the same things. I want to report to you what we are hearing from the outside world. Several constituencies of UCLA are distressed and upset about the very low numbers of African American freshmen. The political angst and concern is enormous. I don't feel the pressure. I sublimate very well. But there *is* pressure exerted *upon* me. The numbers of underrepresented minorities on campus are too small. . . .

"I ask that you make the whole admissions process holistic," Abrams concluded. "Not only that, I have a further request: This is that you adopt the exact same process that Berkeley currently uses."

After some minor debate, the committee did exactly that.

Recall that the *Los Angeles Times* article quotes Darnell Hunt, the sociology professor and director of the Ralph Bunche Center for African American Studies. He was a coauthor of the report that advocated that UCLA adopt a "holistic" system like UC Berkeley's.

Within three months of the *Los Angeles Times* article, UCLA adopted exactly the system that Hunt advocated.

Coda

Twelve days after the committee voted to implement the holistic system, Rebecca Trounson wrote another article about UCLA for the *Los Angeles Times*. This one focused on Abrams, the new chancellor.

The headline was "UCLA's Interim Chief Is Shaking Things Up: In Less Than Two Months on the Job, Norman Abrams Has Shown That He Is Unafraid of Making Difficult Decisions."

The article was very flattering, and it contained many complimentary quotes. One noted Abrams's "galvanizing" leadership. Another noted the "bold, forward progress" he was making.

The "Daily Planet" Theory of Story Selection, and Why It's Wrong

According to many people's worldview, journalists choose topics according to a *Daily Planet* theory. That is, like Clark Kent, Lois Lane, and other reporters in the old Superman television show, journalists do not select their own stories; their editor selects them for them. Or, in the rare cases where he does not select them, the topics just magically appear, as if Nature has an official process for determining which events should and should not be covered in the news. According to the *Daily Planet* theory, the creativity and judgment of journalists have no bearing on the topics they report.

However, the truth is almost exactly the opposite. Instead, reporters are usually assigned specialty beats, and they are allowed much freedom to decide which stories they write about, as long as the stories fall within their beat. For instance, Trounson verified to me that no editor assigned her to do a story about African American students and UCLA admissions. That choice was hers.

Between sips of coffee in the cafeteria at the Los Angeles Times Building, Trounson answered my background questions, such as why she'd entered journalism and how long she'd worked at the *Los Angeles Times*. She was not completely comfortable. She was aware that I had done research on media bias, and although she was convinced that she was not guilty of it, she knew that I would eventually ask a question such as the following: "Three of the people you quoted were Karume James, Jenny Wood, and Darnell Hunt. Every person I've talked to says that their political views are far left. The other three you quoted were . . ."

"But their political views have nothing to do with the story I was writing," said Trounson.

"What about their views on affirmative action," I responded. "Isn't that relevant?"

"I don't see how I could possibly write the story without quoting them," she said. "Karume James was the president of the Afrikan Student Union. Jenny Wood was the student-government president, and she had created a work group to study race and admissions. They are student leaders at UCLA. How could I not ask for their observations? Darnell Hunt's group was writing a report about UCLA admissions. Of course I'd quote him."

As I now write from the solitude of my own office, let me respond to Trounson's statements.

SHE'S RIGHT. If a journalist is writing a story about the declining number of freshmen African Americans at UCLA, it's true, it would be irresponsible for her *not* to seek quotes from those three people.

The problem is the "if" part of the statement. Once she chose to focus on the 96 figure—the number of African Americans expected to enroll as freshmen—there is almost no way the story would not have a liberal bias. In such a story it is natural, perhaps imperative, to quote leaders of far-left student racial groups, to ask questions of university officials that make them look defensive, and in general to present a picture that causes many readers to believe that UCLA creates obstacles for black students to be admitted.

At this point, you may be thinking, "How can you say that such a story has a liberal slant? It's either true or it's not. No one denies that the 96 statistic is true. Therefore, the story has no bias."

But that is the whole point of distortion theory. Any person with pro-affirmative-action opinions strongly wants you to read Trounson's article. If you are on the fence on affirmative action, the article would probably even tilt you toward favoring affirmative action. Meanwhile, a person with an anti-affirmative-action view would prefer that you not read the article.

"Sweetie, You Missed the Real Story"

"Oh, standard academic liberal. Just like everyone else," said Professor Barbara Packer when I asked about her political views.

Packer teaches English at UCLA. Like me, she was on the UCLA faculty oversight committee for admissions. While I thought the Trounson article was biased, I realized that maybe that perception was due to my conservative views. Maybe moderates or liberals would not see a bias. That was why one spring afternoon I visited Packer's office to interview her.

"Oh, not Hubert Humphrey," she exclaimed, as I searched for a public figure who might represent her views. "He couldn't distance himself from Johnson and the war. I voted for the Peace and Freedom candidate. But look what that got us: Nixon."

Packer grew up near Fresno, California; attended Stanford during the 1960s, where she participated in "my share of anti-war protests"; and continued her studies at Yale, where she earned her PhD.

She is left-of-center on affirmative action and genuinely wishes that UCLA could increase its number of African American students. "I know parents of minority students are furiously angry, and I don't blame them," she said.

But at the same time, she did not have many compliments for the *Los Angeles Times* article.

"It wasn't so much that," she explained when I asked if she was outraged by it. "It was 'Not again.' I almost wrote the author and said, 'Sweetie, you missed the real story.' There's a total disconnect between what's really happening and what you read in the papers. What's frustrating is what they're *not* talking about—the decline in white enrollment. I think that's the real story. The media always portrays it as if it's white versus black. The real story is the increase in Asian students.

"White students are only something like 33 percent," continued Packer. "I bet forty years ago it was like 80 or 85 percent. What would happen if one day you picked up an *L.A. Times* and saw 'Anglo Enrollment Plummets at UCLA.' That's the real story."

She mentioned an annual awards ceremony at UCLA, hosted by an alumni association. "The people in the audience were nearly all Anglos," she said, "older people who attended UCLA when it was mostly white. And all the award winners were nonwhite. Lots of Asians. But also some blacks and Latinos. And also lots of Persians and Russian Armenians. We used to announce all the winners. But it got so hard to pronounce the names. We now just put a microphone on stage and let the students state their own name.

"Twenty years ago North Campus [where humanities and social-science classes are generally taught] used to be a place where you'd see a bunch of blond surfer types," said Packer. "They've vanished.

"But [the journalists] beat the same old dead horse. They put their pie charts in, and they don't even look at them. It's as if the truth is visible, but at the same time invisible. It's like those posters that were popular five or ten years ago. There would be some picture, but then you'd stare at it for a long time and you'd see a hidden design, like 'Oh, I see it now; it's a seven.' I could never see those things. That's the way reporters seem to be."

"I Don't Know. Give Me an Example of a Conservative Topic"

Although Trounson refused to tell me her political views, I am willing to bet that they are left-of-center. Her choice to make the 96 number the focus of a story, although not proof, is evidence.

If she had been a conservative, she more likely would have focused on a different topic. For instance, she might have written a story on (i) the record *increase* in black transfer students, (ii) the motivation behind the Life Challenge Index and how it might have violated the spirit, if not the letter, of Proposition 209, (iii) how few Republican students enroll at UCLA, (iv) the special problems that home-schooled students face in the UCLA admissions process (e.g., they do not receive grades, which makes it difficult for admissions staff to evaluate them), or (v) the surprisingly large number of UCLA applicants who reveal their race on their personal essays.

Or if she had been just a "standard academic liberal," who thought Hubert Humphrey was not liberal enough, yet had taught at UCLA long enough to know the whole story about admissions, she might have decided to write a story about the declining number of white students.

All the latter stories are just as true as the one she did write, but they have different political implications. Further, they influence the political views of readers in different ways.

Even if a reporter has no ideological axe to grind, his or her political views can still cause a bias. We all have a tendency to associate with people who agree with us. Thus, a liberal reporter, who is more likely to run in circles with fellow liberals, is more likely to learn facts that liberals are more aware of—facts such as that UCLA was enrolling fewer black freshmen. Meanwhile, a conservative reporter is more likely to learn facts such as that the number of black *transfer* students had increased, that UCLA was employing a Life Challenge Index, and that racial minorities often revealed their race on admission essays.

I have talked to many reporters, and almost all of them are completely convinced that as long as they report only true statements, then their reporting has no bias. The main aspects of distortion theory, I suspect, will genuinely be things they never have considered.

Indeed, when I talked to Trounson, just after she refused to tell me her political views, she said, "I don't see how they affect what I write."

"What about the *topics* you write about?" I responded. "Don't your political views influence whether you choose conservative or liberal topics?"

She paused for a moment. "I don't know. Give me an example of a conservative topic."

My goal in the next chapter is to answer that question, to provide some examples of conservative topics, to show that such things as conservative and liberal topics really do exist.

7. Hidden Under a Bushel

Distortion Theory and News Topics

Below are four stories that conservatives would like you to learn. Each would cause a moderate to become slightly more conservative. Each is a story that in my judgment is not just true, but also important enough that it should have been covered by *all* mainstream media outlets. However, with each, a significant number of mainstream outlets—usually ones that my methods estimate as liberal—ignored it.

1. An Inefficient, and Possibly Corrupt, New Orleans City Government During the Cleanup of Hurricane Katrina

The following are the first three paragraphs of a front-page story that appeared on March 19, 2006, in the New Orleans *Times-Picayune*.

> Katrina turned New Orleans into an auto junkyard and flooded cars are still everywhere, mementos of the storm and of the city's continuing failure to clean itself up.
>
> Almost seven months after Hurricane Katrina, the [Mayor Ray] Nagin administration still dickers over details of a contract that would gradually rid the cityscape of those vehicular eyesores—at a cost of $23 million over another six months.
>
> Which makes it more than passing interest to discover that the largest car crusher east of the Rockies, K&L Auto Crushers of Tyler,

> Texas, offered in October to do the job in 15 weeks and actually pay the city for the privilege of hauling the junk away. How much? How about $100 per flooded car. With an estimated 50,000 vehicles on the street at that time, the city would have netted $5 million, rather than shelling out four times that sum, as it plans to do now.[1]

For at least three reasons this story is, I believe, a conservative one. First, it contrasts the inefficiency of government with the efficiency of private enterprise. Second, it suggests that the city government of New Orleans—headed by Democrats—was inept and possibly corrupt. (Indeed, three days later the *Times-Picayune* ran another story revealing that out of fourteen bids to remove the cars, the city government chose the one with the *highest* cost.[2]) Third, it suggests that people may have misplaced blame for the inept initial response to Hurricane Katrina. That is, most liberals blamed George W. Bush for the poor response. However, many conservatives blamed Louisiana governor Kathleen Blanco and Mayor Nagin, both Democrats. The story suggests that Nagin may deserve more blame than he actually received—that his administration was less competent than we initially thought—and that Bush and Blanco were more competent than we initially thought.

The story, I believe, was interesting and important enough that it should have been covered by all major national media outlets. It was covered, however, by only one, *Special Report with Brit Hume.*

2. "No, no, no, not God Bless America, God damn America"

On April 13, 2003, Jeremiah Wright, Barack Obama's pastor for twenty years, gave a sermon that included the now-famous passage:

> When it came to treating her citizens of African descent fairly, America failed. . . . The government gives the drugs, builds bigger prisons, passes a three-strike law and then wants us to sing "God Bless America." No, no, no, not God Bless America. God damn America.[3]

For five years, few outside Wright's church knew about the sermon. But then, on March 13, 2008, during the heat of the Democratic primary, ABC's *Good Morning America* broke the story and showed clips of the sermon. That day, Fox News and a handful of other outlets echoed the report.

The next day, Barack Obama released a written statement denouncing the sermon. "I vehemently disagree and strongly condemn the statements that have been the subject of this controversy," he wrote. "In sum, I reject outright the statements by Rev. Wright that are at issue."

However, the day before, Obama had struck a slightly different tone. He said that he had not attended the sermon. He also indicated that he was surprised at the words—that they were uncharacteristic of the usual sermon by Wright. "[H]ere is what happens," said Obama, "when you just cherry-pick statements from a guy who had a 40-year career."[4] "It's as if we took the five dumbest things that I've ever said or you've ever said in our lives and compressed them and put them out there—I think that people's reaction would, understandably, be upset."[5]

In a moment, I'll explain why this story is a conservative one, and I'll also explain how the media treated it. But before I do that, it's worthwhile to discuss an aspect that, as far as I am aware, no journalist or pundit has ever noted: this is *how the parishioners reacted* when Wright uttered the passage. Namely, they did not act as if the sermon was unusual.

If you watch the tape, you see six choir members behind Wright. Prior to the "God damn" part of the speech, all sit quietly and listen attentively.

But then Wright's fervor builds: "The government gives the drugs, builds bigger prisons, passes a three-strike law . . ."

A member of the audience shouts, "Yeah." One of the six choir members in camera view begins shaking his fist in agreement.

Wright continues, ". . . and then wants us to sing 'God Bless America'. No, no, no." A second choir member raises her hand, waving it rhythmically. A few more members of the audience yell in agreement. Several more begin to clap.

Wright, who has begun waving his own hand rhythmically and pointing to his printed sermon, continues, "God *damn* America." The fist-pumping choir member stands up and begins clapping.

Wright points to his Bible on the pulpit. "It's in the Bible, for killing innocent people. God damn America for treating her citizens as less than human." The camera pans to show several members of the audience. Approximately one quarter are standing. Several more are clapping or waving their hands.

The camera pans back to Wright. By now, a third member of the choir is clapping. "God damn America," Wright continues, "as long as she tries to act like she is God and she is supreme. The United States government has failed the vast majority of her citizens of African descent."

The parishioners, in sum, did not seem surprised by the sermon or act as if it were unusual. Indeed, their reaction suggested that Wright's controversial passage agreed with their own views.

In contrast, from my vantage point, Barack Obama genuinely seems to love America and to be proud of it. I do not believe, for instance, that he thinks that God should damn America—even if, as Wright claims, it is guilty of social-justice shortcomings.

Accordingly, it is a mystery how Obama could attend the church for twenty years and be comfortable with the views of his fellow parishioners.

This news story, few will disagree, is one that conservatives want you to hear and liberals don't want you to hear. Indeed, Obama quickly denounced the sermon. The reason, I believe, was to make the story disappear from the news cycle as fast as possible. Further, as we now know, far-left members of the JournoList listserv tried to squelch the story.[6] For instance, Chris Hayes of *The Nation* urged his colleagues, "particularly those in the ostensible mainstream media," to ignore it. "I'm not saying we should all rush en masse to defend Wright," wrote Hayes. "If you don't think he's worthy of defense, don't defend him! What I'm saying is that there is no earthly reason to use our various platforms to discuss what about Wright we find objectionable."[7]

In addition to hurting Obama's campaign, there's another reason why Wright's sermon is a conservative story. It bolsters the famous dictum of Jeane Kirkpatrick—that liberals are often members of the "blame America first" crowd. For instance, Wright criticized the United States for bombing Japan, but he failed to mention why the United States might deserve praise for the act—e.g., that it helped end World War II, on net might have saved lives, and possibly saved the world from tyranny.

The video revealed that Wright's views are caustic and extreme. However, before ABC broke the story, almost no pundit or journalist had discussed this fact. The major exception was Sean Hannity. Between March 1, 2007, and March 10, 2008, he or a guest on his show had criticized Wright on fourteen different occasions.

Indeed, of all members of the media, Hannity I believe, held the most suspicion of Wright. However, contrary to conservative folklore, Hannity did not break the story of the "God damn America" sermon. That was done by Brian Ross of ABC News.

Ross reported the story on the morning of March 13, 2008. That afternoon and evening, Fox covered it extensively. ABC covered it again on its evening news show. However, it was ignored by almost all other major outlets, including CBS, NBC, NPR, the *NewsHour,* and the Drudge Report.

Although CNN covered it, albeit just barely, its anchor Anderson Cooper discussed on air his reluctance to cover it. He said:

> All this seems to have nothing to do with the actual issues that the country is facing, which these candidates should be talking about and we probably should be talking about. . . . On the one hand, I mean,

> people are talking about it. It's clearly an issue that is building up in the campaign trail, so we end up covering it. But at the same time, it does feel just completely off track.[8]

The next morning, the story was ignored by nearly every major newspaper, including the *Los Angeles Times, USA Today,* and *The Washington Post.* Although the editorial page of *The Wall Street Journal* discussed some of Reverend Wright's remarks (but not the "God damn America" passage), its news pages ignored the story. *The New York Times* wrote only four sentences about Wright—and buried them on page eighteen. The *Times* did not mention the "God damn America" passage, only that Wright made "stinging social and political critiques in the pulpit."[9]

The next afternoon, Obama condemned the words of Wright. After he did this, nearly all the major outlets did a U-turn and covered the story. Even MSNBC's Keith Olbermann reported it. However, by that point the focus of the story was not Reverend Wright but rather, the fact that Obama had condemned him. Given that many people had already seen the clip—and many more were sure to see it in the future—the new focus made it a liberal story. That is, a liberal would have *wanted* you to learn that Obama condemned the words of Wright. Meanwhile, a conservative would have preferred that you *not* learn that.

3. Van Jones, Green Jobs Czar

On September 5, 2009, *The New York Times* ran a half-page, twenty-five-paragraph story about Betsy McCaughey, the Republican former lieutenant governor of New York.[10] The article was very critical; one could even call it a hit piece. For instance, the first two paragraphs discussed her divorce from billionaire Wilbur Ross and her failed bid to become governor. The fourth paragraph noted that because of statements made by McCaughey, her friend author Erica Jong had resigned in protest from a charity that McCaughey had founded.

The story was very factual—e.g., not one sentence would I describe as an opinion of the writer. Further it was accurate. For instance, the article noted that McCaughey had made a false claim about a Democratic health care bill. Specifically, she had said that the bill would "absolutely require" counseling sessions for Medicare recipients "that will tell them how to end their life sooner." The statement is indeed false in my judgment. In fact, as the *Times* noted, the statement drew a "Pants on Fire" rating from PolitiFact, a fact-checking Web site.

What is most curious is why *The New York Times* would devote so much space to a *former* politician, who was almost completely unknown to anybody outside of New York. Her only newsworthy event—and the focus of the story—was that she had made some critical statements about the Democrats' health care plan, at least one of which turned out to be false.

Meanwhile, during the week before the *Times* published the article about McCaughey, the newspaper ignored a very explosive story: the controversy surrounding President Obama's Green Jobs Czar, Van Jones.

For several weeks, a number of conservatives—most prominently, Glenn Beck—had been reporting inflammatory revelations about Jones. These included:

- At least for a time, Jones was a self-avowed communist. Specifically, he told a reporter, "[In jail] I met all these young radical people of color. I mean, really radical, communists and anarchists. And it was, like hey, this is what I need to be a part of. . . . I spent the next ten years of my life working with a lot of those people I met in jail, trying to be a revolutionary. . . . I was a rowdy nationalist on April 28th, and then the verdicts came down on April 29th. By August, I was a communist."[11] (Jones had been arrested while protesting the Rodney King beating; charges against him were later dropped.)
- Jones was a founding member of STORM (Standing Together to Organize a Revolutionary Movement). A book written by its members noted, "STORM was never formally a Marxist-Leninist organization, and we never had a systematic Marxist theoretical framework. But we did have a poltical commitment to the fundamental ideas of Marxism and Leninism. We upheld the Marxist critique of capitalist exploitation. We agree with Lenin's analysis of the state and the party. And we found inspiration and guidance in the insurgent revolutionary strategies developed by third-world revolutionaries like Mao Tse-Tung and Amilcar Cabral."[12]
- In a public speech, Jones noted: "The white polluters and the white environmentalists are essentially steering poison into the people-of-color communities."[13]

Here, briefly, is the timeline of the final few days of the Van Jones controversy. It culminated with a middle-of-the-night resignation. This occurred early Sunday morning, just past midnight, approximately eighteen hours after the *Times* ran its story on McCaughey.

On the Tuesday before, the Web site DefendGlenn.com posted a video of Jones giving a speech in which he called Republicans "a**holes."

On Wednesday, Jones sent a written statement to *Politico*. "I apologize for the offensive words I chose to use during that speech," he wrote.[14] "They do not reflect the views of this administration, which has made every effort to work in a bipartisan fashion, and they do not reflect the experience I have had since I joined the administration."

On Thursday, the blog Gateway Pundit reported that in 2004 Jones had signed a petition circulated by the group 911Truth.org. The petition suggested that members of the Bush Administration knew that the 9/11 attacks would occur. As it stated, "people within the administration may indeed have deliberately allowed 9/11 to happen; perhaps as a pretext to war."[15]

On Thursday evening, Jones issued another apology, this one for the 911Truth petition. "In recent days," he said, "some in the news media have reported on past statements I made before I joined the administration—some of which were made years ago. If I have offended anyone with statements I made in the past, I apologize. As for the petition that was circulated today, I do not agree with this statement and it certainly does not reflect my views now or ever."

On Friday, Rep. Mike Pence (R-Ind.) called on Jones to resign or be fired.[16] "His extremist views and coarse rhetoric," Pence wrote, "have no place in this administration or the public debate."

On the same day, Sen. Christopher Bond (R-Mo.) urged Congress to investigate Jones.[17] "Can the American people," Bond wrote, "trust a senior White House official that is so cavalier in his association with such radical and repugnant sentiments?"

Also on Friday, White House press secretary Robert Gibbs offered extremely faint praise for Jones. As *The Washington Post* reported,

> Gibbs said Friday that Jones "continues to work for the administration"—but he did not state that the adviser enjoys the full support of President Obama, instead referring all questions to the environmental council where he works.[18]

A day and a half after Gibbs's statement, shortly after midnight, Jones resigned. He timed his resignation, I believe, so that the Sunday morning newspapers could not cover it.

Nevertheless, on Monday, even *The New York Times* covered it. Indeed, it placed the story on its front page. "White House Official Resigns After Flood of G.O.P. Criticism" was the headline.[19] It noted all the major aspects of the controversy, including that Jones had signed the 911Truth petition and that he had "used a vulgarity to refer to Republicans." In general, the article, I believe, had not a hint of liberal bias.

Yet it had one major problem: If the *Times* had been your only source of news during the prior week, then you would have known nothing about the controversy. When you saw Monday's article, you would have wondered, "How'd I miss all this?"

The Van Jones saga, no doubt, is a conservative story. It makes the Obama administration look bad, possibly filled with closeted far-left radicals. During the week before Jones resigned, very few national news organizations covered his saga. Of the twenty outlets that I examined in my article with Milyo, only six covered it: Fox News *Special Report, The Washington Times,* CNN, the Drudge Report, *The Washington Post,* and *CBS Evening News.* The other fourteen ignored it.[20]

Meanwhile, the Betsey McCaughey story, no one will doubt, is a liberal story. During the five days before Van Jones's resignation, *The New York Times* was the only national news organization to report a story focusing on her.[21]

4. Voting According to Skin Color in the 2008 Election

Among political scientists, many of us suspect that a significant number of voters base their choices, at least partly, on the skin color of candidates. However, because voters are reluctant to say this to pollsters, the suspicion is difficult to test.

Simon Jackman and Lynn Vavreck, political scientists at Stanford and UCLA respectively, have devised a clever way to test such suspicions.[22] Following the "list experiment" method introduced by James Kuklinksi, Michael Cobb, and Martin Gilens, they constructed a sample of white adults who said they voted against Obama.[23] They split this sample into two groups, a "treatment" and a "control" group. To each member of the treatment group, they asked the question, "How many of the following characteristics are important to you as reasons not to vote for Obama?[24]

1) His public speaking ability.
2) Iraq policy.
3) Environmental policy.
4) Health care plan.
5) He's a Democrat.
6) He's black.

For the control group, the researchers asked the same question, but listed only the first five choices. Most important, they eliminated "He's black" as a possible reason to vote against Obama.

By comparing the difference in the average (numerical) answer between the two groups, the researchers could calculate the probability that a random respondent had voted against Obama because "He's black." For instance, suppose that the treatment group, on average, said that 4.43 of the characteristics were important, while the control group said that 4.10 of the characteristics were important. Then the researchers would estimate that of the people who voted against Obama, 33 percent (=4.43–4.10) did so partly because "He's black."

The researchers found, however, that the average answer across the two groups was the *same*. Namely, the average member of the treatment group said that 3.3 of the characteristics were important; while the average member of the control group also said that 3.3 of the characteristics were important. Although the researchers (and probably all other knowledgeable observers) expected the former number to be greater than the latter, it was not. The result suggests that the fraction of people who voted against Obama because "He's black" was 3.3 minus 3.3, or *0*.

The researchers also conducted the opposite experiment. That is, they asked the same question to white *supporters* of Obama. In their control group (i.e. those who were not offered the "He's black" choice) the subjects on average said that 4 of the choices were important. Meanwhile, the average member of the treatment group said 4.2 of the choices were important. The difference in the two numbers, 0.2, suggests that 20 percent of white Obama supporters had voted for him partly because "He's black." Thus, the Jackman-Vavreck study suggests that, if anything, Obama's skin color *helped* him in the 2008 election.[25]

This news story, the findings of the Jackman-Vavreck study, is a conservative one, I believe, for at least two reasons. First, it suggests that reverse racism in America is stronger than traditional racism. Such a fact weakens the case for affirmative action, which liberals tend to favor.

Second, it undermines a claim that liberals commonly make: This is that the mandate for Obama's policies was stronger than his vote totals indicated. That is, according to many liberals, Obama proposed wise and popular policies; however, his vote totals understated this fact because of voters' racism. The results of Jackman and Vavreck, however, undermine that claim.

To date, no national media outlet has reported the results of the Jackman-Vavreck study.

Race, Ethnicity, and the Stories Journalists Choose to Pursue

Besides their conservative nature, did you notice a common theme to the four conservative stories? All of them, at least indirectly, involved race or ethnicity. Each portrayed an oppressed minority in an unflattering light. Accordingly, each story, if people learned about it, could harm, at least in minor ways, the advancement of the oppressed minority.

For instance, in the first story New Orleans mayor Ray Nagin, who is African American, looks mildly incompetent. The second and third stories suggest poor judgment by Barack Obama, the first African American president. Namely, they suggest that he has surrounded himself with far-left radicals. The fourth story suggests that reverse racism is more prevalent than traditional racism,

In addition to these four stories, recall a fifth story, in chapter 6, where I report how UCLA was practicing reverse racism. On top of this, in the next chapter I'll discuss a sixth story involving race and ethnicity—one about "flying imams" getting kicked off an airplane because they were acting suspiciously. As you'll see, the latter story portrays Arab Muslims, another oppressed minority, in a bad light.

If you have even weak preferences for "racial justice," then you should be bothered when oppressed minorities are portrayed so unflatteringly. In your mind, you might even have called me a racist for reporting the stories. At a minimum, you may think it improper or immoral for me to mention the stories.

THERE. IF YOU had any of those thoughts, you have just admitted that factors besides the truth are important for deciding whether an author should report a story. Even if you didn't have such thoughts, you have to admit that other people, especially progressives, will have such thoughts. Further, given that journalists are more progressive than average people, it is natural that they will have such thoughts. And even if a particular journalist doesn't personally have such thoughts, she surely realizes that her colleagues, and many of her readers or viewers, will have such thoughts.

Here, for instance, is how Spencer Ackerman, writing on JournoList, urged fellow reporters to react to the Reverend Wright Story:

> I do not endorse a Popular Front [a term commonly used by communists and socialists indicating a coalition with liberals and centrists], nor do I think you need to. It's not necessary to jump to Wright-qua-Wright's defense. What is necessary is to raise the cost on the right of going after the left. In other words, find a rightwinger's [*sic*] and smash it through a plate-glass window. Take a snapshot of the bleeding mess and send it out in a Christmas card to let the right know that it needs to live in a state of constant fear. Obviously I mean this rhetorically.

> And I think this threads the needle. If the right forces us all to either defend Wright or tear him down, no matter what we choose, we lose the game they've put upon us. Instead take one of them—Fred Barnes, Karl Rove, who cares—and call them racists.[26]

Now consider a journalist, thinking about whether to report a story such as one of the four I listed. The thought will naturally cross her mind, "Should I report this story? Do I really want to be called a racist?"

Further, it's not just race and ethnicity. There are *lots* of factors—besides the truth of a story—that can influence a journalist's decision to pursue it. Consider a comment by another participant of JournoList, Michael Tomasky:

> Listen folks—in my opinion, we all have to do what we can to kill ABC and this idiocy in whatever venues we have. This isn't about defending Obama. This is about how the [mainstream media] kills any chance of discourse that actually serves the people.[27]

Consider his phrase "discourse that actually serves the people." When I use that phrase, I mean discourse that helps to: (i) decrease people's taxes, (ii) strengthen the U.S. military, (iii) protect unborn babies, and (iv) relax environmental regulations that harm business. In contrast, I'm certain that Tomasky means something very different when he says "discourse that serves the people." If you've interacted with progressives enough, you soon learn that phrases such as "serves the people" are really just synonyms for liberal policies.

Now consider a journalist thinking about reporting a story that harms the progressive agenda. She will naturally think, "Do I want my progressive colleagues and readers to accuse me of things like killing 'any chance of discourse that actually serves the people'?" She likely will think twice about reporting the story.

8. An "Alien" Conservative Injected into a Liberal Newsroom and the Topics She Might Cover

ON NOVEMBER 20, 2006, six Muslim imams boarded US Airways Flight 300, traveling from Minneapolis to Phoenix. According to many accounts, the imams acted suspiciously as soon as they boarded the plane.

For instance, as *The Washington Times* reported: (i) They left their assigned seats and instead sat in a pattern associated with the 9/11 terrorist attacks. (ii) Some of them asked for seatbelt extensions, yet none was fat enough to require one; nor did any of them actually use the extensions. (iii) Although the imams claimed that they never spoke about politics and only spoke in English, witnesses contradicted that, noting that they mentioned al Qaeda and Osama bin Laden and that they criticized the Iraq War and President Bush. Witnesses also said that part of the time they talked in Arabic.[1]

After several passengers complained, US Airways removed the imams and refused to reschedule them on another flight. The imams retaliated with a lawsuit against US Airways.

More interesting—and outrageous in my view—the imams also sued some of the passengers on the plane. Specifically, when they filed the lawsuit, they made accusations against a number of "John Does"—passengers whom they planned to name during the discovery part of the trial.

This story, that the imams were suing the passengers on the plane, in my judgment is a conservative one. One reason is that this was a case where it was perhaps reasonable and rational to engage in "racial profiling," an exercise that liberals tend to oppose more strongly than conservatives. Another reason is that the story suggests that terrorism is still a real threat within the United States. Liberals often claim that the threat of terrorism is not so large, even at times making fun of the phrase "war on terror."

The journalist who broke the story, Katherine Kersten of the Minneapolis *Star Tribune*, as you might suspect, is conservative.

Suppose you could peer inside her head at the time she chose that topic. In what ways, if any, did her conservative views give her extra motivation to pursue the story? In what ways, if any, did her conservative views give her special knowledge or expertise to pursue the story?

Now consider the "corporate media" view of journalism—that the personal views of journalists are unimportant; instead, what are most important are the personal views of the journalists' corporate bosses. If that's true, however, consider a liberal reporter, who perhaps has a conservative corporate boss. Could that reporter serve as an adequate substitute for Kersten? That is, is it really possible for a liberal to don the skin of a conservative, muster similar motivation and knowledge as Kersten, and pursue the same story that she pursued?

An Alien Conservative in a Liberal Newsroom

Katherine Kersten, it turns out, obtained her job at the Minneapolis *Star Tribune* because of a special "experiment" at the newspaper. Brian Lambert, writing in *The Rake* magazine, described the experiment:

> When the tinny tinkle of "Joy to the World, the Lord Is Come" begins playing on the cell phone, everyone in range in the *Star Tribune* newsroom knows who's getting a call. It is Katherine Kersten, the paper's unapologetically religious and fiercely conservative metro columnist.
>
> Since May 2005, the *Star Tribune* has been engaged in what its top editor freely describes as "an experiment." The test has Katherine Kersten, a fifty-five-year-old former banker, and think-tank denizen, now an opinion writer, playing the role of an alien element injected into a tradition-bound newspaper culture.
>
> Long battered by conservative critics as the "Red Star" for its alleged knee-jerk liberalism . . . the *Star Tribune* decided it had to answer. For the last twenty months, Kersten has been a one-woman solution, applying a decidedly different, and perhaps revolutionary, face to the role of big-city reporter and metro columnist.[2]

Personality Traits, Worldviews, and Other Factors That Influence the Topics a Journalist Pursues

"Oh, that just happens all the time," said Kersten when I asked if her conservative views ever influence the topics that she covers. "I'd only been on the job a few weeks when I told [an editor], 'You know, you guys are missing half the stories out there.' [The liberal reporters at the *Star Tribune*] don't know the people I know. They don't have the same sources. They all move in the same circles. Many of the stories that I'd just jump on wouldn't interest them at all."

Brit Hume, in an interview on C-SPAN's *Q&A,* echoed her sentiment:

> [If you are willing to pursue the stories that traditional, liberal reporters aren't interested in,] it gets to be like picking up money off the street . . .
>
> We had a wonderful example last week, when the report came out from the [George W. Bush] Administration . . . that fifteen of the eighteen political benchmarks were now showing satisfactory progress in Iraq. And you say, well, that's just the Administration. Well maybe so. But a year earlier the same Administration had said that satisfactory progress had been made only on eight of eighteen. Something had obviously happened. . . . That's a big story. We've made it a big story. I led my broadcast with it. And it was virtually ignored everywhere else. Everywhere else.[3]

Kersten's Article and Its Impact

Before Kersten wrote the "flying imams" story, several journalists had reported aspects of it. What they failed to note, however, was that the lawsuit targeted not just the airline but also unnamed "John Doe" passengers on the flight. "Many of the stories" said Kersten, "did little more than copy facts from the press release of the CAIR [the Council on American-Islamic Relations, an ally of the imams].

"With that story," said Kersten, "the typical reporter would investigate a little and say, 'Nope, nothing more there.' But I did some research on those guys, and there was one, Omar Shahin, who had a very checkered background. When I researched him, it took *so* much time. I worked *so* many hours. Yeah, my conservative perspective definitely contributed. If you're not interested, if you don't see a story, you won't do it. To do these sorts of things, you need to have a sort of antenna up—that there may be something fishy about those guys. Most reporters didn't have that antenna.

"I think I was the only one who actually read that whole court document," she said. "And then, there it was, in that one paragraph. They were suing the 'John Does' on the flight. I thought, 'This is awful.'"

"The Real Target of the 6 Imams' 'Discrimination' Suit," was the headline of her article, which she soon published after reading the court document. Kersten wrote:

> Who are these unnamed culprits? The complaint describes them as "an older couple who was sitting [near the imams] and purposely turn[ed] around to watch" as they prayed. "The gentleman ('John Doe') in the couple . . . picked up his cellular phone and made a phone call while watching the Plaintiffs pray," then "moved to a corner" and "kept talking into his cellular phone."
>
> In retribution for this action, the unnamed couple probably will be dragged into court soon and face the prospect of hiring a lawyer, enduring hostile questioning and paying huge legal bills. The same fate could await other as-yet-unnamed passengers on the US Airways flight who came forward as witnesses.[4]

Within hours after the *Star Tribune* published her article, Power Line, the Web log that helped expose Dan Rather's "Memogate," reported a summary of the article. That evening, John Gibson of Fox News reported the story. The next morning, *The Washington Times* and *The New York Sun* reported it. The *Sun* gave credit to Kersten and noted that it had learned of the story through Power Line. Several days later, Bill O'Reilly mentioned the story on his show, and soon after that, several newspapers—including the *Boston Globe*, *USA Today*, and *The New York Times*—ran opinion pieces about it.

As Kersten hypothesized, all evidence suggests that she was the only reporter to read the entire court document. First, the timing agrees with her hypothesis. Before her article, several news stories mentioned the lawsuit against the airline, but none mentioned that the lawsuit targeted passengers. But then after Kersten wrote the article, many reporters mentioned the passengers-being-sued fact. Second, some of the latter reporters gave credit to Kersten. Third, my research found no reporters claiming to have discovered the passengers-being-sued fact on their own.

Impact of the Story

Days after Kersten's article appeared, Rep. Steve Pearce, a Republican from New Mexico, wrote legislation to shield the John Does from the imams' lawsuit. On the House floor he described his motivation:

> Sadly, a lawsuit has been filed in Minnesota which named as defendants the Americans who were simply trying to protect themselves and their country. . . .
>
> If we are serious about fighting terrorism, if we are serious about protecting Americans and asking them to help protect each other, then we must pass this motion.
>
> If I leave my colleagues with one message about this motion, it is simply, no American should be sued for trying to stop terrorism.[5]

On March 27, 2007, Pearce offered his measure as an amendment to the Rail and Public Transportation Security Act of 2007. The Democrat-dominated Rules Committee, however, responded with a procedural motion that disallowed Pearce's measure to be considered. This is a tactic that the majority party often executes when it fears that wavering members might join with the minority party and pass a measure that it opposes.

However, House Republicans responded with a countertactic. The official jargon for their countertactic was "opposing the motion to order the previous question on the resolution to consider the bill." As you can see, it's difficult even to pronounce the countertactic. It is even more difficult to explain to constituents what the Republicans' motion really meant—that it was the key to shielding the innocent witnesses from the imams' lawsuit.

The roll call vote on the Republican's countertactic is important because it reveals how House members felt in their heart for Pearce's motion—that is, how they would vote *when they knew that constituents would not understand the implications of their vote.* On this roll call vote, all Republicans and two Democrats voted with Pearce. The remaining Democrats, which comprised a majority, voted against Pearce.

In a speech on the House floor Rep. Bennie Thompson, a Democrat from Mississippi and the chair of the Committee on Homeland Security, explained why many Democrats opposed Pearce's measure. His speech, I believe, also explains why many liberal *journalists* did not pursue the story.

> For the sake of discussion, Madame Speaker, all of us in this body don't look alike, and it is clear that people could be profiled because of their religion or their race.
>
> I think the record is clear in this country that some people are profiled, and I am wondering if people are profiled illegally, not charged with a criminal act, they absolutely should have the ability to seek redress in a court of law.[6]

The Democrats' procedural motion succeeded, and the Republicans' countertactic failed. It appeared that Pearce's measure was dead. But moments before the vote on final passage of the Rail Act, Rep. Peter King, a Republican from New York, attempted an arcane parliamentary maneuver. "Madame Speaker, I offer a motion to recommit," he said.

In plain English, his "motion to recommit" would direct the Committee on Homeland Security to have an instantaneous meeting on the House floor. The members would not discuss anything. They would simply follow the instructions that King gave the clerk of the House. These instructions were physically to attach Pearce's amendment to the Rail Act, and then return the amended version of the act to the House clerk.

Motions to recommit are often attempted, but they rarely are successful. The reason is that they thwart the power of the majority party. As a consequence, the majority party fiercely pressures its members to vote against such motions. Further, it is generally easy for the members to vote against such a motion. Even if they worry that their constituents might favor such a motion, they can always claim, "Oh that was just a procedural motion. Trust me, I voted your interests. "

This time was different, however. The reason was that Kersten and other journalists had brought so much attention to the issue. Even more important was the threat that they would bring *more* attention to the issue. Wavering Democrats realized that if they didn't vote as their constituents desired, they could be exposed by such journalists.

King's motion passed overwhelmingly, 304–121. All Republicans and almost half the Democrats supported it.

Before it passed, though, it had to survive a final obstacle, one that further revealed the influence of Kersten and other members of the media. Moments before the 304–121 *recorded* vote, Speaker Pro Tempore Hilda Solis (D-Calif.) asked for a *voice* vote. Most remarkable, if you watch the C-SPAN video, you see that the "noes" on the voice vote were much louder and more numerous than the "ayes." Solis proclaimed, "In the opinion of the chair, the 'noes' have it."[7] This is strange given that approximately three quarters of the House voted "aye" on the recorded vote. It means that a significant fraction of the House acted schizophrenically—voting "no", when the media and constituents could not discern their (voice) vote, yet voting "aye" when the media *could* discern their (recorded) vote.

King appealed the voice vote, and the recorded vote became official. The Senate agreed to the act, and by late summer of 2007, President Bush signed it into law. It included Pearce's provision to protect the John Does.

Shortly after Bush signed the act, the imams dropped their lawsuit against the John Does.

Missing Conservative Stories

One of the most moving tributes that a person can witness is a "missing man" formation of fighter jets, sometimes performed at funerals for fallen military pilots. The jets form an upside-down V, except that in one leg of the V a jet is missing. To observers, it's easy to imagine where the missing jet would fit. It's also easy to tell how many jets are missing (namely, one) and what the missing jet would look like if it appeared in the formation (namely, just like the others).

The opposite is true with *missing conservative news stories.* The four stories that I listed in the previous chapter are ones I could find. There surely are many more; however, they don't get reported because there are so few conservative journalists to report them. It is almost impossible to know how many such missing conservative stories there are, or what those stories would look like if we could see them.

However, with a little deeper analysis of the Katherine Kersten case, we can obtain a better idea.

At first glance it seems a huge coincidence that the flying imams happened to perform their antics in the same city, Minneapolis, where the Katherine Kersten "experiment" occurred. However, let me suggest an alternative explanation: Maybe radical Islamists are doing similar antics in many other cities. The problem is that those cities have no Katherine Kersten to expose them.

Few reporters share the views of Kersten, yet about half of the country does. If journalists were to be truly representative of United States, the *Star Tribune* "experiment" would have to be repeated thousands of times at newsrooms across the country.

Now consider that during her first two years at the *Star Tribune,* Kersten, virtually a novice at journalism, wrote a "scoop," which inspired Congress to pass a new law. Further, during the same period, she wrote a half dozen or so other scoops that changed policy at the local level. If U.S. journalists were truly to become representative of the American people—that is, if the Katherine Kersten experiment were repeated thousands of times—then each year, I believe, Americans would see hundreds of additional conservative news stories, stories that would be at least as interesting and important as the "flying imams" story. However, those stories are simply missing.

What If Katherine Kersten Had Been Missing from the Newsroom?

"This is remarkable," I said near the end of my interview with Kersten. "*You* were the reason for the fortunate outcome—all because of that one article."

"Oh, come on," she said. "I think Congress had a little something to do with it."

She has a point. Lots of people contributed to the outcome—in addition to Congress, the editors at the *Star Tribune* deserve much credit, perhaps especially Anders Gyllenhaal, not just for agreeing to publish the article but also for deciding to conduct the conservative-in-the-newsroom experiment in the first place.

But it is also clear that—although Kersten's efforts maybe weren't sufficient to save the innocent passengers—they *were* necessary. If she hadn't written the article, then Congress wouldn't have passed the new law, the imams wouldn't have dropped their lawsuit, and, perhaps most troubling, *future* passengers would have been intimidated and dissuaded from reporting potential terrorist activity.

The experiment at the *Star Tribune* gives us a glimpse of an alternative world, one in which newsrooms move in the direction of hiring a balance of liberals and conservatives. It gives a tiny sample of the topics, currently hidden, that might be brought to light. It also gives an indication of how, in such an alternative world, the views of news consumers might be altered and how public policies might change. Such views and policies, I suggest, would look very different from those of our current world.

"I'm not so sure," I responded to Kersten after she tried to downplay her influence. "Have you ever seen the movie, *It's a Wonderful Life,* where Jimmy Stewart gets to see what the world would look like if he had never existed?"

"Oh, stop it," she interrupted.

PART III

Evidence of Liberal Media Bias

9. Political Views in the Newsroom

VIVA HOMOGENEITY

"IF, IN SOME cataclysm," wrote the great physicist Richard Feynman, "all of scientific knowledge were to be destroyed, and only one sentence passed on to the next generations of creatures, what statement would contain the most information in the fewest words?" As Feynman explained:

> I believe it is the *atomic hypothesis* (or the atomic fact, or whatever you wish to call it) that *all things are made of atoms—little particles that move around in perpetual motion, attracting each other when they are a little distance apart, but repelling upon being squeezed into one another.* In that one sentence, you will see, there is an *enormous* amount of information about the world, if just a little imagination and thinking are applied.[1]

If you ask a similar what's-the-most-important fact about media bias, here's my answer: In a typical presidential election, only about 7 percent of Washington correspondents vote for the Republican.

Perhaps the most famous study to document this was conducted in 1995 by Elaine Povich, a fellow at the Media Research Center's Freedom Forum and a former reporter for *Newsday* and the *Chicago Tribune*. She surveyed 139 Washington bureau chiefs and congressional correspondents. Seven percent said they'd voted for George H. W. Bush, while 89 percent said they'd voted for Bill Clinton.[2]

In 2004, *New York Times* columnist John Tierney found similar results when he conducted an "unscientific survey" among his colleagues. He asked, "Who would make a better president, John Kerry or George W. Bush?" Among Washington-based journalists, about 8 percent said Bush and 92 percent said Kerry.[3]

If, however, you surveyed *all* journalists—not just Washington correspondents—then you'd find their voting behavior not quite as liberal. For instance, in 1981, Robert Lichter and Stanley Rothman surveyed 240 journalists at the most influential national media outlets—including *The New York Times, The Washington Post, The Wall Street Journal, Time, Newsweek, U.S. News & World Report,* ABC, CBS, NBC, and PBS. In the elections of 1964, 1968, 1972, and 1976, the journalists reported voting for the Republican at rates, respectively, of 6, 14, 19, and 19 percent.[4]

When the surveys include reporters of local news, they generally find even more Republican support. For instance, when John Tierney polled journalists *outside* of Washington, D.C., he found that 25 percent preferred Bush and 75 percent preferred Kerry. In March and April 2005, the University of Connecticut's Department of Public Policy surveyed three hundred journalists nationwide. Of the journalists who reported voting for one of the two major-party candidates, 27 percent chose Bush and 73 percent chose Kerry.[5]

It should be noted, however, that many local reporters cover subjects, such as weather and sports, that have nothing to do with politics. Thus, if our concern is the *political* bias of the media, then it is appropriate to focus on the journalists who report on political subjects. Accordingly, it is more appropriate to focus on Washington correspondents—or at least those who work at the major national news organizations—than on local reporters. The surveys that exclude local reporters consistently show that journalists vote for the Democratic candidate at rates of 85 percent or higher.

It is possible that some journalists are lying on the surveys. As I will show, this means that the surveys likely *understate* the degree to which journalists vote Democratic. Indeed, when you look at non-survey-based evidence, as I will present, journalists tend to choose Democrats at extremely high rates, usually higher than 95 percent.

Later in the chapter I will discuss how significant—and astounding—these results are, but for now I ask you to ponder two thoughts. First, people sometimes treat the press as if it were a fourth branch of government. Suppose, however, that one of the actual three branches were as unrepresentative of the people as the press is. For instance, suppose that 93 percent of Congress were Democratic. Or suppose the opposite—that 93 percent were Republican. Or suppose that one party tended to win the presidency 93 percent of the time. If this were the case, then it would not be an exaggeration, I believe, to say that such a situation would produce a revolution. A government that unrepresentative of the people cannot remain stable.

Second, a number of journalists and social scientists have studied the benefits of "diversity." One of the main conclusions of such studies is that newsrooms and other groups are aided in problem solving and information gathering if they receive the input from many different types of people. However, when such studies suggest real-world prescriptions, almost always they focus on a diversity of races, not a diversity of political viewpoints.[6] Such studies, I suggest, are "choking on gnats while swallowing camels."[7,8]

Criticism I: Surveys of Journalists' Political Views Are Irrelevant

Probably the most frequent criticism of such surveys is not that they are inaccurate but that they don't matter—that is, that the personal political views of journalists are largely irrelevant to any bias in their reporting.

For instance, so goes a frequent claim by the left: "Journalists report only the way their corporate bosses tell them." In another paper I examine this claim and show how silly it is.[9] But, for now, if you are inclined to believe it, I ask you to consider three things.

First, if journalists are really nothing more than dupes of their boss, then why do they seek such jobs? Second, if corporate bosses really are so conservative, then why do they hire so many liberals? Third, even if corporate bosses had the time and inclination to monitor and control their journalists, how could they do this under a distortion theory of bias? That is, for instance, think back to the *Los Angeles Times* article that I described in chapter 6, and put yourself in the shoes of the corporate bosses of Rebecca Trounson, the author of the article. How would you know the facts she *omitted*? How, for instance, would you know that the number of African American transfer students at UCLA had increased in 2006? How would you know that UCLA was employing a Life Challenge Index as a backdoor route for affirmative action?

Criticism II: Such Surveys of Journalists' Political Views Are Inaccurate

I am aware of only one analyst who makes the bolder claim that the surveys are inaccurate. This is Eric Alterman, a writer for Media Matters and the author of *What Liberal Media?* For instance, in an appearance on MSNBC's *Scarborough Country,* he explained his view:[10]

> JOE SCARBOROUGH: . . . I want to look at a 1995 poll that I know that you are aware of. This is of Washington reporters; 89 percent in that poll said they voted for Bill Clinton in 1992; 7 percent voted for Bush.
>
> (crosstalk)
>
> SCARBOROUGH: And only 4 percent of the journalists in the polls identified themselves as Republicans. And half of those polled said they were Democrats. And 37 percent said they were independents. Do you not find that to be persuasive in the least, that at least the Washington press corps leans to the left seriously? . . .
>
> ALTERMAN: If you had read [my book], gotten as far as chapter two, you would see that I take that poll apart. It's not a very good poll. It doesn't tell us much of anything. That poll had such a low response rate that no responsible social scientist would ever use it. The fact is, is that journalists, by and large, are liberal socially and conservative economically. But these corporations that own them, like GE, like Rupert Murdoch, like Viacom, they're conservative. And so, even if journalists happen to be liberal, the news is conservative.
>
> (crosstalk)
>
> SCARBOROUGH: And Viacom employs Dan Rather, correct? Are you saying Dan Rather, the *CBS Evening News,* owned by Viacom is rather conservative?
>
> (crosstalk)
>
> ALTERMAN: Joe, how many shows have you done on the FCC decision?
>
> . . .
>
> SCARBOROUGH: I have been all over [FCC chairman Michael] Powell, because I think it's very dangerous what companies like Viacom are able to do.
>
> ALTERMAN: Good for you. I'm proud of you for that, Joe. I'm glad to hear that.

Here's the relevant part of chapter 2 to which Alterman was referring:

> Even with all those caveats, the case is not closed on the Freedom Forum poll. The study itself turns out to be based on only 139 respondents out of 323 questionnaires mailed, a response rate so low that most social scientists would reject it as inadequately representative.[11]

Note that the response rate of the survey that Alterman criticizes is 43 percent (=139/323). In the same chapter, Alterman discusses two other surveys—one by David Croteau, a sociologist at the Virginia Commonwealth University in Richmond, and another by the Pew Research Center.[12] The latter two surveys support Alterman's main conclusions; it is therefore not surprising that he does not criticize their methodology. He does not mention, however, that their response rates were respectively only 30 and 32 percent.[13,14]

Notwithstanding his criticism of the Freedom Forum poll, Alterman actually seems to agree with its main conclusions. That is, after he criticizes the response rate, he provides the following caveat in his book:

> Then again, let's not kid ourselves. The percentage of elite journalists who voted for Bill Clinton in 1992 was probably consistent with the percentage of well-educated urban elites, which was pretty high.[15]

Alterman did not mention the caveat when he debated Joe Scarborough.

But That Was Just a Lie—Why Surveys May Understate the True Liberalness of Journalists

Adam Meirowitz, in my judgment, is the greatest political scientist of his generation. Raised in New Brunswick, New Jersey, he attended the University of Rochester, then Stanford University, where he received his PhD from the Graduate School of Business's political economics program. At Stanford, his fellow graduate students sometimes considered him a little odd. Instead of focusing on the standard classes in politics and economics, he often ventured "across the street" and took PhD courses in mathematics and statistics. "I realized that I love theory; that's what I wanted to do," said Meirowitz. "It was clear that if I wanted to be good at it, I had to take all those classes."

One of Meirowitz's greatest research contributions is a highly complex mathematical model that examines a person's incentive to lie when taking a survey.[16] Meirowitz's model begins with the reasonable assumption that survey respondents often care about policy. Add to this assumption the fact that lawmakers are often influenced by such surveys. As a consequence, survey respondents often have an incentive to be strategic about their responses—that is, to give not necessarily the true answer but the answer that helps move policy in the direction they prefer. Meirowitz showed that, *in general*, for a large class of surveys, all respondents have an incentive to give such strategic responses—that is, to lie.

Here is how the Meirowitz principle would apply to the surveys of journalists I've just cited. Suppose that you're a liberal journalist, and suppose you understand that if most journalists report that they are liberal, then this will cause people to believe that the media have a liberal bias.

Now consider that the latter result can influence policy. That is, if a voter believes that the media have a liberal bias, then he might believe that he's not getting the whole truth about the benefits of conservative policies. This, in turn, may cause him to vote more conservatively in the next election, which ultimately leads to more conservative policies.

As a consequence, if you're a liberal journalist, and you care about policy, then you have an incentive, when answering such surveys, to lie about your political beliefs—that is, to say that you're conservative. Similar logic implies the opposite: that if you're a conservative journalist, then you have an incentive to say that you're liberal.

In practice, however, I don't believe that many journalists lie when they answer such surveys. That is, I believe that most journalists don't think as strategically as the Meirowitz principle assumes that they do.

However, what if a small fraction of the journalists behave as the Meirowitz principle assumes? What if, say, 5 or 10 percent of the journalists lie about their political views when they take such surveys? As I'll show, this means that the surveys likely *understate* the true liberalness of journalists.

But before I do that, let me take a detour and explain the *equal virtue* principle—a principle I try to use whenever I conduct statistical analyses in this book. Applied to the above surveys, it means that I will not assume that liberals are any less virtuous, honest, or intelligent than conservatives—nor are conservatives any less virtuous, honest or intelligent than liberals.[17] Most important, for my analysis of the surveys, I'll assume that a randomly chosen conservative journalist is just as likely to lie as a randomly chosen liberal journalist.

As an example, let me now apply the principle to one of the surveys: the one by Lichter and Rothman. Recall that this survey found that in the 1964–76 elections journalists voted Republican at rates of 6, 14, 19, and 19 percent, which gives an average of 14.5 percent.

Now suppose that a small percentage—say, 5 percent—of the journalists lied when they took the survey. That is, consistent with the equal-virtue principle, 5 percent of the Republican-voting journalists said they'd voted Democratic, and 5 percent of the Democratic-voting journalists said they'd voted Republican.

Here's what this means: Although 14.5 percent of the journalists *said* they voted for the Republican, a fraction of this percentage actually consists of journalists who voted for the Democrat. I now examine: "What fraction?"

The answer can be found by solving an algebra problem.[18] If indeed 5 percent of the journalists lied, then it must be the case that the 14.5 percent figure can be broken down as follows: (i) 10.03 percent of the journalists voted Republican and told the truth about their vote, while (ii) 4.47 percent of the journalists voted Democratic but said they'd voted Republican. Meanwhile, (i) 84.97 percent of the journalists voted Democratic and told the truth, and (ii) 0.53 percent of the journalists voted Republican but said they'd voted Democratic.

This means that the true percentage who actually voted Republican is 10.56 percent—much less than the 14.5 percent who *said* they'd voted Republican.

If we apply the same analysis to the Elaine Povich/Freedom Forum poll (and continue to assume that 5 percent of all journalists lied), then the true percentage of Washington correspondents who voted for George H. W. Bush would be 2.22 percent—once again, much less than the 7 percent who *said* they'd voted for Bush.

When Talk Is Not Cheap

The reason why these surveys are plagued by the Meirowitz principle—and thus why the journalists have an incentive to lie—is that their answers are "cheap talk." That is, when answering the surveys, journalists face no penalty for misreporting their true political preferences.

There are ways to eliminate, or at least diminish, the cheap talk problem. One is to analyze campaign contributions instead of survey responses. Another is to examine the journalists' *publicly expressed* preferences for presidential candidates.

With these two methods journalists still might misrepresent their political preferences, but their incentives to do so are diminished. For instance, suppose you're a liberal journalist and you want to make researchers believe that you're conservative. With the campaign-contribution method, you'd have to donate money to the McCain campaign to fool the researchers. This comes at a cost: your donation, at least in small ways, helps to elect the candidate you oppose.

Similarly, a journalist could lie when she publicly states her political preferences. But if she does, this would come at a cost: her friends will know she is lying.

Campaign Contributions of Journalists

I am aware of only four studies that examine the campaign contributions of journalists. Consistent with the implications of the Meirowitz principle, these studies find that journalists are more liberal than the survey data suggest. Specifically, the average result of the four campaign-contribution studies suggests that the Democrat-to-Republican voting rate of journalists is more like 96–4 or 95–5, instead of 93–7.

The following are summaries of the four studies:

- In July 2004, PoliticalMoneyLine (now CQ MoneyLine) found that the ratio of (i) journalists who gave to the Kerry campaign, to (ii) journalists who gave to the Bush campaign was 93:1. Thus, of the journalists who gave to one of the campaigns, 98.9 percent gave to Kerry.[19]
- In 2008, William Tate of *Investor's Business Daily* searched federal records for the campaign contributions of journalists. He found that for every journalist who contributed to the McCain campaign, twenty contributed to the Obama campaign. Thus, of journalists who gave to either campaign, 95.2 percent gave to Obama.[20]
- In June 2009, Jennifer Harper of *The Washington Times* examined campaign contributions of ABC employees during the 2008 presidential campaign. She found that they gave 80 times as much money to the Obama campaign as the McCain campaign. Thus, of the money that ABC employees gave to one of the campaigns, 98.8 percent went to Obama.[21]
- In 2007, Bill Dedman, an investigative reporter for MSNBC, identified 144 journalists who had made political contributions between 2004 and the start of the 2008 campaign. Of these, he found that 123 journalists gave exclusively to Democrats and liberal causes, while 15 gave exclusively to Republican and conservative causes. (Two gave to both parties, and apparently the remaining four gave to causes that could not be identified as partisan.) Thus, of those who gave exclusively to one side of the political aisle, 89.1 percent gave to Democratic or liberal causes.[22]

Publicly Expressed Preferences of Journalists

I am aware of three additional cases where, because journalists publicly revealed their own views or a colleague revealed the views for them, we can learn the voting choices of a newsroom. The three cases involve *Slate* magazine, NBC News, and CBS News. In each case the evidence suggests that in a typical presidential election, approximately 99 percent of the newsroom votes for the Democrat.

CASE 1

In October 2008, *Slate*, an online magazine founded by Michael Kinsley and Microsoft, asked its contributors and staff to reveal for whom they planned to vote in the presidential election. Their responses were as follows:[23]

- Barack Obama: 55
- John McCain: 1
- (Libertarian) Bob Barr: 1
- "Not McCain": 1
- Non-citizen, can't vote: 4

Thus, of those who chose one of the two major-party candidates, 98.2 percent chose Obama.

Slate conducted similar polls in 2004 and 2000. The respective two-party Democratic vote share in those years was 90.2 and 90.6 percent.[24]

CASE 2

On January 5, 2007, Bill O'Reilly interviewed veteran NBC News reporter Andrea Mitchell. He challenged her to name one conservative at NBC News. Mitchell would not, or perhaps could not, meet the challenge:[25]

O'REILLY: All right, you've been thirty years at NBC. Can you tell me one conservative thinker at NBC News?

MITCHELL: How do you define conservative?

O'REILLY: I don't know—traditional values, maybe supports . . .

MITCHELL: Are you talking about commentators? Are you talking about . . .

O'REILLY: Anybody. Give me anybody. Is there anybody who's conservative in your opinion?

MITCHELL: Well yes, I think there are a lot of people—

O'REILLY: Give me one.

MITCHELL:—who are privately conservative or privately liberal.

O'REILLY: Give me one.

MITCHELL: But I—we don't judge ourselves by how we approach the news.

[As O'Reilly and Mitchell continue the exchange, O'Reilly mentions particular NBC employees, asserting that each is liberal. Mitchell does not concede that any are liberal.]

O'REILLY: When Katie was there, she admitted she was liberal. Come on.

MITCHELL: That's not the way we approach the news.

. . .

O'REILLY: [What about] Chris Matthews? . . .

MITCHELL: I don't think he's a liberal thinker.

O'REILLY: He's not? He worked for Tip O'Neill. How much more liberal can you get?

MITCHELL: He worked for Tip O'Neill how many years ago?

O'REILLY: I don't think he's changed his spots. I am giving you way too much of a hard time.

MITCHELL: No, but—

O'REILLY: And I apologize. It's not your fault.

CASE 3

A similar case occurred, on October 19, 2009, on MSNBC's *Morning Joe*. Host Joe Scarborough asked co-host Mika Brzezinski how many conservatives worked at her former network, CBS.[26]

SCARBOROUGH: How many Republicans do you see running around ABC? You worked at CBS . . . How many around CBS? How many around NBC? They aren't here.

BRZEZINSKI: Yes, although I don't think that CBS and NBC are actually pushing a perspective.

. . .

SCARBOROUGH: Well, but, Mika, based on what you've argued, through the years, Fox is more intellectually honest than every other network, because you say, since we all have biases we should put it out on the table. What, what is more dangerous: a network that says, "Yes, we're center-right" or a news organization—let's just take one, CBS—that says, "Oh, we're objective; we're down the middle"?

BRZEZINSKI: But we're all liberals.

SCARBOROUGH: You know that everyone you worked for—they were all liberals; they were all pro-choice.

BRZEZINSKI: Not all of them, but—

. . .

SCARBOROUGH: Okay, how many people you worked for at CBS do you think voted for George W. Bush? Of all the thousands you worked for, how many people at CBS voted for George W. Bush?

BRZEZINSKI: A very small percentage.

SCARBOROUGH: Maybe 1 percent?

BRZEZINSKI: I don't know.

SCARBOROUGH: Can you think, seriously—just use your inside-head voice here—can you think seriously of one correspondent, of one producer, of one anchor that was a George W. Bush fan?

BRZEZINSKI: Uhh, I can. I can think of one, yes.

SCARBOROUGH: How many people did you work for?

BRZEZINSKI: Uhh, many more than that.

Criticism III: Surveys of Journalists' Political Views Tell Us Nothing New

Almost all serious media observers are aware of these surveys and other evidence that reveal how overwhelmingly liberal U.S. newsrooms are. With many of these observers, however, their main criticism is not that the surveys are faulty; it's that they don't tell us anything new. That is, according to the observers, "Everybody already knows that most journalists are liberal. Why do we need a survey to tell us that?"

Let me suggest however, that the results of the surveys are more remarkable and surprising than people realize. That is, for example, suppose you were asked, "What percentage of reporters are liberal?" You'd probably say "A lot." However, you might also consider 70 percent or 80 percent "a lot."

My goal for this section is to show you how qualitatively different 93 percent is from 70 or 80 percent.

Here is one illustration. Suppose you visited some of the most liberal places in America, such as Berkeley, California, or Cambridge, Massachusetts. The residents of those places are actually more *conservative* than Washington correspondents. For instance, in the Ninth Congressional District of California, which contains Berkeley, 10 percent voted for John McCain in 2008, approximately one and a half times the percentage of Washington correspondents who usually vote Republican. In the Eighth Congressional District of Massachusetts, which contains Cambridge, 14 percent voted for McCain, approximately double the percentage of Washington correspondents.

Here's another set of facts that show just how large and remarkable 93 percent is. A December 2008, Zogby survey examined how various liberal demographic groups voted in the 2008 election.[27] The following are some of the results of the survey:

- Union members voted 63–27 for Obama.[28]
- Nonreligious people voted 65–35 for Obama.[29]

- Low-income people voted 63–27 for Obama.[30]
- People who have never shopped at Walmart voted 80–20 for Obama.

All of the above groups were significantly more conservative than Washington correspondents. Note, for instance, that each group voted for McCain at levels approximately three or four times greater than those of Washington correspondents.

In fact, if you combine two or more of these liberal groups—that is, take the *intersections* of the groups—then you still don't get a group as liberal as Washington correspondents. For instance, suppose you gathered a group of people such that all of them belonged to a union, *and* were nonreligious. Then that group, as the Zogby data show, would vote about 76–24 for Obama. Note that this group votes for the Republican at a rate approximately three times the rate of Washington correspondents.

The following are the results of all such two-way combinations of the groups:

- Unionized, nonreligious people voted 76–24 for Obama.
- Unionized, low-income people voted 70–30 for Obama.
- Unionized, anti-Walmart refuseniks voted 87–13 for Obama.[31]
- Nonreligious, low-income people voted 72–28 for Obama.
- Nonreligious, anti-Walmart refuseniks voted 85–15 for Obama.
- Low-income, anti-Walmart refuseniks voted 88–12 for Obama.

In fact, if you take the three-way intersections of the groups, or even the four-way intersection, then, again, you still don't get a group that is quite as liberal as Washington correspondents. Specifically:

- Unionized, nonreligious, low-income people voted 76–24 for Obama.
- Unionized, nonreligious, anti-Walmart refuseniks voted 88–12 for Obama.
- Unionized, low-income, anti-Walmart refuseniks voted 92–8 for Obama.
- Low-income, nonreligious, anti-Walmart refuseniks voted 88–12 for Obama.
- Unionized, nonreligious, low-income, anti-Walmart refuseniks voted 90–10 for Obama.

10. The Second-Order Problem of an Unbalanced Newsroom

AS THE PREVIOUS chapter illustrates, U.S. newsrooms are extremely one-sided. One consequence of this is what I call the *first-order problem* of an unbalanced newsroom. This is the simple fact that if you read a newspaper article or watch a television news clip, then almost surely it will have been written or produced by a liberal.

But another consequence, which I call the *second-order problem,* may be worse. This is that any reporter, even if she is a conservative, will be surrounded at her work environment almost entirely by liberals.

While most of this book focuses on the politics and economics of the news industry, this chapter focuses on the *sociology* of the newsroom. I'll examine two effects of the second-order problem, effects that seem to afflict any organization that becomes overwhelmingly dominated by one political group.

One is the *minority-marginalization* principle. Here, members of the majority group sometimes treat members of the minority group as if they don't exist. And on the occasions when they do remember that the minority group exists, they sometimes treat the members as if they are mildly evil or subhuman.

Another effect is the *extremism-redefined* principle. Here, the terms "mainstream" and "extreme" take on new meanings within the group. When the group is, say, very liberal, mainstream Democratic positions begin to be considered centrist, and positions that would normally be considered extremely left wing become commonplace.

As a university professor, I happen to work in an environment that is as politically imbalanced as a newsroom. Economists Christopher Cardiff and Daniel Klein have conducted an extensive examination of the political beliefs of university professors. They found that, in general, Democratic professors outnumber Republican professors by a 5:1 ratio. However, this varies considerably by field. For instance, in sociology the ratio is 44:1; in ethnic studies, 16:1; political science 6.5:1; physics 4.2:1; economics, 2.8:1; electrical engineering 2.5:1; accounting, 1.2:1; and finance, 0.5:1.[1]

At the UCLA political-science department, where I work, only about four professors—out of a total of about forty-eight—voted for McCain in the 2008 election. Thus, our voting pattern, 92.5–7.5 percent, is very similar to that of Washington correspondents.

According to my experience, the second-order problem has a very nonlinear effect. That is, for instance, when a group has a perfect, 50–50 balance of conservatives and liberals, then the second-order problem doesn't exist at all. If the imbalance rises to 70–30, then the problem becomes small. However, if the imbalance rises to 90–10, then the problem becomes huge. Although the imbalance doubles when you move from 70–30 to 90–10 (that is, note that 90 minus 10 is twice as large as 70 minus 30), the *effect* of the imbalance more than doubles.

The following thought experiment helps to illustrate the second-order problem, and why its effects are nonlinear. The thought experiment also illustrates why, I believe, the problem would greatly diminish if the political imbalance of a newsroom were only, say 60–40 or 75–25, instead of 93–7.

Suppose you randomly chose three colleagues at your work to join you for lunch. What's the chance that all three of them would be right-of-center politically? The answer, if your workplace has a perfect 50–50 political balance, is one out of eight ($=0.5\times0.5\times0.5$).

Average people find themselves in such a situation several times a year. For instance, if you engage in such a social interaction twice a week—that is, you randomly invite three people from a politically balanced group for lunch—then approximately once a month your three lunchmates would be conservative.

Now suppose that you're a Washington correspondent and you conduct the same experiment. Then the chance that all three of your lunchmates would be right-of-center is approximately 1 in 3,000 ($=0.07\times0.07\times0.07$). If you engage in this social interaction twice a week, then only once every thirty years will all three of your lunchmates be conservative.

Meanwhile, the probabilities would change significantly if liberals comprised only 60 or 75 percent of the newsroom. The probabilities that all three of your lunchmates would be conservative change from 1 in 3,000 to 1 in 16 or 1 in 64. These frequencies change from "virtually never" to "a few times a year."

That's the crux of the second-order problem. Journalists almost never find themselves in a situation where they are outnumbered by conservatives. Consequently, they naturally think, "Only fringe extremists believe that people join the military out of pride, that high taxes are bad, that abortion is bad, etc."

Remember, the same principle applies to a conservative journalist. It will be extremely rare for her to be in a group where her conservative colleagues outnumber her liberal colleagues. As a consequence, imagine that she is thinking of writing a story that, say, reveals that a university is illegally engaging in affirmative action or that most soldiers join the military out of pride, not lack of career options. Although her story may be true, if all her colleagues tell her that it is not—or, perhaps instead, they chide her that it is irresponsible or hurtful or racist to report it—then she will need a strong dose of courage and persistence to continue to pursue it.

Minority Marginalization in a Group as Liberal as a Newsroom

In *The Blues Brothers* movie, Elwood asks the waitress at Bob's Country Bunker, "What kind of music do you got here?"

"Oh, we got both kinds," she answers, "country *and* western."

The waitress, if she were to describe a newsroom, would only slightly exaggerate if she said, "Oh, we got both kinds of political views: liberal and progressive."

That's the first lesson to learn about the minority-marginalization principle. Similar to the patrons at Bob's Country Bunker, liberals, when they overwhelmingly dominate a group, can sometimes act as if conservatives don't exist at all. (And likewise, as I'll discuss in the next chapter, the opposite can happen when conservatives overwhelmingly dominate a group.)

Perhaps the most famous illustration of this occurred after Richard Nixon won the 1972 presidential election. Pauline Kael, a film critic at *The New Yorker*, proclaimed "I can't believe it. I don't know a single person who voted for him."[2] Notwithstanding her claim, Nixon won 61 percent of the popular vote—a near record—and he won every state in the Electoral College except Massachusetts.

A similar illustration occurred during the 2000 presidential campaign.

In a political-science class at Stanford University, a professor, whom I'll call Jack Healy, had the following exchange with his student, whom I'll call Matt:

MATT: How can George Bush possibly win? I don't know a single person at Stanford who will vote for him.
HEALY: (after a long silence) Matt, you know when you're on the airplane, flying back to the East Coast, and you look down and see all those green square patches?
MATT: Yeah.
HEALY: You know who lives there?
MATT: No.
HEALY: Republicans.

As mentioned earlier, a related aspect of the minority-marginalization principle is that in groups, such as a newsroom, where conservatives are so outnumbered, liberals sometimes regard conservatives as subhuman or mildly evil.

"In the eyes of most journalists," said Ethan Bronner, a reporter for *The Boston Globe*, "opposing abortion . . . is not a legitimate, civilized position in our society." Many journalists, he added, regard abortion opponents as "religious fanatics" and "bug-eyed zealots."[3]

Marianne Rea-Luthin, president of the Value of Life Committee of Boston, confirmed such attitudes: "Reporters often say to me, 'Gee, you're reasonable,' as if all pro-life people are unreasonable." She also noted that journalists sometimes—trying to perpetuate the stereotype of the pro-life activist—tell her to "make sure you look angry," when they interview her on television.[4]

Liberal journalists sometimes hold the same contempt for conservative journalists. When the Minneapolis *Star Tribune* hired Katherine Kersten as part of its experiment to bring a conservative into the newsroom, some of her colleagues called it a "sick joke." One emailed her to tell her she didn't belong.

"The elephant in the room is our narrowness," said Marie Arana, a *Washington Post Book World* editor.[5] "Too often, we wear liberalism on our sleeve and are intolerant of other lifestyles and opinions . . . We're not very subtle about it at this paper: If you work here, you must be one of us. You must be liberal, progressive, a Democrat."

Another aspect of the minority-marginalization principle is how the minority responds to being so outnumbered. As I have witnessed, when the minority is outnumbered at 90–10 rates or greater, its members become beaten down. They begin to downplay their differences with the majority—

usually by keeping their views to themselves, but sometimes by emphasizing, or even pretending, that some of the majority's views are similar to their own.

For instance, I have witnessed political-science colleagues say publicly that they are moderates, libertarians, or "old-line Southern Democrats" but admit privately that they are genuine, true-blue conservatives.

As *The Washington Post*'s Deborah Howell noted:

> [S]ome of the conservatives' complaints about a liberal tilt are valid. Journalism naturally draws liberals; we like to change the world. I'll bet that most *Post* journalists voted for Obama. I did. There are centrists at the *Post* as well. But the conservatives I know here feel so outnumbered that they don't even want to be quoted by name in a memo.[6]

Recall the poll at *Slate* magazine, where only one employee said she planned to vote for McCain. Here is the defense she gave for her choice. Note how reserved, even squeamish, she was about defending conservatives and conservative principles:[7]

> This is a difficult election for me. But voting for John McCain is an easy choice. He's a man I admire, I agree with many of his policy positions, and, since I am a moderate but loyal Republican, I feel a kind of kinship with him. Barack Obama is an exciting candidate, and I wish I could share the enthusiasm so many Americans feel for him . . .
>
> . . . I don't hate President Bush like so many do, but even I can say his presidency has been a disappointment. . . . I'm hopeful that an Obama victory would be a wakeup call as well as an opportunity [for more libertarian-minded conservatives] to take back the party from the religious right and social conservatives. . . . So regardless of what happens on Nov. 4, I won't be too upset. But neither will I be too excited.

In contrast, here are some of the explanations her liberal colleagues gave for voting for Obama:

- "I'm voting for [Obama] to support an energy and transportation policy that will focus on creating viable sources of renewable energy and reducing carbon emissions; to support a cautious and multilateral foreign policy that ensures American security with diplomacy, not a cowboy hat; and to support economic policies that benefit all Americans instead of just the wealthy."

- Two more *Slate* employees quoted David Sedaris when explaining why they prefer Obama: "I think of being on an airplane. The flight attendant comes down the aisle with her food cart and, eventually, parks it beside my seat. 'Can I interest you in the chicken?' she asks. 'Or would you prefer the platter of sh*t with bits of broken glass in it?' So, yes, I'm having the chicken."

Here's a final illustration of the minority-marginalization principle—and some more insight about what it's like to be a conservative in a very liberal newsroom. After spending two and a half years as almost the lone conservative at the *Star Tribune*, Katherine Kersten offered the following advice to any conservative considering a career in journalism:

> At first there was significant resistance [about my hire]. But over time you become more accepted. Part of it is when the ribbing—that sort of thing—comes, I just smile and take it in stride. People can actually see that I'm human. You have to be nice. You have to have a good sense of humor. And you have to be firm in your convictions, or you'll just become liberal like everyone else.

Extremism Redefined in Groups as Liberal as a Newsroom

As mentioned earlier, another effect of the second-order problem is the extremism-redefined principle. According to it, when groups become overwhelmingly liberal, *mainstream* and *extreme* take on new meanings. Mainstream Democratic positions begin to be considered centrist, and positions that would normally be considered far left begin to be considered mainstream.

Despite the title of the previous chapter, in such overwhelmingly liberal groups, the liberals within the group are not so homogenous. Despite what many outsiders might imagine, they do not all hold standard Democratic views, such as those by Hillary Clinton, Harry Reid, or Joe Biden. Many are much more liberal. Some, in fact, hold contempt for people like Clinton, Reid, and Biden.[8]

As I mentioned, the department in which I work voted approximately 92.5–7.5 for Obama in 2008, which means our voting rate was very similar to that of a newsroom. One of my colleagues, a genuine Marxist, taught a class on Marxism, and on the wall of his office he displayed a poster of Angela Davis—the feminist, civil-rights activist, and two-time vice-presidential candidate for the American Communist Party. Another 10–15 percent of the department hold similar views. On any politically charged issue that the department has faced, they almost always have voted with the Marxist.

Two other colleagues are very left wing, yet they are not as left wing as the Marxist sympathizers. One is a former leader of Greenpeace. During one protest he was interviewed by CNN while he was suspended by a cable from the Golden Gate Bridge. Another is an admirer of the left-wing anarchist Noam Chomsky. He even met his wife at a Noam Chomsky speech. On his door he displays a photo of his four-year-old daughter that appeared in the *Los Angeles Times.* She had accompanied him to a rally that occurred twelve days after the 9/11 attacks. The purpose of the rally was to protest the possibility that the United States might invade Afghanistan.

The latter two colleagues, although very liberal, are actually relatively moderate when compared to the Marxist sympathizers. Despite their far-left views, such views are approximately average in my department. That is, if there is an issue that is political in nature (say, to change our hiring standards to increase the racial diversity of the department) and splits the department approximately 50–50, then those two will be approximate fence sitters on the issue. The dean once asked the Chomsky admirer to be the chair of the department, since he believed that the Chomsky admirer had the "least divisive" views in the department.

My colleague Byron B. Bright, whom you may recall from the preface, is a staunch Democrat and thinks that only ignorant extremists listen to Rush Limbaugh. He is considered a relative *conservative* in the department.

As I have witnessed, when groups are this liberal, the left-of-center members of the group see significant distinctions among themselves, and the distinctions become more salient to them over time. Consider, for instance, the following exchange that Bill O'Reilly had with Marc Lamont Hill, a professor of education at Columbia University:[9]

O'REILLY: Right. There is a perception among many Americans, and I'm included in this, that Barack Obama is a hard-core leftist. I could be wrong. I could be wrong.

HILL: You are wrong, Bill. I wish he were a hard-core leftist. I'm a hard-core leftist. Barack Obama is not a hard-core leftist.

O'REILLY: But he hangs with people who are.

HILL: That's more—

O'REILLY: What did your mom say to you? You're defined by your friends.

HILL: Absolutely. Barack Obama has surrounded himself with people on both sides of the aisle. He's shown enormous flexibility on everything from drilling to school reform. He is not a leftist. Dennis Kucinich is a leftist. He's not a leftist. I wish he were, but he's not.

Within any group it's natural for members to magnify their differences of opinion. Indeed, I'm sure that if Bob's Country Bunker, from *The Blues Brothers* movie, actually existed, then at some point a heated, angry argument would pit the country-music fans against the western-music fans.

In such overwhelmingly liberal groups, the far-left members sometimes feel disgust for the mainstream Democrats. At times, they will even accuse them of being *conservative*. For instance, as William Greider wrote in *The Nation*:[10]

> [Obama's] victory, it appears, was a triumph for the cautious center-right politics that has described the Democratic Party for several decades. Those of us who expected more were duped, not so much by Obama but by our own wishful thinking.

Meanwhile, the disgust by the far left, at least partially, achieves their intent. The mainstream Democrats, at least in small degrees, feel guilty. "Maybe our far-left brethren have a point," they think. "Maybe we don't have sufficient compassion for the poor or concern for the environment. Maybe we *are* sellouts for corporate interests. Maybe we do lack courage for true, revolutionary change."

Given their disagreement with the far left, however, with whom they interact often—and given their simultaneous disagreement with conservatives, with whom they interact very little—they feel that they have struck a balance. In their mind, their views are a reasonable compromise.

The above points illustrate the most important aspect of the extremism-redefined principle. This is that mainstream Democrats, once they are injected into a group as overwhelmingly liberal as a newsroom, naturally begin to consider their views centrist.

But another aspect of the principle is almost as important. This is that, within such an overwhelmingly liberal group, far-left views begin to be considered mainstream.

The city of San Francisco is a group which, if anything, is slightly more conservative than a typical newsroom. For instance, in 2008 it voted 86–14 for Obama. Thus, its McCain share was approximately double that of Washington correspondents.

Two issues in San Francisco reveal just how extreme mainstream members of a group become once the group's voting pattern begins to mirror a newsroom's. In November 2005, 58 percent of the voters in San Francisco voted for Proposition H, which banned the sale of guns and required all existing gun owners to turn in the guns that they already owned. Notwithstanding the proposition's violation of the Second Amendment, a *majority* of San Francisco favored the measure. The same was true of Proposition I, which banned military recruitment in the city's public schools. At the time of the vote, the United States, so it appeared, was stuck in an unpopular and unsuccessful war in Iraq. Accordingly, it's not surprising that many people opposed the war. But Proposition I was more extreme than that. It opposed not just the war but also the troops, since it hampered their ability to recruit reinforcements for the battle zone.

Related, in groups that are so overwhelmingly liberal, far-left conspiracy theories become accepted. For instance, a common conspiracy theory of the left is that "9/11 was an inside job." I can attest that a non-trivial number of my university colleagues subscribe to this theory. For instance, the following passage—from the group Scholars for 9/11 Truth—is representative of the views of such colleagues.

> [W]e are convinced, based on our own research, that the [Bush] administration has been deceiving the nation about critical events in New York and Washington, D.C. We believe these events may have been orchestrated by elements within the administration to manipulate Americans into supporting policies at home and abroad they would never have condoned absent "another Pearl Harbor."[11]

An excellent source for far-left conspiracy theories is Pacifica Radio, which can be heard in most urban centers on the East and West Coasts. I first learned about it from my neighbor Andy in 2001. "You gotta check out this frickin' hilarious radio station," he told me one day. "It's always talking about 'social justice' and the news you won't hear from the corporate media. They call George Bush 'the so-called president.' And once a week they get an update from their special correspondent, who's this guy who killed a cop in Philadelphia. They call him a 'political prisoner.' He gives his report from jail."

I began listening to the station, and Andy was right, it is hilarious. If anything, he understated how outrageous it is. The station has reported, for instance: that George W. Bush invaded Iraq because Saddam Hussein was about to begin listing the price of Iraqi oil in euros, instead of dollars; that George W. Bush is a "drunk"; and that bombs planted inside the building, not a hijacked plane, were the cause of the damage to the Pentagon on 9/11.

Shortly after Andy told me about Pacifica, Georgia congresswoman Cynthia McKinney granted an interview to the station in which she insinuated that the Bush administration knew in advance that 9/11 would occur.[12]

Although I listen to the station for humor, several of my university colleagues consider it a legitimate news source. I'm certain that the same is true of journalists—and I once obtained evidence of that. A producer from the *The Newshour with Jim Lehrer* contacted me to see if I would comment on any biases in the U.S. news coverage of the 2006 Israeli-Hezbollah conflict. She asked me about the news outlets that I frequently read or watch. I mentioned a few, and then said, "I also listen to Rush Limbaugh. And, on occasion, I even listen to Pacifica Radio."

I was about to explain that I listen to Pacifica for humor, but before I could, she said, "Oh, I do, too," and then she started naming some of her favorite Pacifica programs. Remember, she worked at an outlet that I and many others consider centrist. I'm sure that at more liberal outlets, even more journalists and producers listen to Pacifica.

Consequences of the Second-Order Problem

Occasionally members of the mainstream media admit their liberal bias. And sometimes they explain that the bias is caused by the second-order problem.

One such admission occurred on September 27, 2009. During the prior few weeks, James O'Keefe and Hanna Giles had released some of their now-famous undercover videos of ACORN employees. In the videos, O'Keefe and Giles dressed as a pimp and prostitute. Their videos show ACORN employees giving advice on how to set up a brothel that would involve fifteen-year-old girls.

While conservative talk radio, Fox News, and many Internet sites devoted a huge amount of coverage to the videos, *The New York Times* was silent on the subject.

Despite this, two days after the first video aired, the U.S. Census Bureau severed all ties to ACORN.[13] Robert Groves, the Census director, said that ACORN had become "a distraction." The *Times* ran a story about the Census Bureau's decision but it mentioned nothing about the videos.

As O'Keefe and Giles released more videos—and other outlets began making the videos the lead story of the day—the *Times* finally began to mention the videos.

The *Times*'s public editor criticized his paper's response. "Tuning in Too Late" was the title of his piece on September 27, 2009.[14]

> [F]or days as more videos were posted and government authorities rushed to distance themselves from ACORN, *The Times* stood still. Its slow reflexes—closely following its slow response to a controversy that forced the resignation of Van Jones, a White House adviser—suggested that it has trouble dealing with stories arising from the polemical world of talk radio, cable television, and partisan blogs. Some stories, lacking facts, never catch fire. But others do, and a newspaper like *The Times* needs to be alert to them or wind up looking clueless or, worse, partisan.
>
> Some editors told me they were not immediately aware of the ACORN videos on Fox, YouTube and a new conservative web site called BigGovernment.com.
>
> . . .
>
> Jill Abramson, the managing editor for news, agreed with me that the paper was "slow off the mark," and she blamed "insufficient tuned-in-ness to the issues that are dominating Fox News and talk radio.

Two decades earlier, David Shaw of the *Los Angeles Times* wrote a Pulitzer Prize–winning series of articles about abortion and how unfairly his fellow journalists generally treat pro-life activists and their arguments. One of the most egregious examples involved an April 1989 abortion-rights rally in Washington, D.C. As Shaw wrote,[15]

> *The Washington Post* gave it extraordinary coverage, beginning with five stories in the five days leading up to the event, including a 6,550-word cover story in the paper's magazine on the abortion battle the day of the event. The Post even published a map, showing the march route, road closings, parking, subway, lost and found and first-aid information.

However, a year later, when pro-life activists held their "Rally for Life," the *Post* gave it only a tiny fraction of the coverage that it gave to the previous year's abortion-rights event. Nor did the *Post* publish any aids to the rally's participants, such as a map or parking information.[16]

Leonard Downie, the *Post*'s managing editor, explained that the culprit for the asymmetric coverage was the second-order problem: "When the abortion-rights people held their rally [last year]," he said, "we heard about it from our friends and colleagues."[17] However, the *Post* did not benefit from the same kinds of interactions with the pro-life side. The result, as the *Post*'s ombudsman admitted, was "embarrassing."[18]

"I am concerned," said Downie, "about whether we are paying enough attention to the other side of the argument. . . . People as high as me should have been aware of what was happening."[19]

11. The Anti-Newsroom, Washington County, Utah

MOST JOURNALISTS, I have found, aren't bothered that the typical newsroom is so liberal. One reason is that they often don't realize how liberal they are. As Bernard Goldberg has noted, journalists are like fish. Having lived their entire lives in water, they don't realize they're wet.

In this chapter, to illustrate just how liberal journalists are, I ask you to imagine a counteruniverse—one where 93 percent of journalists vote *Republican.* To make such a universe tangible, I have searched for a county within the United States that votes at least as conservatively as Washington correspondents vote liberally. The idea, to borrow Goldberg's analogy, is that if you want to show a fish that he's wet, the best way to do that is to bring him to the desert.

As it turns out, however, there is only one county in the entire United States, King County, Texas, that votes as conservatively as Washington correspondents vote liberally. Located approximately 200 miles west of Dallas, King County has a population of only 281. In 2008, 151 of its residents voted for John McCain; 8 voted for Barack Obama; and 3 voted for Libertarian Bob Barr. Thus, the county's two-party vote share for McCain was 95 percent.

An argument can be made, however, that even King County is not quite as conservative as Washington correspondents are liberal. Namely, in the three previous elections, 1996, 2000, and 2004, the two-party Republican share was respectively 68, 90, and 88 percent.

If we focus only on U.S. counties that have at least 100,000 people, then only a handful come even close to achieving a 93 percent Republican vote share. For instance, the following are all U.S. counties that (i) have at least 100,000 people, and (ii) voted for McCain at a rate of at least 75 percent.

TABLE 11.1

Conservative Counties with Populations Above 100,000

County	State	Description	Population	McCain Vote %*
Livingston	La.	Baton Rouge suburb	120,000	86.6
Randall	Tex.	Amarillo suburb	114,000	81.6
Utah	Utah	Provo and suburbs	531,000	80.9
Forsyth	Ga.	North Atlanta exurb	168,000	79.7
Midland	Tex.	Midland and suburbs	129,000	78.9
Washington	Utah	Southwest Utah	138,000	78.4
Parker	Tex.	Fort Worth exurb	112,000	77.8
St. Tammany	La.	New Orleans exurb	228,000	77.2
Montgomery	Tex.	North Houston exurb	430,000	76.6
Canadian	Okla.	Western Oklahoma	106,000	76.1
Baldwin	Ala.	Coastal Alabama	134,000	76.0
Cherokee	Ga.	North Atlanta exurb	211,000	75.0
Hall	Ga.	NE Atlanta exurb	185,000	75.7

* In this column, as I do throughout the chapter, I list the share of the *two-party* vote—that is, the share among people who voted only for the Democrat or Republican.

Of the thirteen counties in the table, only one, Washington County, Utah, is within a day's drive of Los Angeles. I therefore chose it for a case study—to illustrate the political mirror image of a newsroom.

A Group as Conservative as a Newsroom Is Liberal

Straddling Interstate 15 and located in the southwest corner of Utah, Washington County is about 120 miles northeast of Las Vegas. Named after a Mormon apostle, the county seat, St. George, was settled around 1856. Brigham Young, living in Salt Lake City, had a vision that the United States would soon engage in a civil war, and he determined that Salt Lake needed a source of cotton closer than the southeastern United

States. He gathered approximately three hundred families, some of whom had grown cotton in the Southeast, and persuaded them to settle in southwest Utah.

Eventually, the settlers abandoned the quest to grow cotton, mainly because the near-desert climate was too harsh. However, the influence of the Confederate sympathizers remains. About a half mile from the center of St. George is a large hill; jutting from it is a large, flat rock with the word "Dixie" painted in large letters. About two miles west of the center of town, on another hill, is a large "D," which is illuminated at night; it also stands for Dixie. A mile southeast of the center of town is Dixie State College. Near the center of the college is a statue of a Confederate soldier carrying a Confederate flag and aiding a fallen comrade.

John Shelton Reed, a world-famous sociologist at the University of North Carolina, has devised methods to define where the South ends and the rest of the United States begins. For instance, one of his methods analyzes where kudzu does and does not grow. Another, more statistical method looks in the phone books of towns and counts the businesses whose names begin with "Dixie" and compares those whose name begins with "American." By his definition, a town is part of the South if for every one hundred "American" businesses, there are at least six "Dixie" businesses.

By this definition, not only is Washington County part of the South, it is the most "southern" of all towns in the United States. Specifically, for every 100 "American" businesses in Washington County, there are 214 "Dixie" businesses. In fact, Washington County is more than twice as southern as the most southern town that Reed examined: Macon, Georgia. The latter town lists only 86 "Dixie" businesses for every 100 "American" businesses.

Remember these facts when thinking about media bias. Take an area founded by Confederate sympathizers and filled mostly with Mormons. That area is still not as conservative as Washington correspondents are liberal.

"Now, Franklin Delano Roosevelt Did Some Good Things"

Between bites of a cheese omelette at St. George's Bear Paw restaurant, Mike Empey described the moment he first realized that he might be a Democrat.

"It was at a family picnic," he said. "I was about ten years old. Just about everyone there was Republican. At one point some people started bashing FDR. My grandmother, who is usually this mild little woman, broke in and said, 'Now, Franklin Delano Roosevelt did some good things, some things that made all of you better off. And if you don't understand that, you weren't alive during the Depression.'"

I was interviewing Empey as part of my quest to find the most liberal resident of Washington County—and to see the county through his eyes. However, as I would soon learn, Empey, although a Democrat, is not that liberal.

If it weren't for a dirty trick by the Republican state legislators in Utah, I would not have been eating breakfast with Empey that day. Empey, at the time, was the lone Washington County staff member for U.S. congressman Jim Matheson. Matheson, a Democrat, was first elected to the U.S. House in 2000. At the time, his district lay completely within the Salt Lake City area, which is not quite as conservative as the rest of the state. Shortly after the 2000 Census, however, Republican state legislators redrew district lines to try to oust him. The new district stretched more than 250 miles from Matheson's home to the southeast and southwest corners of the state. This made it difficult for him to campaign and visit constituents. Worse for him, the new district contained some of the most conservative areas of the state, including Washington County.

The dirty trick failed, however. Matheson won reelection in 2002—albeit just barely, by less than 1 percent of the vote. Since then, however, he has managed to make the seat almost safe. In 2004, 2006, 2008, and 2010 he won by margins of 12, 22, 29, and 5 percent, respectively

"My main job is to show up at community and political functions and maintain a presence for Jim [Matheson] in Washington County," said Empey. Empey washed down his omelette with occasional sips of water. Unlike me, he ordered no coffee. He, like approximately 61 percent of Washington County, is Mormon.[1]

"Can you get people to vote for Matheson in this area?" I asked.

"Well, we'll always lose Washington County. But if we can just maintain 30 or 35 percent, we'll make it up in other counties.

"I try to convince people that we [Matheson and his staff] are not like the national Democratic Party. We're not extreme environmentalists, we're not rabid George Bush haters. And I try to explain to people that you can be Mormon and still be a Democrat."

"I'm sure he'd oppose it," said Empey when I asked how Matheson would vote on a hypothetical gun-control issue. "Anything against Second Amendment rights around here is political suicide."

More interesting than Matheson's position was Empey's language to describe it. In a later chapter I'll discuss how liberals and conservatives use different language. Gun issues are an example. Conservative politicians almost never say that they are "pro-gun" or that they "oppose gun control." Instead, their preferred phrase is that they are "pro-Second Amendment rights." Although Empey is a Democrat, on gun issues he talks like a Republican.

The voting record of Matheson, Empey's boss, agrees with Empey's description. His PQ is 67.4. Out of the twelve "key votes of the 108th Congress" listed in the *Almanac of American Politics,* Matheson favored the conservative position seven times. This included supporting Bush's tax cuts, a ban on partial-birth abortion, and a ban on gay marriage.

Christine Blum and Etta Cheeney are two leaders of the Republican Women of Washington County. When I talked to them, they were surprisingly critical about Utah's two Republican senators, Orrin Hatch and Bob Bennett ("too soft on illegal immigration" and "[had been] too buddy-buddy with Ted Kennedy"). Yet they were surprisingly *un*critical about Matheson, even though he's a Democrat. "He's not bad," said Cheeney. "He probably votes with us most of the time," said Blum.

When I mentioned that I had talked to a member of Matheson's staff, Cheeney asked, "Was it Mike Empey?"

"Yes, how'd you guess?" I responded.

"His mom lives across the street from me," she said. "Real nice guy. Visits her often."

EMPEY WAS BORN in Hurricane, a small town northeast of St. George, and raised in St. George. He graduated from Dixie High School and Dixie College (which was later renamed Dixie State College). Until recently, the college flew a Confederate flag at sports events and called its teams the Rebels. Amid significant controversy, however, the college abandoned the flag and the mascot.

"During college, I had a rebel-flag sticker on my car," Empey said. "But never did I intend that to mean anything racial. To us, it symbolized Dixie College and Southwest Utah, nothing else. If I had known that anyone was offended by its racial overtones, I would have taken it down immediately."

On many weekends Empey helps to train Boy Scout leaders. "You're aware," I asked, "that many on the left are calling for a boycott of the Boy Scouts?"

"Why is that?" he asked.

"Because they exclude gays," I said.

"Oh, yeah. I heard about that," said Empey. "Well, it doesn't affect me. I'm proud of my work with the Scouts."

In Los Angeles, especially on the UCLA campus, it is fashionable among the far left to wear T-shirts with the image of Che Guevara, the guerilla fighter who helped lead the communist revolution in Cuba. "Suppose a student at Dixie State has left-of-center political views," I asked Empey, "and suppose he wants to show how rebellious he is. What does he do?"

Empey laughed. "He wears a 'Democrats of Southern Utah' T-shirt." (There really was such a T-shirt, and it really was fashionable among some Democratic students for a time.)

American Exceptionalism Personified

American exceptionalism personified. There's probably no better phrase to describe Tom Seegmiller. Seegmiller is the owner of two successful businesses in Washington County, Dixie Gun and Fish, a store catering to hunters and fishermen, and the Locker Room, an athletics supply store.

The phrase "American exceptionalism" was first coined by Alexis De Tocqueville in his classic study of the early United States, *Democracy in America*. As De Tocqueville and many later scholars noted, the United States is fundamentally different from other economically advanced countries. For instance, compared to Europeans, Americans go to church more, are more entrepreneurial, earn more money, have more children, own more guns, and have much more favorable views toward capitalism.

The first thing you notice as you enter Seegmiller's office is the eight-by-ten picture of Jesus. It's at eye level, just to the right of his desk. Below that is a similar-size picture of George Washington. Below that is a plaque, given to him by one of his eight children, proclaiming him the "World's Greatest Dad." The office is littered with stacks of papers, and at the front of his desk is a small poster, "A clean desk is a sign of a cluttered mind."

Behind the desk Seegmiller keeps a police riot shotgun. "Have I ever shot it?" he asked. "No. But there was a time when there were a few robberies in the area. I felt comfortable just knowing it was around."

"Well, my daughter got a little buck just two days ago," he said, when I asked if deer hunting was popular in Washington County. "All of my sons have gotten a deer. And all but one of my daughters has gotten one also. I'm sure it's just a matter of time before she does, too."

Although he likes deer meat, and he enjoys shooting, those are not the main reasons he hunts. "It's not like we're shooting everything in sight. Half the fun is just being together. It's just something you enjoy doing as a family."

"All Your Turkey and Duck Hunting Needs"

Dixie Gun and Fish is the primary retailer in Washington County for Legacy Sports, a gun supplier and manufacturer. I first learned about Legacy from the following radio commercial. The commercial was my first step on the path that led me to Seegmiller.

> Legacy Sports International is a premier importer of affordable, high-quality rifles and shotguns. From their tact-driving M-15 series of Howa rifles, to their Italian-made Silma over-and-under shotguns, the quality just screams at you. . . . If you fancy a pump-action or semi-auto shotgun, Legacy's Escort series will exceed your expectations without emptying your bank account. Check out their Camouflage Escort semi-auto with two barrels and a high-vis' fiber optic sight to handle all your turkey and duck hunting needs. . . .[2]

One of the main points of this chapter is to explain to liberals how a conservative might feel in a newsroom filled with liberals. Occasionally, liberals use phrases that sound foreign to a conservative. "White male power structure," "Christian intolerance," and "American colonialism" are some examples. While we all can imagine what such concepts mean, it is not clear that the concepts actually exist in practice—that is, it's not really clear that white males are so powerful, that Christians are so intolerant, or that America is truly practicing colonialism. If you are an urban-dwelling liberal, consider that such phrases sound approximately as foreign to conservative ears as "your duck and turkey hunting needs" probably sound to yours.

To my ears, Seegmiller sometimes sounded like that commercial. In the course of a conversation about home defense, he discussed "double ott" and "triple ott" shells; why I should avoid "number seven and a half or eight shot," which is primarily used for small game; and why instead I should use "number two shot," which is primarily used for geese or turkey. The main reason, he explained, is that the pellets are large enough to kill the intruder, but too small to penetrate your wall and hurt a neighbor.

"Now that is an absolute fallacy," said Seegmiller. "In fact, that's almost a Hillary Clinton–like cliché."

I had just asked him, "Isn't a gun more likely to kill a family member accidentally than to kill an intruder? Aren't you better off just using alarms and police for protection?"

"Even if you're lucky," said Seegmiller, "the police will get there in two minutes. What good are they if the intruder kills you in thirty seconds? The people who say things like that have almost no knowledge about guns. It's as if you take someone with a kindergartner's knowledge but for some reason you give him a podium."

Nothwithstanding all our talk about guns and how to kill home intruders, there is a tangible gentleness about Seegmiller. Between answering my questions, he helped a young mother load a trampoline into her minivan. "I bet you're gonna want to assemble it as soon as you get home," he said as he gave a nod to her young sons. As he gave me a hunter's inside account of Dick Cheney's hunting accident, two spry sixty-something men began looking at softball bats near the register. Washington County was hosting the World Senior Games, and the softball competition would begin that afternoon. "Now what *you guys* do is dangerous," Seegmiller exclaimed, as he broke from our conversation about hunting. "Pitching—I'd never do that."

Unusual for him, Seegmiller was sporting a short beard that day. "He's got the Moses-from-the-Mountain look today," one of his employees joked.

Another of his office decorations is a photograph of an African toddler, severely malnourished, who has collapsed on her way to a feeding center in Sudan. Behind her, a plump vulture is eyeing her. "I keep it there," said Seegmiller, "so that I see it every time I look at my file cabinet. It's to remind me of how much we have and how much we should be doing for other people in the world . . . definitely food and money, but also to help them to be free, to lift them up."

Perhaps the best example of his gentle nature occurred during our first phone call. In between answering my questions, he'd place me on hold as he attended customers. Amid our discussion about guns and how to kill home intruders, the music that came from his phone system was an instrumental version of the Christmas carol "What Child Is This?" Yet the call took place well outside of the Christmas season.

If it isn't obvious already, Seegmiller is right-of-center politically. Indeed, that's understating things. In my judgment, if not far right, he is at least as conservative as the average Republican in Congress.

In any East- or West-Coast city his political views would seem extreme, even strange. Meanwhile, however, he feels the same way about East- and West-Coast cities. "Now if I lived in Los Angeles," he said, "I'd keep a gun in every room."

But in Washington County his views are mainstream. "I'd say I'm probably slightly more conservative than the average person around here," he said. "But on just about any issue, 90 percent of the people would be in accordance with me."

Many, if not most, of the residents share his hunting passion. In fact, the county has *three* deer hunting seasons: one for bow hunting, one for muzzle-loading guns (like the guns used during the Civil War), and one general season.

"In the old days, before deer season was split into three," said Seegmiller, "it would always start on a Saturday. Eventually, the schools realized that about half the kids wouldn't show up the next Monday, so they just made it a holiday."

Gun ownership is very common in Washington County. "Most people own a gun," said one resident, "and maybe everybody does in rural areas."

"A woman once told me," said Seegmiller, " 'I'm so glad to live in a place where there are no guns. Back in New York all the time we used to hear gangs shooting at each other. You never hear that here.' "

Seegmiller explained that despite the woman's beliefs, the reason gun crimes are so rare in Washington County is *because* so many people own guns.

"I told her, 'Lady, there are guns all around you. Nearly every pickup around here has *two* guns in it.' Now that's probably exaggerating things. But there probably was a time when most pickups had a gun in them. The first gun crime I'd ever heard about around here was when a cop shot his wife's boyfriend. We used to have a saying, 'If everybody had a gun, and no cops had them, everything would be fine.' "

Cyril Noble, the president of the Washington County Democrats, echoed that sentiment. "You have to understand, this is a rural area. There are lots of hunters, and guns are just a way of life around here. I don't have a problem with guns."

In Washington County not only are Seegmiller's views mainstream, compared to some residents, he's liberal.

Extremism Redefined in Washington County

As Empey finished his omlette, he described a local political group, the Citizen's Council on Illegal Immigration, which vehemently opposes illegal immigration. "Now that group makes the Republican Women of Washington County seem liberal," he joked.

The John Birch Society is another far-right group that has a presence in the County. "Just drive about ten miles south on Highway Fifty-nine," said Empey, "and you can't miss the sign, 'United States Out of the U.N.' That's theirs."

While San Francisco banned guns in the home and military recruiters in the schools, La Verkin, Utah, a town fifteen miles northeast of St. George, declared itself a United Nations–free zone. According to an ordinance passed by the town council, (i) UN personnel and facilities are banned inside the town limits, (ii) no UN flag can be flown on town property, and

(iii) any resident who works for a UN-financed project must post a sign declaring "United Nations Work Conducted Here."

As for other extreme groups, if you keep traveling south on Highway 59, just before you reach the Arizona border, you find Hildale Utah, home to several members of the Fundamentalist Church of Jesus Christ of Latter Day Saints. The Church, which split from the mainstream Mormon Church during the early 1900s, encourages its members to practice polygamy. As Empey and I ate at the Bear Paw, Warren Jeffs, the leader of the Church, sat in a prison a few miles north of us. Jeffs was awaiting trial, for being an accomplice to rape—specifically arranging marriages for underage members of his church.[3]

Empey told me about another extreme group in Washington County, the Dixie Republicans. Members of the group had split from the Washington County Republicans because they felt it was not conservative enough. Their main complaint was that George W. Bush and other prominent Republicans were not tough enough on illegal immigration.

Just as the far left has its conspiracy theorists, Washington County has its far-right conspiracy theorists. For instance, Empey has received phone calls from people concerned that the contrails from jet airplanes are part of a master plan, orchestrated by the UN, to eliminate the white race.

Minority Marginalization in Washington County

What about the minority-marginalization factor? Do conservatives in Washington County ever treat Democrats as if they're subhuman or don't exist at all?

"Nothing major," said Empey. "But every once in a while I'll get a small slight. Once at a gathering of political leaders of Washington County, the guy leading the meeting said, 'I'm glad to see that everybody's here . . . even Brother Empey.' He was singling me out because I was the only Democrat. He said 'Brother' because that's the way we address each other in the LDS church. He was hinting that good Mormons aren't Democrats."

Cyril Noble, the president of the Washington County Democrats had the same reaction: no major ostracism but maybe an occasional slight. Once, when a neighbor learned he was a Democrat, the neighbor playfully formed his fingers into a cross, as if warding off a vampire.

How about hostile reactions? "Every once in a while we'll get an angry call at the office," said Empey. "But, again, nothing major. I think it's partly because it's just not my style to be confrontational."

A Newsroom of Washington County Residents

While the people of Washington County are conservative, very friendly, and maybe the truest practitioners of family values I have witnessed, I should not overstate things.

Like any other place, couples on occasion get divorced. There's a restaurant that's almost considered a gay bar. Although the local Walmart has a special "LDS Entertainment" section (mainly DVDs with Christian themes), the section is tiny compared to the regular entertainment section. At a Dixie Rebels football game, my five-year-old daughter and I watched pregame warm-ups, up close, from the back of the end zone. As I thought how family-friendly the area is, an assistant coach yelled at his defensive back, "When he crosses the middle like that you need to knock the sh*t out of him!"

But the region is tangibly different from New York or Los Angeles, or even Atlanta or Phoenix or Albuquerque. And if you filled a newsroom with its residents, that newsroom would seem vastly different, even alien, to the observer of the usual newsroom.

The Second-Order Problem in a Conservative Newsroom

Consider again my theory about the second-order problem of a liberal newsroom. One of its implications is that if liberal journalists just interacted more with moderates and conservatives, then their perspectives would change.

But what about the counter-theory? In an overwhelmingly conservative area such as Washington County, would conservatives change their perspective if they interacted more with liberals?

Cyril Nobel, the president of the Washington County Democrats, certainly *thinks* that is true. "I'm the most optimistic person I know," he responded after I kidded him about how difficult it must be to recruit people to become Democrats.

Further, in this chapter you've already seen a case where a liberal in Washington County changed the perspectives of conservatives—Mike Empey's grandmother. Not only did she remind conservatives that FDR "did some good things," but she also influenced her grandson to become a Democrat.

Moreover, I believe that Empey himself may have changed the perspectives of some conservatives in Washington County. About a year after our breakfast at the Bear Paw, I visited him again. Between visits, the illegal immigration issue had become extremely heated. The U.S. Senate had narrowly voted down a bill that would have given partial amnesty to illegal aliens. This was the bill that led some conservatives to dub Lindsey Graham "Senator Grahamnesty." Many voters, anticipating that the bill would reach the House, called Empey to relay their opinion to his boss, Congressman Matheson.

"Some of those calls were the most vile and vicious that I've ever received," said Empey. "A few were even racist. During the first part of this summer, I felt like I had this dark cloud around me—all because of illegal immigration."

One of the most vicious of the calls began like many of the others. The caller announced his name and address and said that he was concerned about the immigration bill. Eventually, however, he became angry. "But then the politicians go to Washington, and they lose touch with what the people want," he continued.

Empey went into hyper-professional mode, calmly taking notes and only saying things like "Yes, sir. I appreciate that." "I will relay those concerns to Congressman Matheson."

The caller continued: "I would rather pay more for a head of lettuce than have one American job be lost to an illegal immigrant." Empey suspected that the caller had talking points in front of him, mainly because he repeated some of the same things that other callers had said. For instance, lots of callers mentioned the part about the price of lettuce, but none mentioned the price of cabbage or carrots or any other vegetable.

The caller began to scream. Empey responded with more rounds of "Yes, sir. I'll tell Congressman Matheson." Then the caller suddenly became calm and friendly, as if it suddenly occurred to him that there was a real person at the other end of the phone.

"Boy, you must have a lousy job," he said. Empey just laughed and continued to take notes.

"Corporate Media" and Washington County as a Newsroom

In a more academic piece, I examine and critique the "corporate media" theory.[4] This theory says that despite the liberal views of journalists, their reporting will be centrist—and maybe even conservative—because of pressure from their corporate bosses. I place little credence in the theory, and indeed the point of my academic piece is to document the overwhelming evidence against it.

But as a final thought experiment, suppose that the theory were true. Suppose, however, that the tables were turned—that the newsroom had adopted political views like those of Washington County. Meanwhile, you, as the corporate boss, have liberal views. Your job, in this thought experiment, is to make your journalists report in a centrist or left-leaning fashion.

Imagine how difficult that would be—to persuade them to write stories about why the government should ban guns like it did in San Francisco; why abortion rights are important for the careers of working women; why tax increases are good for the economy; why humans are causing "climate change"; and so on.

Imagine doing this when the average person in the room is an admirer of George W. Bush; keeps a tact-driving M-15 series Howa rifle in his home; is a devout Mormon; refrains from alcohol, coffee, and R-rated movies; and thinks that Democrats are mildly evil. Moreover, he is convinced that his views are reasonable and mainstream. After all, he is a member Washington County Republicans, not the Dixie Republicans or the John Birch Society. He is a member of the mainstream Jesus Christ Church of Latter Day Saints, not the *Fundamentalist* Jesus Christ Church of Latter Day Saints.

Now imagine that you want to hire someone who is not so conservative. But if you do, whom do you hire? If you want a reporter with experience, then you must hire from the pool of already-working reporters, which in this thought experiment has a distribution of political views like those of Washington County. The most liberal person you can find is someone like Mike Empey. Although a Democrat, he is "pro-Second Amendment rights." Although pro-choice on abortion, he opposes partial-birth abortion. He attended Dixie College and cheered for the Rebels. On weekends he is an active leader in the Boy Scouts. His inspiration for becoming a Democrat, his grandmother, described FDR not as an icon who worked for "social justice," only as a person who "did some good things."

Once he is in the newsroom he feels less than comfortable among the other reporters. Sarcastic salutations such as "Brother Empey" make him feel like an outsider.

Through watchful oversight, salary incentives, and threats of firing people, however, you, as corporate boss, attempt to make the other reporters think and report like him, instead of the other way around.

It's an understatement to say that that would be a difficult task.

12. Walk a Mile in the Shoes of a Centrist

IN A SCENE from *Raiders of the Lost Ark,* Indiana Jones watches a crowd part to reveal a menacing, black-clad swordsman. The swordsman begins swinging his sword, simultaneously showing off his skills and challenging Jones to a fight. The original script called for Harrison Ford, the actor playing Jones, to fight the swordsman. However, Ford had developed a severe case of dysentery. Instead, he pulls out a gun, flashes a "I don't have time for this" grimace, and shoots the swordsman.

I felt a little like Jones when I gave an interview to an NPR station in Madison, Wisconsin. The host wanted me to answer questions about the *QJE* article that Milyo and I had written. The interview was conducted via phone while I was visiting my mother-in-law in the Philippines. Because of the time difference, the interview took place at 3:00 AM Philippines time.

I was tired and cranky, and I became even crankier when a caller to the show, whom I'll call "Tiffany," snidely asked, "How can you say that *The New York Times* and Dan Rather have a liberal bias? They're all part of the corporate media."

My first thought was to explain the arguments I made at the end of the last chapter, and the critiques that I made in my academic piece on "corporate media." But that would have taken a long time, and, like Indiana Jones, I didn't feel like a fight. Instead, I pulled out a metaphoric gun.

"Look," I said, "my results show that *The New York Times* and CBS News are about as liberal as Joe Lieberman. I bet you probably think that he's conservative."

"Yes," said Tiffany.

"Then we agree. We only disagree on semantics—on how to define 'conservative'," I responded.

"Moderate" According to the Far Left

Many on the left agree with Tiffany. They do not dispute my result that the average *New York Times* article has approximately the same slant as the average Joe Lieberman speech. In fact, many of them might claim that I understated things—that *The New York Times* really is to the *left* of Joe Lieberman.

Where they disagree is how you should describe the politics of Joe Lieberman.

"I might agree with you," I explained to Tiffany, "that Joe Lieberman is probably more conservative than the average European voter or the average *world* voter. But you can't claim that he's more conservative than the average *American* voter. There are too many measures in political science that dispute that."

A weakness of nearly all humans is that we tend to overestimate the degree to which other people agree with us. If, for instance, it's clear to you that abortion should be legal, then it's natural for you to think, "Surely, most others think the same." If it's obvious to you that the rich should pay a greater share of the taxes, then you'll also probably think, "Of course, most other people can see that."

On top of all this, if you live in a place like Manhattan, San Francisco, or just about any college town in the United States, then your belief—that most people have "progressive" views like you—will usually be reinforced whenever you talk to friends and neighbors.

Recall Mike Empey, the Washington County staff member for Congressman Jim Matheson. In August 2010, Matheson had just survived a serious primary challenge. Some left-wing activists in his district thought his voting record was too moderate, so they sponsored a far-left challenger for the primary. "What are they thinking?" I asked Empey. "Everybody knows that 2010 is gonna be a good year for Republicans. How does a far-left left person win a general election in 2010—*in Utah*?"

Empey told me about some pockets of far-left voters in Utah, such as the "Avenue area" of Salt Lake City. "I think what happens" he said, "is you kind of get in your own little world. If the other three people in your golf foursome agree with you, then you think that must be the way the rest of the world thinks."

Joe Lieberman Is *Left* of Center

If you have far-left views, and you're angered by Joe Lieberman's occasional agreement with Republicans, then it's natural for you to believe that most others share that anger. If someone asked you, you'd say, "Yeah, it's gotta be the case that Joe Lieberman is more conservative than the average American voter."

Let me dispel that myth.

First, Joe Lieberman's PQ is approximately 74—this is, well left of 50, the PQ of the average voter. He is much closer to 84, the PQ of the average congressional Democrat.

It's true that on a few issues Lieberman leans right, including the Iraq and Afghanistan wars, capital gains taxes, and free trade. But on the vast majority of issues he leans left. These include abortion, the minimum wage, unions, gun control, environmental regulation, privatizing Social Security, and the constitutional amendment against flag burning. Although he usually favors lower capital gains taxes (perhaps partly because of the financial interests that he represents in Connecticut), on *income* taxes he generally favors higher rates. For instance, he voted against George W. Bush's tax cuts in 2003, choosing not to join the thirteen Democratic senators who voted for them. During the 2004 Democratic presidential primary, he gave a quasi-Marxist explanation for why he opposes a tax break for the wealthy: "They don't need it."[1]

Although he switched party affiliation in 2006—from Democratic to Independent—his policy stances hardly changed. Namely, as a Democrat his PQ was 75. As an Independent, it only dropped to 74.

Although he campaigned for McCain in 2008, this was largely due to personal reasons and less because of any broad policy agreement with McCain. In all other presidential elections during his political career he has endorsed the Democrat. In 2000 he didn't just endorse Al Gore; he became his running mate. This is perhaps the most damning evidence of all to any claims that Lieberman is right of center. If Lieberman is really so conservative, then why did Al Gore, the great liberal icon, ask him to be his vice president?

Most journalists, I believe, have a similarly misguided view about what it means to be centrist in America. Like Tiffany, they consider Lieberman at least centrist, if not right of center. Meanwhile, they consider true moderates—those with a PQ near 50—as conservative. The following are a few examples where journalists have revealed these misguided views:

- In 2001, *Washington Post* staff writers John F. Harris and Dan Balz noted that "Democrats such as *conservative* [my emphasis] freshman Ben Nelson (D-Neb.) . . . could command attentive audiences from Senate leaders and [President Bush]."[2]

  Although it would be reasonable to call Nelson "a conservative Democrat"—that is, conservative relative to other Democrats—that was not the way *The Washington Post* writers described him. They described him as conservative in the absolute sense. With a PQ of 56, however, Nelson would best be described as a left-leaning moderate. "Conservative" is simply not accurate.

- In June 2007, *Pittsburgh Post-Gazette* writer Jerome L. Sherman wrote an in-depth and flattering article about Rep. Jack Murtha (D-Pa.). It began with a description of Murtha's impressive record as a soldier in the Vietnam War, and then it discussed his opposition to the Iraq War. "Many anti-war activists," Sherman wrote, "credit Mr. Murtha's switch as a turning point in the debate about the war, citing his credibility as a *conservative* [my emphasis] lawmaker with a good track record on defense issues."[3]

  Although it is true that Murtha sometimes voted with conservatives, including perhaps often on defense spending, usually, however, he voted with liberals. This is revealed by his 59 PQ. Further, he was well known as a strong ally of Speaker Nancy Pelosi and a vocal critic of President George W. Bush. It is inaccurate to call him a "conservative."

- In November 2005, *New York Times* reporter David S. Cloud wrote a similar piece about Jack Murtha. Here is how Cloud described Murtha's rural, western Pennsylvania district: "Though most voters lean Democratic in this blue-collar region, they are generally conservative. President Bush only lost the district by 8,000 votes in 2004."[4]

  Indeed, in 2004 the district voted against Bush 48–52, while the country voted for Bush 52–47. This makes the district slightly more liberal than the average U.S. congressional district. Further, as Cloud himself notes, most voters in the district "lean Democratic." Yet, strangely, he called the district "generally conservative."

What It Means to be Centrist in America

Most journalists, I believe, try to write in a centrist fashion. The problem, however, is their perception of what it means to be "centrist." To them, it often does *not* mean sounding like a politician with a PQ near 50—e.g., a Ben Nelson (D-Neb.) or an Olympia Snowe (R-Me.). Instead, to them, centrist means sounding like a person with a much higher PQ—e.g., a Joe Lieberman or someone to his left. As a consequence, it should be no surprise that the slant quotients of such journalists are closer to 74 than 50.

Indeed, if you are a journalist, the remaining sections of this chapter are perhaps the most important of the book. They give some lessons about how centrists in America think.

The first lesson is that a true centrist has a PQ of approximately 50.

The second lesson is that America is approximately a 50–50 nation—that is, in a typical election approximately just as many people vote Republican as Democratic. One implication of this is obvious once you think about it—however, I believe, it is not so obvious to many on the left: The average voter in America is not a supporter of the Democratic Party. Rather, he is *on the fence* between supporting the Democratic and Republican parties.

To illustrate this further, suppose, as a thought experiment, that during the 2008 election you lined up all Americans according to their support for the two candidates—that is, you placed the most pro-Obama voters on one end and the most pro-McCain voters on the other end. What would be the views of the middle person in the line? Recall that Obama won 53–46. Thus, the median voter—the one with 50 percent of the voters on one side of him and 50 percent on the other—would have preferred Obama over McCain, but just barely. In fact, among the Obama voters he would have been among the 3/53 fraction who had the weakest enthusiasm for Obama.

The great political scientist Donald Stokes discussed the importance of *valence* factors in an election. These are things such as charisma, intelligence, youth, vigor, and leadership skills—factors that give a candidate an advantage but are unrelated to policy positions. Most people would agree that Obama had a *valence* advantage over McCain. Indeed, few candidates since World War II, I believe, come close to matching Obama's charisma, oratorical ability, youth, or academic credentials. On top of this, many voters were excited about making history—to vote for the first ever African American president. Such excitement added to Obama's valence advantage.

If, as I claim, Obama possessed a large valence advantage over McCain, then this means that a significant number of voters were what I have elsewhere called *Stokes voters.* These are voters who vote for the valence-advantaged candidate (Obama), although they prefer the policy positions of the valence-disadvantaged candidate (McCain). Indeed, because Obama had such a large valence advantage, yet the election was so close, it is reasonable to believe that the median voter was a Stokes voter. Accordingly, a true centrist in America is a person who slightly preferred Obama over McCain in 2008, yet if he had based his decision strictly on policy, he would have slightly preferred McCain.

Similar reasoning implies that since George W. Bush barely defeated John Kerry in 2004, a true centrist would have slightly preferred Bush over John Kerry in 2004. Further, since the 2000 election was almost a perfect tie, a true centrist would have been almost perfectly indifferent between George W. Bush and Al Gore.

Centrist Regions in America

A third lesson is that if you are truly centrist, then you would be at home in a region that is politically representative of the country—that is, in a region that voted approximately 53–46 for Obama in 2008 or approximately 52–47 for Bush in 2004.

An example of such a region is Suffolk County, New York (located in eastern Long Island). It voted 51–47 for Obama in 2008 and 50–49 for Kerry in 2004.[5] Another example is Dallas County, Texas (which contains the city of Dallas). It voted 57–42 for Obama in 2008 and 50–49 for Bush in 2004.

Meanwhile, a true centrist would feel out of place in a region such as Manhattan, New York City. It voted 84–13 for Obama in 2008 and 82–17 for Kerry in 2004. For opposite reasons, a true centrist would feel out of place in Washington County, Utah, which voted 76–21 for McCain in 2008 and 81–17 for Bush in 2004.

By using regression analysis and data from presidential elections, I can estimate the PQ of the average *voter* in a region—that is, I do not have to restrict my analysis to PQs of politicians. To illustrate this, consider Figure 12.1:

FIGURE 12.1

Estimating the PQs of Congressional Districts

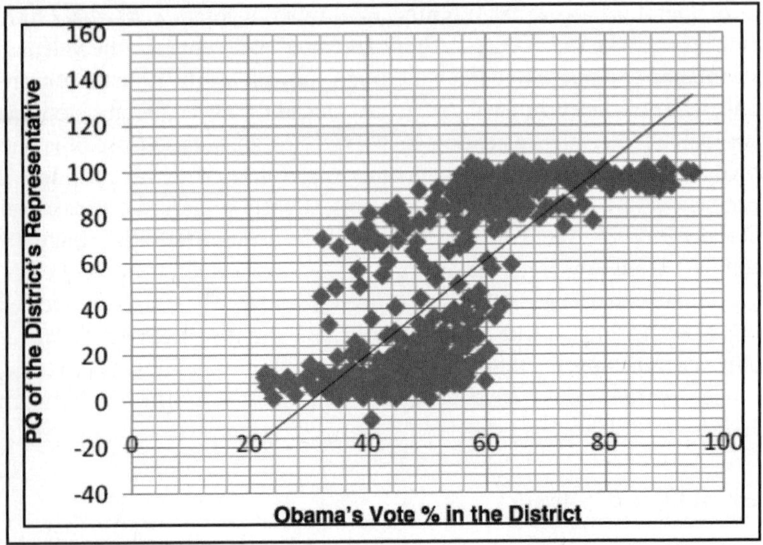

The horizontal axis represents President Obama's share of the two-party vote in a congressional district, and the vertical axis represents the PQ of the district's representative. Each dot represents a congressional district and its representative. For instance, consider the graph's most "north-western" dot. It represents the Seventeenth District of Texas. In that district Obama received 32.3 percent of the two-party vote. (Note that the horizontal position of the dot is at 32.3.) The House member of the district was Chet Edwards, whose PQ was 70.7. (Note that the vertical position of the dot is at 70.7.).

Using the dots on the graph (which represent data), regression analysis finds the line that best "fits" the dots. The line solves the following thought experiment: Suppose you knew the share of the vote that President Obama received in a particular congressional district. Using only that information, what is the best prediction of the PQ of the district's House member?

The regression line in the above graph, which answers that question, is represented by the following equation:

$$[\text{Predicted PQ}] = -61.04 + 2.040 \times [\text{Obama's vote \%}]$$

Thus, for instance, consider, once again, the Seventeenth District of Texas. Once we substitute 32.3 for "[Obama's vote percentage]," we get a predicted PQ of 4.9. This number is the vertical position of the line (corresponding to the 32.3 horizontal position). Note that Chet Edwards's actual PQ is about 66 points higher. Thus, the regression line implies that Edwards is, if anything, too liberal for his district. (Indeed, although Edwards is a Democrat, his district contains George W. Bush's ranch in Crawford.) The above analysis predicts that if Edwards were to lose his seat in an election, then his replacement would more likely be to his right than his left. (This actually happened in 2010.)

Now recall from chapter 5 that I assume that, on average, legislators are representative of their district. If true, then this means that the predicted PQ from the above equation is a good estimate of the PQ of the average voter in a district.

Further, the equation allows me to estimate the PQ of the average voter in *any* region, not just congressional districts, as long as I have data about how the region voted in the 2008 presidential election.

For instance, consider the state of Georgia. In 2008 Obama's two-party vote share in the state was 47.4 percent. Substituting this into the above equation gives 35.6 as the PQ of the average Georgia voter in 2008.

I have computed similar PQ estimates with data from the prior presidential election, in 2004.[6] Thus, for any region I can compute the 2004 PQ of its average voter, and the 2008 PQ. I take the average of those two PQs and call it the PQ of the region. Using this method, I have computed the PQ of all fifty states:

TABLE 12.1

PQ of the Average Voter in U.S. States

	State	PQ
1	Utah	5.8
2	Wyoming	7.0
3	Idaho	11.7
4	Oklahoma	13.1
5	Nebraska	19.9
6	Alaska	20.4
7	Alabama	20.9
8	Kansas	24.3

(continued)

TABLE 12.1 (continued)

	State	PQ
9	North Dakota	26.4
10	Kentucky	26.8
11	Texas	27.5
12	Louisiana	28.5
13	Mississippi	28.5
14	South Dakota	29.8
15	Arkansas	30.4
16	Tennessee	30.5
17	South Carolina	32.1
18	West Virginia	32.2
19	Montana	33.5
20	Georgia	34.3
21	Indiana	35.3
22	Arizona	36.0
23	North Carolina	39.5
24	Missouri	42.1
25	Florida	44.8
26	Virginia	44.9
27	Ohio	47.4
28	Colorado	48.2
29	Iowa	50.7
30	Nevada	51.2
31	New Hampshire	51.9
32	Pennsylvania	52.9
33	Minnesota	53.4
34	New Mexico	53.5
35	Wisconsin	53.6
36	Michigan	56.6

TABLE 12.1 (continued)

	State	PQ
37	Oregon	57.0
38	New Jersey	57.9
39	Washington	59.1
40	Maine	60.2
41	Delaware	63.2
42	Connecticut	63.5
43	California	64.2
44	Illinois	64.9
45	Maryland	66.5
46	New York	70.2
47	Rhode Island	72.2
48	Massachusetts	73.6
49	Hawaii	74.4
50	Vermont	76.7

As Table 12.1 indicates, the five most centrist states in the United States (in order of their centrism) are: Iowa, Nevada, Colorado, New Hampshire, and Ohio.

I have also computed the average PQ for each *county* in the United States. For instance, the following are the twenty most centrist counties in the United States. (Although, in chapter 5, I reported 50.4 as the PQ of the average U.S. voter, that number had been rounded to the nearest tenth. The more accurate number is 50.3504.)

TABLE 12.2

The Twenty Most Centrist Counties in the United States

	County	Description	PQ
1	Rowan, Ky.	rural, 60 miles east of Lexington	50.36
2	Washoe, Nev.	contains Reno, "biggest little city in the world"	50.37
3	Pinellas, Fla.	St. Petersburg & suburbs	50.33
4	Chester, S.C.	small town, northern S. Carolina	50.32
5	Somerset, Me.	small town, central Maine	50.40
6	Tillamook, Ore.	rural, coastal, 60 miles west of Portland	50.30
7	Baker, Ga.	rural, southwest Georgia	50.29
8	Cedar, Iowa	rural, eastern Iowa	50.43
9	Big Stone, Minn.	rural, western Minnesota	50.45
10	Menifee, Ky.	rural, 50 miles east of Lexington	50.21
11	Yazoo, Miss.	small town, 50 miles north of Jackson	50.50
12	Arapahoe, Colo.	southeast Denver suburbs	50.19
13	Skagit, Wash.	north Seattle exurbs	50.18
14	Alger, Mich.	rural, northern Michigan	50.16
15	Las Animas, Colo.	rural, southern Colorado	50.56
16	Marshall, Iowa	small town, 50 miles NE of Des Moines	50.58
17	Fayette, Pa.	small town, 50 miles SE of Pittsburgh	50.12
18	Sullivan, N.Y.	small town, 100 miles NW of NYC	50.08
19	Essex, N.Y.	small town, 60 miles east of Syracuse	50.07
20	Ventura, Calif.	northwest Los Angeles exurbs	50.06

Because many these counties have small populations, and therefore you might not have heard of them, I have conducted a similar exercise with larger counties. The following table lists all U.S. counties that contain at least 700,000 people and have an average PQ between 35 and 65. I divide these counties into three groups: (a) right-leaning centrist, (b) centrist, and (c) left-leaning centrist, where I define the latter terms according to whether the county's average PQ is between: (a) 35 and 45, (b) 45 and 55, and (c) 55 and 65.

TABLE 12.3

Large, Right-Leaning-Centrist Counties

County	Description	PQ
Duval, Fla.	Jacksonville and suburbs	36.6
Fresno, Calif.	Fresno (city) and suburbs	37.7
Riverside, Calif.	far southeastern L.A. suburbs	38.5
Harris, Tex.	Houston and suburbs	41.3
San Bernardino, Calif.	far northeastern L.A. suburbs	42.2
Bexar, Tex.	San Antonio and suburbs	43.2
Hillsborough, Fla.	Tampa and suburbs	43.6

TABLE 12.4

Large, Centrist Counties

County	Description	PQ
Hamilton, Ohio	Cincinatti and suburbs	45.9
DuPage, Ill.	western Chicago suburbs	46.4
San Diego, Calif.	San Diego (city) and suburbs	47.7
Suffolk, N.Y.	eastern Long Island	49.2
Macomb, Mich.	far northeastern Detroit suburbs	49.8
Ventura, Calif.	far northwestern L.A. suburbs	50.1
Pinellas, Fla.	St. Petersburg and suburbs	50.3
Pima, Ariz.	Tucson and suburbs	52.7
Nassau, N.Y.	western Long Island	53.1
Bergen, N.J.	far northern NYC suburbs	53.1
Dallas, Tex.	Dallas (city) and suburbs	53.4
Pierce, Wash.	southern Seattle suburbs	53.8
Oakland, Mich.	far northwestern Detroit suburbs	53.9

TABLE 12.5

Large, Left-Leaning-Centrist Counties

County	Description	PQ
Sacramento, Calif.	Sacramento (city) and suburbs	55.7
Orange, Fla.	Orlando and suburbs	55.8
Baltimore, Md.	environs of, but not including, Baltimore City	56.0
Monroe, N.Y.	Rochester and suburbs	56.5
Fairfield, Conn.	far northeastern NYC suburbs	57.7
Miami-Dade, Fla.	Miami (city) and suburbs	58.1
Clark, Nev.	Las Vegas and suburbs	58.7
Worcester, Mass.	Worcester (city) and suburbs	61.1
Franklin, Ohio	Columbus and suburbs	61.2
St. Louis, Mo.	St. Louis (city) and suburbs	61.5
Marion, Ind.	Indianapolis and suburbs	61.9
Allegheny, Pa.	Pittsburgh and suburbs	62.3
Montgomery, Pa.	far northern Philadelphia suburbs	63.2
Erie, N.Y.	Buffalo and suburbs	63.3
New Haven, Conn.	New Haven (city) and suburbs	64.0
Middlesex, N.J.	far southwestern NYC suburbs	64.7

A final set of centrist regions are what I call NASCAR counties. These are counties that host a Sprint Cup NASCAR race. The following is a list of those counties as well as the PQ of the county. Note that the average PQ of all the counties is 44.4—that is, NASCAR counties are just slightly more conservative than the average American voter.

TABLE 12.6

NASCAR Counties

Racetrack	County of Racetrack	Town of Racetrack	PQ of County
Atlanta Motor Speedway	Henry, Ga.	Hampton	23.7
Auto Club Speedway	San Bernardino, Calif.	Fontana	42.2
Bristol Motor Speedway	Sullivan, Tenn.	Bristol	4.6
Charlotte Motor Speedway*	Cabarrus, N.C.	Concord	17.8
Chicagoland Speedway	Will, Ill.	Joliet	49.8
Darlington Raceway	Darlington, S.C.	Darlington	42.6
Daytona Intl. Speedway	Volusia, Fla.	Daytona Beach	49.9
Dover Intl. Speedway	Kent, Del.	Dover	43.2
Homestead-Miami Speedway	Miami-Dade, Fla.	Homestead	58.1
Indianapolis Motor Speedway	Marion, Ind.	Speedway	61.9
Infineon Raceway	Sonoma, Calif.	Sonoma	92.3
Kansas Speedway	Wyandotte, Kans.	Kansas City	84.6
Las Vegas Motor Speedway	Clark, Nev.	North Las Vegas	58.7
Martinsville Speedway	Henry, Va.	Ridgeway	32.5
Michigan Intl. Speedway	Jackson, Mich.	Brooklyn	40.5
N. Hampshire Motor Speedway	Merrimack, N.H.	Loudon	56.1
Phoenix Intl. Raceway	Maricopa, Ariz.	Avondale	32.5
Pocono Raceway	Monroe, Pa.	Long Pond	54.9
Richmond Intl. Raceway	Henrico, Va.	Richmond	47.9
Talladega Superspeedway	Talladega, Ala.	Eastaboga	23.8
Texas Motor Speedway	Tarrant, Tex.	Fort Worth	26.1
Watkins Glen International	Schuyler, N.Y.	Watkins Glen	32.3
Average			44.4

* In 1999, Charlotte Motor Speedway was renamed Lowe's Motor Speedway. After the 2009 NASCAR season, Lowe's chose not to renew its contract for the naming rights, and the stadium reverted back to its original name.

Thus, to summarize the third lesson, if you want a good idea of what it means to be centrist in America, you won't find it in New York City, nor in Washington County, Utah. The key is visit a few NASCAR counties, or a place like Reno, Long Island, Tucson, or Dallas.

13. "Wise Men from the Center on Budget and Policy Priorities Say . . ."

JUST BECAUSE JOURNALISTS' personal opinions are liberal, so goes a common claim, that doesn't mean that their reporting will be biased. As Michael Kinsley, the founding editor of *Slate*, notes, "But—for the millionth time!—an opinion is not a bias! The fact that reporters tend to be liberal says nothing one way or another about their tendency to be biased."[1]

I agree with Kinsley. The survey evidence that I presented in earlier chapters does not prove that the *reporting* of journalists is biased. Further, to some extent, I also agree with the "corporate media" theorists: That is, many corporate bosses pressure their journalists not to report in the far-left manner the journalists desire. This may happen because the boss is conservative and has a personal stake in the news that his company reports. More benignly, he may want to maximize profits, which usually means reporting the way his moderate consumers desire.

I also agree with Kathleen Hall Jamieson, a communications professor at the University of Pennsylvania. She has noted, "Another explanation would hold that norms of journalism, including 'objectivity' and 'balance' blunt whatever biases exist."[2]

In sum, although the personal views of journalists, in general, pull their reporting to the left, countervailing forces pull their reporting the other way—toward the center, and maybe even past the center to the right.

But even if such countervailing forces exist, that by no means implies that they are stronger than the personal views of the journalist.

Notwithstanding the claims of the far left—even if the journalist works for a corporation, and even if her boss is conservative—this does not end the argument. The net effect of all the forces is an empirical question.

And the only way to answer that question is to examine the *content* of the media. As Don Quixote noted, the proof of the pudding is in the eating.

This and the next three chapters are devoted to such proof of the pudding. I discuss three methods, all of which measure the bias of the content of the media.

Quotations from Experts as Data to Judge Bias

In his book *Bias*, Bernard Goldberg, a former CBS News correspondent, reveals a tactic that journalists can use to disguise their bias:

> Well, news fans, here's one of those dirty little secrets journalists are never supposed to reveal to the regular folks out there in the audience: a reporter can find an expert to say anything the reporter wants—*anything*! Just keep calling until one of the experts says what you need him to say and tell him you'll be right down with your camera crew to interview him.[3]

Steve Curnutte is the author of *Mortgage Cocktail* and an expert on the home-loan industry. During 2008, television news shows frequently asked him to comment on the mortgage crisis. "Not only is [Goldberg] exactly right," Curnutte told me, "it's worse than that. They ask you what you're going to say, and if they like it, they send a limo to your office, take you to the satellite uplink studio, and then take you back. All in like forty-five or fifty minutes. It's hysterical that it's like that. It's a shame. But that's the way it is."

Three decades before Goldberg, Timothy Crouse in his classic *The Boys on the Bus*, also gave hints of the tactic.

> The editors in Los Angeles killed the story. They told journalist [Jules] Witcover that it didn't "come off" and that it was an "opinion" story . . . The solution was simple, they told him. All he had to do was get other people to make the same points and draw the same conclusions and then write the article *in their words* [emphasis in original].[4]

While many people might be outraged at the tactic—i.e., when journalists engage in it, they are basically deceiving their audience, disguising their own opinions as ones from experts—Milyo and I are grateful that they do it. The tactic was what provided us data to objectively measure the media's bias, which eventually allowed us to publish our article in the *Quarterly Journal of Economics.*

As I've noted earlier, the slant quotient is defined as the solution to the following thought experiment: If you read a news story, but mistakenly think it is a speech by a politician, what would you guess is the PQ of the would-be politician? That guess is the slant quotient.

Here is how the quotes-from-experts data helps to solve the thought experiment. Suppose, as a simplified example, there were only two think tanks in the world, A and B. And suppose you found that *The New York Times* quoted experts from A twice as often as it quoted experts from B.

Now suppose that you also found that when politicians quoted experts from A and B, they did not do this randomly. Instead, their choice seemed to be related to their PQ—e.g., suppose that, as their PQs rose, they became more likely to cite A instead of B. Given those citation patterns, what is the most likely PQ of a politician who cites A twice as often as B? That PQ, according to the method that Milyo and I developed, is the slant quotient for *The New York Times.*

In practice, our method is more complicated. First, I am leaving out the technical details about how our method decides "what is the most likely PQ of a politician who cites A twice as often as B." Explaining that requires a strong dose of statistical jargon and a few mathematical formulas.[5] Second, instead of two think tanks, our data involved citations from two hundred different think tanks and policy groups.[6]

A feature of our data is that, with only one exception, it does not require us—nor our research assistants—to make any subjective decisions when coding the data. That is, for instance, never did we or our research assistants have to think, "Did that sentence seem liberal, centrist, or conservative?" Instead, all we had to do was note the name of the think tank that was cited.

The one exception was that we excluded cases where a journalist or legislator cited a statement from an expert, but then criticized the statement. Sometimes we had to make a subjective judgment to decide if the expert really was being criticized. However, those cases comprised only a tiny fraction of our data. For instance, of the citations by journalists, only about one percent were cases where the journalist criticized the expert's statement. Further, even if we had adopted an extremely inclusive definition of *criticize,* such cases would have comprised only about 1.5 percent of the data.

Related, we excluded cases where the journalist or legislator gave an ideological label to the think tanks. For instance, we did this if the journalist wrote something like "Mr. Smith of the conservative Heritage Foundation said . . ." In our sample, the media outlets tended to brand conservative think tanks with ideological labels more often than they did liberal think tanks. This caused the slant quotients of the outlets to be more liberal. However, the effect was small. When we re-did the analysis—but this time did not exclude such ideologically branded citations—the average SQ dropped only a half point, from 62.6 to 62.1

Results of the Method

After we gathered all the data and programmed a computer to execute our method, the computer reported the following SQs for the twenty news outlets that we examined.

TABLE 13.1

Slant Quotients of Various Media Outlets

Media Outlet	Period of Observation	Estimated SQ
ABC's *Good Morning America*	6/27/1997–6/26/2003	56.1
ABC World News Tonight	1/1/1994–6/26/2003	61.0
CBS Early Show	11/1/1999–6/26/2003	66.6
CBS Evening News	1/1/1990–6/26/2003	73.7
CNN *NewsNight with Aaron Brown*	11/9/2001–2/5/04	56.0
Drudge Report	3/26/2002–7/1/04	60.4
Fox News *Special Report with Brit Hume*	6/1/1998–6/26/2003	39.7
Los Angeles Times	6/28/2002–12/29/02	70.0
NBC *Nightly News*	1/1/1997–6/26/2003	61.6
NBC *Today Show*	6/27/1997–6/26/2003	64.0
The New York Times	7/1/2001–5/1/02	73.7
The NewsHour with Jim Lehrer	11/29/1999–6/26/2003	55.8
Newsweek	6/27/1995–6/26/2003	66.3
NPR's *Morning Edition*	1/1/1992–6/26/2003	66.3
Time	8/6/2001–6/26/03	65.4
U.S. News & World Report	6/27/1995–6/26/2003	65.8
USA Today	1/1/2002–9/1/02	63.4

TABLE 13.1 (continued)

Media Outlet	Period of Observation	Estimated SQ
The Wall Street Journal	1/1/2002–5/1/02	85.1
The Washington Post	1/1/2002–5/1/02	66.6
The Washington Times	1/1/2002–5/1/02	35.4
Average		62.6

Perhaps the most noteworthy result is that—consistent with the survey results, showing that the personal views of journalists overwhelmingly lean left—most of the outlets were indeed left of center. Only two of the twenty outlets had SQs that were right of center: *The Washington Times* and Fox News *Special Report with Brit Hume.*

However, while the latter two outlets were right-leaning, they were not far-right. For instance, *Special Report* was significantly more centrist than *CBS Evening News.* That is, the difference between the SQ of *Special Report* (39.7) and the center (50.4) was 10.7. The difference between the SQ of *CBS Evening News* (73.7) and the center was 23.3. Since the latter number is more than double the former number, this means that the liberal bias of *CBS Evening News* was more than double the conservative bias of *Special Report.* Meanwhile, *Special Report* and *ABC World News Tonight* were approximately equal in their biases. (*World News Tonight,* was 10.6 units from the center, 0.1 units closer than *Special Report.*) And *Special Report* was slightly less biased than *NBC Nightly News.* (*Nightly News* was 11.2 units from the center, 0.8 units further than *Special Report.*)

The SQ of *The Washington Times* was 15 units right of center. Thus, its bias was approximately equal to that of *The Washington Post,* whose SQ was 16.2 units left of center.

Two additional results may at first appear anomalous, however, they are not so anomalous once you know some context. The first involves the Drudge Report. Although Matt Drudge admits that his personal views are right of center, the SQ of his Web site leans left. One reason is that our data came both from (i) the news flashes that Matt Drudge himself occasionally reports and (ii) the news stories to which his site links. In fact, of the entire 311 think-tank citations that we found for the Drudge Report, only 5 came from reports written by Matt Drudge. Thus, for all intents and purposes, our estimate for the Drudge Report refers *only* to the articles to which his Web site links. Since these come from a broad mix of media outlets, and since the news in general is left-leaning, it should not be surprising that the SQ of the Drudge Report leans left.

A second seemingly anomalous result is *The Wall Street Journal*, which Milyo and I found to be the most liberal of all the news outlets of the twenty we examined. The first piece of context is that all of our data came before News Corp. bought the *Journal*. I expect that News Corp. will try to hire more conservative journalists, which should push the *Journal*'s SQ toward the center, perhaps past it.[7]

Other context is that our data came only from the *news pages* of the *Journal*. If we had included data from the editorial pages, then I'm sure that the *Journal*'s SQ would have been more conservative.

While our finding for the *Journal* might surprise many, some anecdotal evidence explains why the finding perhaps shouldn't be so surprising. Reed Irvine and Cliff Kincaid, for instance, note that "The *Journal* has had a long-standing separation between its conservative editorial pages and its liberal news pages."[8] Paul Sperry, in his article, "Myth of the Conservative *Wall Street Journal*," notes that the news division of the *Journal* sometimes calls the editorial division "Nazis." "Fact is," Sperry writes, "the Journal's news and editorial departments are as politically polarized as North and South Korea."[9] Sperry also documents a former *Journal* reporter, Kent MacDougall, bragging that he used the "bourgeois press" to help "popularize ideas with lengthy sympathetic profiles of Marxist economists." In addition, a poll from the Pew Research Center indicates that a greater percentage of Democrats, 29 percent, say they trust the *Journal* than do Republicans, 23 percent. Importantly, the question did not specify "the *news* division at the *Wall Street Journal*." If it had, Democrats surely would have said they trusted the *Journal* even more, and Republicans even less.[10]

Another result, which will surprise some readers, is that, according to our estimates, the mainstream media are actually not *that* far left, at least under some interpretations. For instance, while the PQ of the average Democrat in Congress is approximately 84, almost none of the media outlets has an SQ that high. Indeed, *The New York Times*, which was the third most liberal news outlet of all those we examined, is only as liberal as the average speech by Sen. Joe Lieberman (D,I-Conn.)—whom many people do not consider very liberal.

Another somewhat surprising result involves NPR's *Morning Edition*. Conservatives frequently blast NPR as an egregious example of liberal bias.[11] However, by our estimate *Morning Edition* hardly differs from the average mainstream news outlet. For instance, its SQ is approximately equal to that of *Time*, *Newsweek*, or *U.S. News & World Report*, and its SQ is slightly more *conservative* than *The Washington Post*'s.

Critiques of Our Method

In this final section I address some of the critiques that left-wing blogs have leveled at the method that Milyo and I developed. It may be a bit pointless to try to respond to these critiques. Many, and perhaps almost all, of the left-wing blogs would criticize the method no matter how sound it was—as long as its results showed a liberal bias in the media.

Nevertheless, it is useful to provide a few general responses to these critiques. One reason is to give you some background into the world of academic publishing. Another reason is that in some cases the critiques, coupled with my response, help you to better understand our method.

My first general response is simply to note the high standards that exist at top-tier academic journals, including the *Quarterly Journal of Economics*. At such journals if someone can expose a major problem in a published article, then the journal almost always allows that person to publish his critique in the journal.

It has now been more than five years since Milyo and I published the article, and the *QJE* has published no such piece. In fact, as far as I am aware, none of the left-wing bloggers has even *attempted* to publish such a piece in the *QJE*. (When someone sends a critique to the journal, the usual courtesy is for the journal editors to send a copy of the critique to the authors of the original article and allow them to write a response to the editors. The *QJE* has never sent Milyo or me such a critique, so I am confident that it has never received such a critique.) This fact makes me think that the bloggers themselves do not believe that they have discovered a major problem in our article—otherwise they would have sent their critique to the *QJE*. Keep in mind that some of the left-wing bloggers are professors. If they could publish such a piece, this would give them a publication in a first-tier economics journal, which would go a long way toward, if not guarantee, their earning tenure at their universities.

Related, a host of blogs adopted the following tactic. They would chip away at some minor aspect of our method. Although the blog's criticism might identify a genuine imperfection in the method, often the imperfection was trivial and had no effect on the main conclusions. Here again, in these cases I don't believe that the bloggers themselves think that they found a major problem. Here's why: As is common among academic researchers, Milyo and I are willing to give, and have given, our data to anyone who asks for them. If such a blogger truly believed that he had found a significant problem in our method, then he could have corrected the problem, re-conducted our statistical analysis himself, and shown how the correction changed the main results. If he did such a project, it would be a significant achievement—almost surely worthy of a publication in the *QJE*. Plus, it would seriously embarrass Milyo and me, which, I am certain would delight many of the bloggers. Yet not one of the left-wing bloggers has even asked for our data, much less executed such a project.

My second general response is more substantive. A common claim of the left-wing blogs goes something like the following: "(i) Left-wing think tanks are generally more scholarly and honest than right-wing think tanks; (ii) consequently, if a media outlet has a preference for honest and scholarly experts, then Groseclose and Milyo's method will spuriously cause it to appear to have a liberal bias."

Although, in terms of explaining our method, part (ii) is the more important part of the claim, let me first address (i). At least for the two hundred-think-tank sample that Milyo and I used, it appears that the opposite is true.

For instance, of the left-wing think tanks in our sample, the most scholarly is the Center on Budget and Policy Priorities.[12] However, if you check their Web site, you'll see that most of their experts do not have a PhD. Meanwhile, at the most scholarly conservative think tanks in our sample—such as the Hoover Institution, American Enterprise Institute, or the Political Economy Research Center—almost all of the experts have a PhD. Further, none of the experts at the Center on Budget and Policy Priorities has received highly prestigious honors such as a Nobel Prize, membership in the National Academy of Sciences, or membership on the President's Council of Economic Advisers. Meanwhile, the Hoover Institution has three Nobel Prize winners: Michael Spence, Douglass North, and Gary Becker. Another scholar, Robert Barro, who holds appointments at both Hoover and AEI, is a near-certain bet to win a Nobel Prize someday. In addition, six Hoover fellows are members of the National Academy of Sciences, and several more are members of the American Academy of Arts and Sciences. Two Hoover fellows, Michael Boskin and Edward Lazear, are former chairs of the President's Council of Economic Advisers. The AEI's Allan Meltzer, who has held faculty appointments at Harvard, University of Chicago, and Carnegie Mellon University, also was a member of the President's Council of Economic Advisers. As part of my job, I frequently read articles from the top four economics and political-science journals. I don't recall *ever* seeing one written by a scholar from the Center on Budget and Policy Priorities. Meanwhile, I frequently see such articles by scholars at one of the three conservative think tanks I've just mentioned. Hoover's Bruce Bueno de Mesquita, in fact, has written more articles in the flagship journal of political science, the *American Political Science Review*, than any other political scientist.

More important, let me address point (ii) of the above left-wing claim. That is, for the sake of argument, let me concede to the left-wing bloggers that (i) is true—that left-wing think tanks really are more scholarly and honest than conservative think tanks. However, even if this is true, it still does not mean that statement (ii) is true. That is, even if left-wing think tanks are more scholarly and honest than right-wing think tanks, then our method will *not* necessarily overstate the liberalness of the media. In fact, it might even *understate* the liberalness of the media.

The best way to illustrate this is with the following thought experiment. First, recall that, according to our results, the SQ of *The New York Times* is approximately equal to the PQ of Sen. Joe Lieberman. That is, the average *New York Times* article is about as liberal as the average speech by Joe Lieberman.

Now suppose that we could magically make the left-wing think tanks in our sample *more* scholarly and honest than before. Naturally, this would cause journalists to cite left-wing think tanks experts more. In turn, this would cause the SQs of the media to become more liberal, right?

The answer is no, and here's why: If such think tanks increased their scholarship and honesty, then this would also cause a politician like Joe Lieberman to cite the left-wing think tanks more. And if he increased his citations of left-wing think tanks just as much as *The New York Times* did, then *The New York Times* would still sound like a Joe Lieberman speech. Accordingly, the *Times*'s SQ would still approximately equal Joe Lieberman's PQ.

Not only that, suppose that this scenario caused Joe Lieberman to cite left-wing think tanks more often than it caused *The New York Times* to cite them. If this happened, then the *Times* would sound *less* liberal than a Joe Lieberman speech. As a consequence, our method would assign the *Times* an SQ less than (i.e., more conservative than) Joe Lieberman's PQ.

A related issue arises if, say, the left-wing think tanks happen to have better publicists than the right-wing think tanks. Yes, the publicists would cause the media to cite left-wing think tanks more, but they would also cause *politicians* to cite left-wing think tanks more. Again, the net effect would not necessarily make the media's SQs more liberal.

Moreover, you could probably think of a host of other nonpolitical factors that might cause the media to increase their citation of left-wing think tanks. Yet, as long as the factor also causes politicians to increase their citations in the same manner, then this will not be a problem for our method. However, what if the factor is not as symmetric as I've presented it? That is, what if the factor affects journalists and politicians in different ways?

For instance, suppose that (a) experts at left-wing think tanks are actually more scholarly than experts at right-wing think tanks, and (b) journalists have a preference for citing scholarly experts, *and their preference for doing so is greater than that of politicians.*

If this happens, then the method that Milyo and I developed indeed faces a problem. We will overstate the true liberalness of the media.

However, at least three points should be noted in response. First, it is by no means clear that (a) and (b) are true. For instance, consider (a). As I've argued, at least when you look at the most scholarly think tanks in our sample, you find that the right-wing think tanks are clearly more scholarly than the left-wing ones.[13] Further, it is not clear that (b) is true—that is, it is possible, and maybe likely, that politicians' taste for citing scholarly experts is higher than that of journalists. For instance, the competition for a job in Congress is much higher than that for a job as a journalist. Further, members of Congress are very well educated (e.g., more than 65 percent have graduate degrees), and I warrant that they are also better paid than journalists.

Second, now suppose that (b) is true, while *the opposite of* (a) is true. That is, suppose journalists prefer to cite scholarly think tanks more than politicians do; and right-wing think tanks are more scholarly than left-wing think tanks. Then this would cause our method to *understate* the true liberalness of the media. To see this, note that under this scenario, part of the reason that media outlets would cite right-wing think tanks is not so much their desire for conservative balance. Rather, it would be artificial—it would be because the right-wing think tanks in the sample happened to be more scholarly. This would cause our method artificially to understate the SQs of media outlets—i.e., to report them as more conservative than they actually are.

For similar reasons, the same thing would happen if (a) is true, but the opposite of (b) is true: Our method would again, understate the true liberalness of the media. Meanwhile, however, if the opposite of (a) and the opposite of (b) are true, then our method would overstate the true liberalness of the media.

Thus, of the four combinations in which (a) and (b) or their opposites can be true, two imply that our method overstates the liberalness of the media, and two imply that it understates the liberalness of the media.

My third point is simply to state that, at least approximately, I don't believe that (a) or (b), or their opposites, are true. That is, I believe that the left-wing and right-wing think tanks in our sample are approximately equal in terms of their scholarliness. Also, I believe that politicians and journalists have approximately equal preferences for citing scholarly think tanks.

But that's only my assertion. I could be wrong. Accordingly, it is important to examine other methods that measure the bias of the media—methods that won't be plagued by the potential problems I've just described. That task is the focus of the next three chapters.

14. The Language of Journalists and the Special Case of Partial-Birth Abortion

"What Opponents of the Procedure Call 'Partial Birth'"

On October 21, 2003, by a vote of 64–34, the U.S. Senate passed the Partial-Birth Abortion Ban Act. While it was a huge victory for conservatives, the next day's news revealed that liberals had won perhaps an even bigger victory—the battle over the language about abortion.

Here's how David Crary, an AP National Writer, began his article: "On Capitol Hill, in the Florida statehouse, even in the boardroom of the YWCA, the *self-proclaimed* [my emphasis] right-to-life movement and its conservative allies are on a winning streak that is deeply troubling to abortion-rights activists."[1]

Note that, according to Crary, the term for the "right-to-life" movement is "self-proclaimed," but the term for "abortion rights" activists is not.

Publishing the same day, a separate AP writer, Will Lester, noted "'When people see *Roe v. Wade* at risk, they vote for the pro-choice position,' said Ellen Malcolm, the president of the pro-choice group EMILY's List."[2]

Although many conservatives would call the EMILY's List "pro-abortion" or "anti-life," note that the AP used the preferred term of liberals, "pro-choice."

Suppose for a moment that advocates of other issues were as successful at influencing the language of journalists as "abortion rights" proponents are.

If so, then mob bosses would proclaim, "I'm not 'pro-murder'; I'm 'pro-revenge-killing rights.'" House speaker John Boehner (R-Ohio) would explain, "I'm not 'pro-tax cut'; I'm 'pro-choice' on tax cuts. After all, under my plan, if anyone wants to pay his former, higher rate, then he can always send a check to the U.S. Treasury." Jefferson Davis would have called himself not "pro-slavery," but "pro-choice on slavery," since he did not advocate that each white person own a slave, only that each white person have the right to own a slave. Alternatively, he might have called his position "pro-slave-owner rights."

Two more sentences, respectively by AP writers Crary and Lester, contain a similarly interesting choice of words:

- "The vote in Congress to ban *what critics call partial-birth abortion* [my emphasis] capped a campaign waged by anti-abortion groups since 1995."[3]
- "Dick Gephardt, the former House minority leader, voted with the Republican majority last year for legislation that would ban *what critics call partial birth abortion* [my emphasis]."[4]

Note that instead of the simple phrase "partial-birth abortion," the AP writers used the more unwieldy "what critics call partial birth abortion." Even when journalists don't have an alternative phrase, they still won't deign to use the language of conservatives.

Fox News anchor Brit Hume made fun of such journalists:

> From some of the wording in news accounts of yesterday's Senate vote on abortion, you might not have known it was about banning a procedure in which a live fetus is partially pulled from the womb before its skull is punctured and brains sucked out. This is commonly referred to as "partial-birth abortion."
>
> But ABC's Peter Jennings called it, quote, "a certain abortion procedure." The AP called it, "a type of late-middle and late-term abortion." CBS called it, quote, "the procedure generally performed between the eighteen and twenty-four weeks of a pregnancy." Today's *Washington Post* called it "an abortion procedure" in a headline and then refers to it as, quote, "what abortion foes call a partial-birth procedure." *The New York Times* refers to it as, quote, a "type of abortion," and then refers to a "partial-birth method."[5]

In fairness to journalists, one reason they might not have called the procedure "partial-birth abortion" is that, as Sen. Barbara Boxer and other opponents of the act noted, "there is no such term in medicine as 'partial-birth abortion.'"[6] The argument, however, is tenuous. First, "partial-birth abortion" *is used*, at least occasionally, as a medical term.[7] Second, to be an official *legal* term, it does not matter whether a phrase is a medical term. After all, by many accounts there are no such medical terms as "manslaughter," "assault," or "stab." Yet journalists still use these terms. Third, not only was "partial birth" precisely defined in the bill, the term was part of the official title of the bill.[8]

No doubt many journalists refused to use the term "partial-birth abortion" for another reason: If they had, it would have helped persuade people to oppose the procedure. Even if you agree that "a woman should have the right to do whatever she wants with her own body," that argument, at best, only partially applies when the fetus has partially left the woman's body. When you agree to the "partial-birth" language, then you implicitly endorse, at least to a partial degree, the notion that the procedure kills a baby.

Words That Work

If you want to persuade someone, so goes the truism, some words work better than others. Frank Luntz, a Republican pollster and the author of *Words That Work,* is perhaps the authority on the principle. In a widely circulated 2005 memo, he advised Republican congressional candidates how best to describe President Bush's proposal to reform Social Security:

> Never say "privatization/private accounts." Instead say "personalization/personal accounts." Two-thirds of America want to personalize Social Security while only one-third would privatize it. Why? Personalizing Social Security suggests ownership and control over your retirement savings, while privatizing it suggests a profit motive and winners and losers.[9]

Combine this fact with another fact—that humans often try to persuade each other—and you get an important corollary: If you want to know a person's stance on an issue, note the words that he uses.

The corollary performed brilliantly in the Senate vote on the Partial-Birth Abortion Ban Act. Of the twenty-three senators who made a speech about the bill, thirteen used the plain-language term *partial-birth abortion.*

All thirteen of those voted *for* the bill. Of the ten senators who used a different phrase, such as "so-called partial birth" or "what opponents call partial birth," all ten voted *against* the bill.

Using Words to Measure Media Bias

Now let us apply this phrasing analysis to the media. For each of the twenty outlets that I listed in the previous chapter, I analyzed the first story that the outlet reported about the Senate bill. The following table lists the percentage of times that the outlet used the plain-language term "partial birth," versus the percentage of times that it used another phrase such as "what opponents call partial-birth abortion."

TABLE 14.1

Language Choice by Various Media Outlets

Media Outlet	% of times the outlet called the procedure: "partial birth"	something else
ABC World News Tonight	0	100
ABC's *Good Morning America*	0	100
CBS Early Show	0	100
CBS Evening News	0	100
CNN *NewsNight with Aaron Brown*	0	100
NBC Today Show	0	100
The New York Times	0	100
The NewsHour with Jim Lehrer	0	100
Time	0	100
U.S. News & World Report	0	100
The Washington Post	0	100
Los Angeles Times	14	86
NBC Nightly News	20	80
NPR's *Morning Edition*	20	80
The Wall Street Journal	25	75
USA Today	40	60
Newsweek	50	50

TABLE 14.1 (continued)

Media Outlet	% of times the outlet called the procedure: "partial birth"	something else
Drudge Report	60	40
Centrist—Ave. U.S. Senator	65	35
The Washington Times	78	22
Fox News *Special Report**	100	0

* The headline on the Drudge Report used the plain-language phrase "partial-birth abortion." That headline linked to the story by *The Washington Post,* which used the plain-language phrase zero times and phrases like "what opponents call..." four times. One method would be to analyze only the words that Matt Drudge wrote. That method would record the Drudge Report as using the plain-language term 100 percent of the time. Another method would be to analyze all words in (i) the headline by Matt Drudge *and* (ii) the story to which it linked. The latter method records the Drudge Report as using the plain-language term 20 percent of the time. The average of the two methods gives 60 percent, which is the figure that I list in the table.

As the table shows, the media overwhelmingly adopted the language of the (minority) opponents of the bill—not that of the (majority) proponents.

To define *centrist* in the table, I conducted the following thought experiment. Suppose that the sample of senators who made speeches accurately represents the language of proponents and opponents. That is, for instance, suppose that the fifty-one senators who voted for the bill, yet did not make a speech, would also call the procedure "partial birth" and not an unwieldy term such as "what opponents of the procedure call partial birth." Suppose also that the two senators who did not vote, Kay Bailey Hutchison (R-Tex.) and John Edwards (D-N.C.), would respectively have voted yea and nay on the bill. Then, by my definition, a news story is centrist if it sounds as if it were written by a cross section of U.S. senators. In such a story, 65 percent of the time the journalist would call the procedure "partial birth" and 35 percent of the time she would use a more unwieldy phrase such as "what opponents call 'partial birth.'"

According to this definition, similar to the results of the previous chapter, eighteen out of twenty media outlets were left of center. The Drudge Report, while left-leaning, was the closest to the center. Unlike the results of the previous chapter, most of the mainstream outlets were *far left* of center. Note that eleven out of twenty outlets *never* used the language preferred by moderates and conservatives.

Further, for many reasons my definition of *centrist* is overly charitable to the media. First, the Senate on this issue was not quite representative of voters. According to a Gallup poll, 70 percent of the American people oppose partial-birth abortion.[10] This suggests that 70, not 65, is the more appropriate number to define centrist in the table.[11]

Second, in coding the language of senators, there were three questionable cases—those involving speeches by Bill Nelson (D-Fla.), Russ Feingold (D-Wis.), and Richard Durbin (D-Ill.). I coded each senator as *not* using the plain-language "partial-birth" term, even though you could argue that I should have. For instance, Nelson said, "I am opposed to the procedure known as partial-birth abortion." Further, in the same speech he called the act by its official name and did not use any qualifier such as "so-called."

Given this, if we could poll all the senators, it is reasonable to believe that *more* than sixty-five senators would call the procedure its plain-language term. I believe that something like five or ten of the nay-voting senators would do this. If so, then the proper number to define centrist in the table would be not 65, but something like 70 or 75.

Third, the official title of the bill was the "Partial-Birth Abortion Ban Act of 2003." It wasn't, as the mainstream media might lead you to believe, the "What-Opponents-of-the-Procedure-Call-Partial-Birth-Abortion Ban Act of 2003." Further, in contrast to what many journalists claimed, "partial birth" *is* the most accurate description of the procedure that the Act banned. Although some journalists argued that "intact dilation and extraction" was the more accurate term, that's not true. The bill precisely defined "partial-birth," and that definition distinctly differs from "intact dilation and extraction."[12]

Now suppose you believe that "unbiased" should be defined according to whether the journalist uses the most accurate term, not whether he or she mimics the language of a cross section of the Senate. Then an unbiased journalist should use the plain-language term 100 percent of the time, not 65 percent. By this standard, only one of the outlets mentioned in the table, *Special Report with Brit Hume*, was unbiased. All the rest, even *The Washington Times*, were biased left.

On top of all this, my analysis, I believe, understates the true bias of the media on this issue. Language was only one symptom of the bias. Other symptoms—such as failing to mention facts that conservatives were emphasizing—may have been much worse.

On my Web site I have posted a copy of the entire Senate debate on the partial-birth bill (see www.timgroseclose.com/partial-birth-senate-speches.pdf), along with several paragraphs of the stories that twenty news outlets reported (see www.timgroseclose.com/partial-birth-media-treatment.pdf). If you read the two treatments, I'm confident that not only will you notice the asymmetry, you'll become outraged by it. You'll see for yourself (i) how informative and balanced the Senate treatment was, yet (ii) how unbalanced the media treatment was. The latter systematically withheld certain facts from their readers and viewers.

One example involved whether the bill allowed an exemption for the health or life of the mother. Here is how NBC's Chip Reid treated the issue on the *Nightly News*:

> VIDEO OF SEN. RICK SANTORUM: These abortions are performed on healthy mothers with healthy children, so these are healthy children—otherwise would be born alive.
>
> CHIP REID: Opponents say that's not accurate and criticize the ban for undercutting the right to abortion and for failing to make an exception for the health of the mother.
>
> VIDEO OF SEN. BARBARA BOXER: She could have blood clots, an embolism, a stroke, damage to nearby organs or paralysis if this particular procedure is not available to her.[13]

It is true, as NBC reported, that the bill did not contain an exemption for the *health* of the mother. However, the bill did contain an exemption for the *life* of the mother, a fact NBC didn't mention.

If your only source of information had been a report such as NBC's or a speech such as Senator Boxer's, then you easily would've been fooled into believing that the bill contained no exemption for the *life* of the mother.

CNN's Aaron Brown, I believe, *was* fooled in such a manner. The following was his report:

> The Senate voted to ban the medical procedure known by abortion opponents as partial-birth abortion. This type of abortion is relatively infrequent. Though, like most of the abortion debate, there is little agreement on that as well, we suppose. It is almost always done late in a pregnancy. The measure drawing fire—*it contains no exception for when the mother's life is in danger* [my emphasis]. It will certainly end up in court after the president signs it.[14]

Sen. Wayne Allard (R-Colo.) responded to Senator Boxer's speech—as well as to misleading media reports—simply by reading from the text of the bill:

> [The ban] does not apply to a partial-birth abortion that is necessary to save the life of a mother whose life is endangered by a physical disorder, physical illness, or physical injury, including a

> life-endangering physical condition caused by or arising from the pregnancy itself.[15]

IF YOU WERE a journalist, there are four ways you could have treated the issues of life and health exemptions: First, if you wanted to distort the story in the conservative direction, then you would have reported that (i) the bill contained a life exemption, but you would have omitted that (ii) it didn't contain a health exemption. None of the twenty outlets did that.

Second and third, if you wanted to provide a balanced treatment of the two facts, then you would have reported *both* (i) and (ii) or reported *neither* (i) nor (ii). Five of the twenty outlets—*Special Report,* NPR, *USA Today, The NewsHour with Jim Lehrer,* and *U.S. News & World Report*—did that.

Fourth, if you wanted to distort the story in a liberal direction, then you would have omitted (i) but reported (ii). Fifteen of the twenty outlets did that.

Finally, if you were a journalist wanting to give a *very* balanced and accurate report, you might also have explained *why* the authors of the bill didn't include an exemption for the health of the mother. If so, you might have quoted a passage such as the following, which Sen. Rick Santorum (R-Pa.) delivered on the Senate floor:

> The interesting point is, why are they pushing so hard for this health exception, and why are we resisting it so much? . . .
>
> [W]hen *Roe v. Wade* was decided, there was a companion case called *Doe v. Bolton,* and in that case "health" was defined as: "Medical judgment may be exercised in the light of all factors: physical, emotional, psychological, familial, and the woman's age relevant to the well-being of the patient." . . .
>
> So what this provision did, and that is what the Court wanted to do, was to give absolute latitude to the doctor . . . So the health exception bars the bill, stops the bill from having any effect.
>
> So that is why we resist.[16]

None of the twenty media outlets—not even *The Washington Times* or *Special Report*—mentioned *Doe v. Bolton*; nor did any outlet explain the broad manner in which judges had treated health exemptions in the past.

15. The Language of Journalists and the Gentzkow-Shapiro Measure of Media Bias

TWO ECONOMISTS AT the University of Chicago, Matthew Gentzkow and Jesse Shapiro, have shown that the main principles of the previous chapter—(i) that words can reveal a person's political views, and (ii) that you can use words to judge the slant of the media—apply more generally to *any* political issue, not just partial-birth abortion.

Gentzkow and Shapiro, who both graduated from the economics PhD program at Harvard, do not think like typical economists. Between obtaining his undergraduate degree at Harvard and entering the university's PhD program, Gentzkow spent two years as a director of theatrical plays. The plays included ones by Shakespeare, Becket, Ionesco, and some that Gentzkow wrote himself.

Much of Shapiro's research involves topics that are not normally studied by economists. Besides the news media, he has examined factors that have caused American obesity rates to rise and factors that contribute to anti-Americanism in the Muslim world. In addition, along with Gentzkow, he has studied the effect of television on adolescent intellectual development. (Surprisingly, they find it has a *positive* effect.)

Just after receiving their PhDs—Gentzkow in 2004 and Shapiro in 2005—both took jobs at the University of Chicago. Quickly, they established themselves as rising stars in the economics profession. In January 2007, *The New York Times* featured them (along with Justin Wolfers—see chapter 3) as two of thirteen young "economists to watch." As the article noted, they were two of the top scholars "doing work that is both highly respected among experts and relevant to the rest of us." They, the article suggested, are "the future of economics."

In their project on media slant they applied principles (i) and (ii), plus an additional insight: The method that Milyo and I constructed—which used think-tank citations as basic data—could instead have used *any* words as its basic data.[1]

Gentzkow and Shapiro began their project by programming a computer to construct a list of all the two- and three-word phrases ever mentioned in a congressional speech during 2005. For instance, if a Senator or House member said, "I favor this bill," then Gentzkow and Shapiro's method would record three two-word phrases: "I favor," "favor this," and "this bill." The method would similarly record two three-word phrases from the sentence ("I favor this" and "favor this bill").

Next, the researchers noted that some phrases were used more often by Republicans and others were used more often by Democrats. Using a precise mathematical algorithm, they programmed a computer to construct a list of "politically loaded phrases." For instance, the following were some of the politically loaded phrases used most often by Democrats:

- veterans' health care
- arctic national wildlife
- outing [a] CIA agent[2]
- oil companies
- civil rights
- Rosa Parks

And the following were some of the politically loaded phrases used most often by Republicans:

- personal retirement accounts
- global war [on] terror
- partial-birth abortion
- stem cell
- death tax
- illegal aliens

Now recall the method that Milyo and I constructed. It allowed you to take a list of think-tank citations that a media outlet made, feed it into a computer, and then the computer would spit out a slant quotient. The computer treated the citations as if they had come from a speech by a politician. It asked, "What is the most likely PQ of the would-be politician, given the think-tank citations?"

Gentzkow and Shapiro's method does the same, except instead of think-tank citations, it uses loaded political phrases as its basic data.[3] By their method, a media outlet received a high SQ if the outlet used mainly liberal loaded phrases, and it received a low SQ if it used mainly conservative loaded phrases. The following table lists some of their results. It ranks—from most liberal to most conservative—the twenty highest-circulation newspapers in the United States.[4] (Unlike Milyo and me, Gentzkow and Shapiro analyzed only newspapers; that is, they ignored television shows, magazines, and radio shows.)

TABLE 15.1

Slant Quotients of the Highest-Circulation Newspapers

SQ Rank	Newspaper	Daily Circulation	Slant Quotient
1	*Detroit Free Press*	330,000	81.5
2	*N.Y. Daily News*	718,000	81.0
3	*Journal-Constitution* (Atlanta)	357,000	74.8
4	*San Francisco Chronicle*	386,000	71.9
5	*Chicago Tribune*	566,000	70.4
6	*Dallas Morning News*	411,000	69.8
7	*USA Today*	2,278,000	68.6
8	*Philadelphia Inquirer*	352,000	68.4
9	*The Boston Globe*	382,000	67.8
10	*The New York Times*	1,120,000	67.3
11	*Los Angeles Times*	815,000	66.1
12	*New York Post*	724,000	66.0
13	*Newsday* (Long Island)	398,000	65.9
14	*The Washington Post*	699,000	65.8
15	*Newark Star-Ledger*	372,000	64.8

(continued)

TABLE 15.1 (continued)

SQ Rank	Newspaper	Daily Circulation	Slant Quotient
16	*Cleveland Plain Dealer*	344,000	64.0
17	*Star Tribune* (Minneapolis)	345,000	59.2
18	*Arizona Republic*	433,000	55.5
19	*The Wall Street Journal*	2,062,000	55.1
20	*Houston Chronicle*	503,000	53.8
	Average		66.9

Similar to Milyo's and my results, Gentkow and Shapiro's results show that the overwhelming majority of media outlets are left of center. Indeed, as the table shows, *all* of the nation's twenty highest-circulation newspapers lean left. Of the one hundred highest-circulation newspapers, only two are right of center, the *Arizona Daily Star* (Tucson) and the *Daily Oklahoman* (Oklahoman City).

The method found that a small number of newspapers could be called centrist. The following are the fifteen newspapers that (i) have slant quotients between 45 and 55 and (ii) are among the one hundred highest-circulation newspapers:

Daily Oklahoma (Oklahoma City)	48.3
Arizona Daily Star (Tucson)	49.2
Daily Herald (NW Chicago suburbs)	51.4
Omaha World Herald	51.6
Las Vegas Review-Journal	52.1
The Washington Times	52.4
Asbury Park Press (New Jersey)	52.5
Honolulu Advertiser	52.5
Tulsa World	52.7
Orange County Register (Southern Calif.)	52.8
Morning Call (Allentown, Pa.)	53.1
Rocky Mountain News (Denver)	53.2
Houston Chronicle	53.8
Albuquerque Journal	54.8
Salt Lake Tribune	54.8

Bias Estimates for Local Newspapers

The following is a claim that people sometimes make about the biases of newspapers: "While perhaps we should expect major national newspapers to have a liberal bias—since their reporters and customers tend to live in large East and West Coast urban areas—we should expect the opposite with local newspapers, since their reporters and customers tend to live in smaller towns in the American Heartland."

To test the claim, I used Gentzkow and Shapiro's results. Specifically, I analyzed a sample of newspapers from "average" towns in the United States—where "average" means that the town is approximately average in population and average in political views.

To decide if a town's population is average, I conducted the following thought experiment. Suppose you lined up all the people in the United States according to the size of the metropolitan area in which they lived. That is, in such a line, the first nineteen million would be New Yorkers (including those who lived in the suburbs of New York City). The next thirteen million people would be Los Angelinos. The next ten million would be Chicagoans. And so on. After you've ordered everybody in this fashion, consider the median (i.e., middle) person in line. In which metropolitan area would he or she live?

The answer is Jacksonville, Florida. But if you guessed Nashville, Milwaukee, Memphis, or Louisville, you would have been very close. The following table lists Jacksonville and the ten metropolitan areas that come immediately before and after it in terms of population. The people living in those areas are thus average in terms of their "cosmopolitanness"—i.e., the extent to which they live in a large urban area.

The table also lists (i) the population of the metropolitan area (in 2008), (ii) the share of the two-party vote that George W. Bush received from the metropolitan area in 2004, (iii) the newspaper in the area with the most circulation, and (iv) the slant quotient of the newspaper, based on the Gentzkow-Shapiro results.

It turns out that this sample is also average in terms of its political views. Note, for instance, that the average two-party Bush vote of the twenty-one metro areas is 52.9.[5] This is only slightly higher than the national vote, 51.2.

TABLE 15.2

Slant Quotients of Newspapers in Average-Sized Cities

Metro Area	Population (in millions)	2004 Bush Vote	Newspaper	SQ
Las Vegas, Nev.	1.87	46.8	*Review-Journal*	52.1
San Jose, Calif.	1.82	n.a.	*Mercury News*	n.a.*
Columbus, Ohio	1.77	52.1	*Dispatch*	55.9
Indianapolis, Ind.	1.72	61.0	*Star*	59.4
Charlotte, N.C.	1.70	56.3	*Observer*	67.1
Virginia Beach–Norfolk, Va.	1.66	53.1	*Virginia Pilot*	61.9
Austin, Tex.	1.65	49.3	*Statesman*	69.4
Providence, R.I.	1.60	37.5	*Journal*	68.2
Nashville, Tenn.	1.55	56.0	*Tennessean*	68.4
Milwaukee, Wis.	1.55	50.2	*Journal Sentinel*	63.9
Jacksonville, Fla.	1.31	63.1	*Florida Times-Union*	67.9
Memphis, Tenn.	1.29	46.9	*Commercial-Appeal*	70.3
Louisville, Ky.	1.24	54.5	*Courier-Journal*	76.8
Richmond, Va.	1.23	55.0	*Times-Dispatch*	58.4
Oklahoma City, Okla.	1.21	66.7	*Daily Oklahoman*	48.3
Hartford, Conn.	1.19	40.4	*Courant*	62.7
New Orleans, La.	1.13	50.0	*Times-Picayune*	71.9
Buffalo, N.Y.	1.12	42.7	*Buffalo News*	65.5
Birmingham, Ala.	1.12	63.2	*Birmingham News*	59.1
Salt Lake City, Utah	1.12	59.8	*Tribune*	54.8
Raleigh, N.C.	1.09	53.2	*News & Observer*	71.4
Average		52.9		63.7

* Gentzkow and Shapiro did not calculate the bias of the *San Jose Mercury News*. Although I did not use it for my average calculations, the two-party Bush vote for San Jose was 35.0.

As Table 15.2 shows, local newspapers were more often biased left than right. Further, on average, they hardly differed from national newspapers. For instance, consider the slants of (i) *The New York Times* (67.3), (ii) *USA Today* (68.6), (iii) *The Wall Street Journal* (55.1), and (iv) *The Washington Post* (65.8). The average slant of these four national newspapers, 64.2, was hardly different from the average slant of the local newspapers, 63.7.

Bias in the Bias-Rating Methods?

The following table lists the six news outlets that were analyzed both by (i) Milyo and me, and (ii) Gentzkow and Shapiro. The table allows you to compare the results of the two methods, which may reveal problems of one method or the other.

TABLE 15.3

Comparing Slant Quotients of Two Different Methods

	Estimated SQ by:	
Newspaper	Gentzkow-Shapiro	Groseclose-Milyo
Los Angeles Times	66.1	70.0
The New York Times	67.3	73.7
USA Today	68.6	63.4
The Wall Street Journal	55.1	85.1
The Washington Post	65.8	66.6
The Washington Times	52.4	35.4
Average	62.6	65.7
Average without *The Wall Street Journal*	64.0	61.7

The results of the two methods, however, are extremely similar. For instance, both methods conclude that the *Los Angeles Times, The New York Times, USA Today,* and *The Washington Post* were left of center (50), yet right of the average Democrat in Congress (84).

If you use all six of these newspapers to compare the two methods, then Milyo and I conclude that the media are slightly more liberal than Gentzkow and Shapiro conclude—specifically the average of the Groseclose-Milyo estimates, 65.7, is 3.1 points more liberal than the average of the Gentzkow-Shapiro estimates.

The largest discrepancy involved *The Wall Street Journal*. However, the discrepancy, I believe, was due more to an idiosyncrasy of the *Journal*—namely, that its news and editorial pages are so politically different—than a genuine inconsistency between the two methods.

Like us, Gentkow and Shapiro based their estimates on the *news* pages of newspapers—that is, like us, they tried to omit opinion pieces and letters to the editor from their data.

However, because their method was completely automated (i.e., Gentzkow and Shapiro programmed a computer to "scrape" text from electronic versions of newspapers, instead of hiring research assistants to hand-enter data after reading news stories), the method was not perfect at excluding data from opinion pieces and letters to the editor. Gentzkow and Shapiro, for instance, report that when they conducted a manual audit, they found that approximately 23 percent of their newspaper data came from opinion pieces.

With other newspapers—which usually have a general agreement between their news and editorial pages—this would not be a problem. However, it causes the *Journal*'s news pages to appear more conservative than they really are, since the Gentzkow-Shapiro data is contaminated with editorial-page data.

If you remove the *Journal* from our data sets, then the results from our two methods agree even more. In fact, it causes the Gentzkow-Shapiro method to conclude that the media are even more liberal—albeit slightly, by only 2.3 points—than the Groseclose-Milyo method concludes.

It is easy to think of problems that, in theory, might cause either of the two methods to understate or overstate the true bias of the media. However, the fact that the two methods find such similar results suggests that the problems, in practice, are very minor.

For instance, many on the left criticized the method that Milyo and I developed because it might have involved two different "data-generating processes." That is, for instance, suppose publicists at right-wing think tanks work harder at delivering their message to politicians than they do to the media, while publicists at left-wing think tanks do the opposite. If so, then this would cause our method to judge the media more liberal than they really are. A similar discrepancy in "data-generating processes" would occur if, say, left-wing think tanks were more honest and scholarly than right-wing think tanks, *and* journalists preferred honesty and scholarship more than politicians did.

Although such arguments are potentially important in theory, as the above results show, they are not in practice. That is, regardless whether these criticisms really apply to the method that Milyo and I developed, note that they do *not* apply to the Gentzkow-Shapiro method—or if they do, they apply in a much diminished fashion. (To see this, note, for instance, that the phrases that journalists and politicians choose—as opposed to the think tanks they cite—do not need to be filtered through a publicist or an expert at a think tank.)

Because the average estimates of our two methods differ by only a few points, this means that the method developed by Milyo and me overstates the liberal slant by at most only a few points, even if you believe that the above criticisms make sense theoretically.

16. Facts About the Bush Tax Cuts

ANOTHER WAY TO MEASURE MEDIA BIAS OBJECTIVELY AND QUANTITATIVELY

AS THE LAST three chapters show, at least two areas of data can reveal media bias: think-tank citations and loaded political phrases. One problem with these data, however, is that they might detect only *symptoms* of media bias. That is, they might miss the underlying, root causes of the bias.

It is like a child who has the flu. One symptom is that the temperature in his mouth (and the rest of his body) is higher than normal. Although you could put ice cubes in his mouth to cure the symptom, the underlying problem, the flu virus, would remain.

Likewise, you could, for instance, mandate that journalists quote conservative think tanks more frequently and use conservative phrases more often. But if they still overreport the facts that liberals want you to hear, and they underreport the facts that conservatives want you to hear, then the journalists would still have a bias—*however, the methods of the last three chapters would fail to detect it.*

For that reason, this chapter constructs a more direct way to measure bias: by examining the underlying fundamental problem, the *facts* that news outlets do and do not report about an issue.

The Bush Tax Cuts and Facts That the Media Reported

The motivation for this chapter grew out of a conversation with possibly the best and most esteemed political scientist on the planet, John Zaller, a colleague at UCLA. His book, *The Nature and Origins of Mass Opinion,* is widely credited with revolutionizing the entire subfield of public opinion.

Zaller is liberal politically, but you wouldn't know it from his scholarly work or his classroom lectures. In fact, I have taught students, who, having earlier taken Zaller's class, were willing to bet that he was conservative.

Partly because his political views usually oppose mine, we are prone to some marathon discussions. One such discussion occurred when Zaller mentioned that he was skeptical of the method that Milyo and I developed—to use think-tank data to measure media bias.

"Maybe left-wing think tanks are more scholarly and truthful than right-wing think tanks?" said Zaller. "If so, then what you're calling a liberal bias might instead be a bias for scholarship and truth."

"But I don't think you'd say that," I responded, "if you actually read a sample of the quotes in our data. Almost none of the quotes are false statements. What they reveal are the facts that journalists want you to learn.

"Here's an example," I continued. "When Congress considered the Bush tax cuts, conservatives kept saying that the cuts would make the tax system more progressive, while liberals kept saying things like 'the richest 10 percent will receive 50 percent of the tax cut.' Well, it turns out both sides were right. But if you're a conservative journalist and you want people to favor the tax cuts, what do you do? You call up someone at the Cato Institute who'll tell you the first fact. And if you're liberal journalist, what do you do? You call up someone at the Center on Budget and Policy Priorities who'll tell you the second fact.

"That's what the think-tank data do," I continued. "They serve as a proxy for the facts that journalists are telling us or not telling us."

"But why don't you just use the facts themselves?" Zaller replied. "Why do you need to use think tanks?"

"But how would you build a database of all the relevant facts that a journalist might state?" I replied. "That'd take forever, and it'd be so subjective."

"Why don't you just use the two you just told me?" said Zaller. "That's the study you ought to do."

I now realize that, as usual, Zaller had a good idea. But at the time, I resisted. Milyo and I were almost finished with our paper, and to incorporate Zaller's idea would have delayed its publication by at least several months.

Then, a few months later, at a lunchtime discussion group at UCLA, I heard the suggestion again. This time it was from the best and most esteemed *economics* professor at UCLA, Arnold Harberger. "There's an interesting case," he said, "that may be relevant to your project. It turns out that with the Bush tax cuts there were two facts that were equally true . . ."

So that's what this chapter does: it conducts the test that Zaller and Harberger suggested.

A downside to the test is that it examines only a very narrow issue, the Bush tax cuts, and not, for instance, a broad sample of issues. For this reason, some may claim that I cherry-picked the issue.

First, let me deny that. In fact, it's more correct to say that the issue was picked *for* me—by the two most eminent social scientists at UCLA.

Second, even if you don't believe my denial, consider this: If you wanted to conduct a test that involved two opposing and politically charged facts, there would be no more natural and appropriate issue than the Bush tax cuts. It is very difficult to think of another issue—and I cannot—that similarly produces two facts that (i) are true, yet (ii) at first glance seem to contradict each other, while (iii) are so cross-wise persuasive. By (iii) I mean that if you learned (a) that a small fraction of rich taxpayers received *most* of the benefit of the tax cut, but failed to learn (b) that the tax cut made the system more progressive, then this would likely cause you to oppose the tax cuts. Likewise, if you learned (b) but not (a), then it would likely cause you to favor the tax cuts.

Why It's True That the Bush Tax Cuts Made the Tax System More Progressive

While many people are aware of fact (a), few are aware of fact (b)—that the tax cut actually made the system more progressive; that is, that it *raised* the share of income taxes that the rich paid.

In fact, many people, even several of my conservative friends, insist that the two facts contradict each other—that is, if (a) is true, then it is logically impossible for (b) to be true.

It is remarkable that so many people were fooled into believing this. In later chapters I'll present more general evidence showing that the media really do have a significant ability to influence people's political beliefs. The fact that so many people were fooled beautifully illustrates, I believe, this general point.

For now, let me explain why the two facts don't contradict each other. As this chapter shows, *The New York Times* was very unfair and imbalanced in its treatment of the Bush tax cuts. However, one of its articles, written by David Rosenbaum, was perhaps *the* most fair, balanced, and informative of all the several hundred reports that I examined about the tax cuts.[1]

Here's how the article began:

> Democrats maintain that President Bush's tax-cut plan would result in a windfall for the wealthy. Republicans say the wealthy would wind up paying a bigger share of the national tax burden than they do now.
>
> Which side is right? Both are. Here's how.
>
> If the entire plan becomes law, the richest 1 percent of taxpayers would get between 22 percent and 45 percent of the tax benefits, depending on how the calculations are done. . . .
>
> That seems to buttress the Democratic position.
>
> The Bush administration counters with these statistics: Under the president's plan, [many low-income taxpayers would see their tax bill drop to 0. Further,] the richest 1 percent of taxpayers [who currently pay] 31.5 percent of all income taxes, would see their share rise to 32.6 percent.

Next using calculations by Deloitte & Touche, the accounting firm, Rosenbaum explained how the tax cuts would affect a hypothetical poor family:

> A young childless couple with an income of $20,000 now pays $990 in income taxes. With the Bush plan fully in place this couple would pay $580, a cut of $410, or 41 percent.

He next explained how the cuts would affect a hypothetical rich family:

> [Consider a couple, ineligible for a child credit, with an income of $1 million. They currently pay] $306,842 in income taxes, according to the Deloitte & Touche calculation. Under the Bush plan, this couple would owe $259,728, a tax saving of $47,114, or 15 percent.

Now, to see how it's possible for facts (a) and (b) both to be true, consider a very simple example. Suppose the above hypothetical rich and poor families were the *only* two families in the United States.

Table 16.1 shows their respective shares of the tax cut:

TABLE 16.1

Effects of Bush Tax Cuts on Two Hypothetical Families

Family	Income	Old Tax Amt.	New Tax Amt.	Tax Cut	Share of Tax Cuts (%)
Rich	1,000,000	306,842	259,728	47,114	0.9914
Poor	20,000	990	580	410	0.0086

Note that, consistent with the claims of liberals, the hypothetical rich family receives a disproportionate share of the cuts. That is, although the rich family comprises only 50 percent of the families, it receives 99.14 percent of the total tax cuts.

Meanwhile, however, as the following table shows, the rich family ends up paying a *greater* share of the taxes after the tax cut.

TABLE 16.2

Effects of Bush Tax Cuts, Continued

Family	Income	Old Tax Amt.	Old Share	New Tax Amt.	New Share
Rich	1,000,000	306,842	0.9967	259,728	0.9977
Poor	20,000	990	0.0033	580	0.0023

Specifically, its share of the taxes increases from 99.67 to 99.77 percent.

This hypothetical example is similar to the actual numbers. For instance, recall that the Rosenbaum article noted that, according to White House calculations, the share paid by the richest 1 percent would rise from 31.5 to 32.6 percent. The Senate's Joint Tax Committee calculated a similar figure—specifically, that the share from the richest 1 percent would rise from 35.6 to 36.5 percent.

In addition, other aspects of the Bush plan made the tax system more progressive. For instance, the plan completely wiped away the tax bill of many of the poorest taxpayers. Further, the new tax system made child credits refundable. This meant that not only would some low-income parents see their taxes decline to 0, they would receive a check from the government, thus paying negative taxes.

Steven Landsburg, an economist at the University of Rochester, wrote an analysis of the Bush plan. He concluded, "But if, on the other hand, you believe that the tax system should soak the rich even more than it already does, . . . then George W. Bush is your guy."[2]

A Fact-Based Measure of Media Bias

Here now are the details of my statistical method—to use facts about the Bush tax cuts as a way to measure media bias.

First, I counted a statement as part of the *liberal family of facts* about the Bush tax cuts if it said something like the following:

- That a disproportionate amount of the tax cut would go to the rich. (This includes making the point in a specific way—e.g., that the richest 10 percent will receive 50 percent of the tax cut.)

- That the richest individuals would receive an extraordinary benefit from the tax cut (including statements such as "the richest 1 percent will receive benefits on average of $50,000").
- That the tax cut would be targeted to the rich (including similar statements where phrases such as "tilted to," "intended for," "favors," and others are substituted for "targeted to.")

And I counted a statement as part of the *conservative family of facts* about the Bush tax cuts, if it said something like the following:

- That, under the Bush plan, the share of taxes paid by the rich would increase. (This included statements that made this point in a specific way—e.g., that the share paid by the richest 1 percent would increase from 35.6 to 36.5 percent.)
- That the tax cut received by the poor and middle class, as a proportion of their taxes, would be higher than the cut received by the wealthy.
- That share of the tax cut received by the rich would be less than the share of the taxes that they currently pay.
- That the bill would make the tax system more progressive.

I examined the media's coverage of the issue over the period January 1, 2001, to June 30, 2001. (Bush signed the bill on June 7, 2001. He touted the tax cuts even before he assumed office on January 20, 2001.)[3]

The following are some examples where a journalist mentioned a fact from the liberal family:

- "[Bush's] budget, however, faces a much tougher test in the Senate next week with Democrats saying the tax cut package is unacceptably big and weighted toward the rich" (Tom Brokaw, *NBC Nightly News,* March 28, 2001).
- "The top 1 percent of taxpayers would get 38 percent of the tax relief" (Linda Douglass, *ABC World News Tonight,* May 26, 2001).
- "But Democrats accused Republicans of ramming through a tax cut for the rich by shortchanging programs and doing it under orders from a president who they say is anything but bipartisan" (Carl Cameron, Fox News *Special Report with Brit Hume,* May 10, 2001).
- "But the top two Democrats in Congress yesterday criticized Mr. Bush's plan as benefiting primarily the wealthy. To highlight their argument, Senate Minority Leader Tom Daschle of South Dakota

and House Minority Leader Richard A. Gephardt of Missouri posed with a luxury automobile outside the Capitol. Mr. Daschle said that the 2000 Lexus GS-300 was 'fully loaded—just like the Bush tax cut.' 'If you're a millionaire, under the Bush tax cut, you get a $46,000 tax cut, more than enough to pay for this Lexus,' Mr. Daschle said. 'But if you're a typical working person, you get $227, and that's enough to buy this muffler.'" (*The Washington Times*, February 9, 2001).[4]

The following are some examples where a journalist mentioned a fact from the conservative family:

- "Mr. Bush promised [a refund to taxpayers], saying that low- and middle-income people, not the rich, would get the largest tax reductions in terms of percentages" (*The New York Times*, March 1, 2001).[5]
- "[The Democrats'] tax cut is not fair. Look, the Bush tax cut is. It makes the tax system more progressive. It means that wealthier people are going to pay a higher percentage of taxes than they do now" (Fred Barnes, Fox News *Special Report with Brit Hume*, March 22, 2001).[6]
- "Though Bush says the wealthy would actually pay a bigger share of the tax burden under his plan, Democrats call it a reverse Robin Hood scheme to help the rich" (Carl Cameron, Fox News *Special Report with Brit Hume*, February 27, 2001).[7] (This first part of the sentence was classified as a member of the conservative family of facts, and the second part of the sentence was classified as a member of the liberal family of facts.)
- "[White House spokesman Ari Fleischer] said those who earn more than $200,000 a year currently pay 41.8 percent of federal income-tax receipts. Under the Bush plan, they will receive 26.9 percent of the tax cut" (*The Washington Times*, February 9, 2001).[8]

Data Analysis

We can use these data to construct another objective measure of media bias. The method behind it is very similar to the think-tank method that Milyo and I developed, and it conducts a similar thought experiment.

For instance, suppose a media outlet mentioned one of the liberal facts eight times and one of the conservative facts two times. The method asks, if these data had instead come from a speech by a politician, then what would be the best guess of his PQ? The answer, as my statistical model estimates, is 74.1, approximately the PQ of Joe Lieberman.

Meanwhile, if a member of Congress mentioned liberal-to-conservative facts at a ratio of approximately two to one, then 64.1 would be the best guess of his PQ. If a member mentioned these facts at a ratio of twenty-six to one or greater, then the best guess of his PQ would be the maximum possible score, 100.[9]

Table 16.3 lists the number of times that each media outlet mentioned a fact from the liberal and conservative families, as well as the slant quotient that my statistical method estimated.

TABLE 16.3

Estimates of Bias Based on Facts Reported About the Bush Tax Cuts

Media Outlet	# of Liberal Facts Reported	# of Cons. Facts Reported	SQ
ABC's *Good Morning America*	13	7	63.5
ABC World News Tonight	8	1	83.7
CBS Early Show	21	8	68.3
CBS Evening News	10	1	86.8
CNN *Wolf Blitzer Reports*	26	5	77.8
Fox News *Special Report*	59	28	65.3
Los Angeles Times	44	7	80.4
NBC Nightly News	11	6	63.4
NBC Today Show	13	7	63.5
The New York Times	89	11	83.9
The NewsHour with Jim Lehrer	21	4	77.9
Newsweek	11	0	100.0
NPR's *Morning Edition*	20	5	74.1
Time	9	0	100.0
U.S. News & World Report	11	0	100.0
USA Today	43	6	82.2

(continued)

TABLE 16.3 (continued)

Media Outlet	# of Liberal Facts Reported	# of Cons. Facts Reported	SQ
The Wall Street Journal	24	6	74.1
The Washington Post	85	15	78.9
The Washington Times	44	18	67.3
Total/Average	562	135	78.5

As you can see, the media are very liberal by this measure. The method even places Fox News *Special Report* and *The Washington Times* slightly *left* of center. Meanwhile, three of the mainstream outlets, *Time, Newsweek,* and *U.S. News & World Report,* received the *maximum possible* liberal score.

The results contradict two common claims of left-wing critics. One claim is that the media's liberal bias is stronger on social issues than economic issues. Some people even claim that the bias on economic issues is actually conservative. For instance, in chapter 7 of *What Liberal Media?* Eric Alterman concedes that the media might have a liberal bias on social issues.[10] However, in chapter 8, he insists that on economic issues the media have a conservative bias.[11]

My results, as seen in Table 16.3, however, do not support the claim. Note that the think-tank and loaded-phrases methods of the prior few chapters capture a mix of economic and social issues. However, the above analysis involves only an economic issue. Yet, it finds the media *more* liberal than the other two methods find.

Another claim, commonly made by the left, is that liberals tend to use fact-based approaches in argument, while conservatives tend to appeal more to emotions. Consequently, so goes the claim, a method such as the think-tank method that Milyo and I developed should find a spurious liberal bias—that is, the media might quote liberal think tanks more, not because they are liberal per se, but because they tend to be more factual than conservative think tanks.

But the method of this chapter uses *only* facts. Any opinions—for example, from think tanks—are omitted.[12] Yet the method finds that the media are biased more leftward than the think-tank method finds.

"But This Ignores the Fact That Liberals Are More Honest Than Conservatives"

Related, many left-wing critics of the think-tank method claimed that liberals are more honest than conservatives. Consequently, so goes their claim, journalists cite liberal think tanks more not because journalists have a taste for liberal quotes, but because they have a taste for honest quotes.

For the sake of discussion, let's suppose this claim is true—that liberals really are more honest than conservatives. But even if that's true, it doesn't affect the fact-based method of this chapter, since the facts that I have selected are all true.

In fact, if anything, the facts from the liberal family are more questionable than those from the conservative family. Namely, many of the facts from the conservative family were basically mathematical truisms, which followed directly from the language of the tax bill. For instance, consider the following instance, listed earlier, of a conservative fact:

> "Mr. Bush promised [a refund to taxpayers], saying that low- and middle-income people, not the rich, would get the largest tax reductions in terms of percentages" (*The New York Times*, March 1, 2001).

To verify that this is true, all you need to do is consult the text of the bill. As the bill stated, the lowest-earning taxpayers would see their tax rate dropped by one third, from 15 to 10 percent. Meanwhile, the very highest-earning taxpayers would see their rate dropped by only 11.6 percent, from 39.6 to 35 percent.[13] Further, although it would involve more complicated calculations, you could also show the same thing for middle-class taxpayers—that, in terms of percentages, the decrease in their taxes would be greater than the decrease for the rich. Again, all you would need to do is consult the language of the bill.

Meanwhile, a large percentage of the liberal facts were *not* mathematical truisms. Instead, they depended upon assumptions, sometimes questionable, about tax revenue from various groups. For instance, consider the following instance of a liberal fact, reported by Linda Douglass of *ABC World News Tonight*, which I repeat from the earlier list:

> "The top 1 percent of taxpayers would get 38 percent of the tax relief."

Although Douglass did not say where she obtained this statistic, almost certainly her source was Citizens for Tax Justice. *The New York Times* reported that the group "has the only computer model in private hands capable of figuring how people at different income levels would be affected."[14] Similarly, *The Washington Post* reported that the group "has the only nongovernmental tax model for analyzing the distribution of tax cuts."[15] In the course of my research, I found no other group reporting statistics such as these.

Citizens for Tax Justice released various versions of the statistic, ranging from 33 percent to 45 percent as the share of the total tax relief that the richest 1 percent of taxpayers would receive. (Part of the reason the estimate changed was because the House and Senate were making adjustments to the bill.)

The first thing you should know about Citizens for Tax Justice is that it is a liberal group. As its Web site notes, it fights "against the armies of special interest lobbyists for corporations and the wealthy." The Web site also notes that the group fights for "adequately funding important government services" and "requiring the wealthy to pay their fair share" of taxes.

The second thing you should know about Citizens for Tax Justice is that it is an advocacy, not a scholarly, group. Unlike groups such as the Rand Corporation, the American Enterprise Institute (AEI), the Hoover Institution, the Cato Institute, and the Brookings Institution, Citizens for Tax Justice does not publish the curriculum vitae of its senior staff on its Web site. When I inquired if any of its members had a PhD or had published in peer-reviewed journals, a representative of the group told me that he knew of only one staff member who had a PhD, and he was aware of only one article from its staff—published in 1999—that has been published in a peer-reviewed journal. In contrast, groups such as AEI, Cato, and Hoover have several senior staff with PhDs, and their members annually publish dozens of peer-reviewed articles.

Although journalists frequently cited statistics such as those from Citizens for Tax Justice, almost never did the journalists reveal the questionable assumptions on which the statistics were based. Unlike the statistics that conservatives were citing about the Bush tax cuts, the statistics from Citizens for Tax Justice were sensitive to projections about who would receive benefits from the cut in the "estate tax" (or what conservatives call the "death tax"). Namely, the projections relied upon projections about how many people would die in a given year and the value of those estates.

Perhaps most questionable, Citizens for Tax Justice assumed that that estate-tax relief would benefit almost exclusively the richest 1 percent of income earners. Although in one sense this is defensible, since the cuts in estate taxes applied mainly to the very largest estates, in another sense it is not. Although most of the people *bequeathing* the estates were rich, it is not clear that we should call those people the beneficiaries, since after all, they have died. It is more proper to call the *heirs* of the estate the beneficiaries. And it is less clear, even if the estate is very large, that these people would be among the top 1 percent of income earners.[16]

Even some liberals were squeamish about citing the group's statistics. One was Sen. Max Baucus, a Montana Democrat with a PQ of 77. He was the ranking Democrat on the Senate Finance Committee. In a speech on the Senate floor, he noted:

> There is an old saying about statistics: Anybody can do what they want with statistics. When senators are arguing their points, they are going to find facts and figures and use statistics that make their case better, the basic problem being in most cases senators do not give the full picture because, correctly, they are advocating their point of view.
>
> That must be very frustrating to the American public. Who is right? Somebody makes one set of claims; somebody else makes another set of claims. The tax legislation is confusing enough as it is, but when people hear different sets of numbers, they seem to be juxtaposed to one another. Who is right? . . .
>
> Let me talk about the Joint Tax Committee analysis. They are the group we look to for honesty and integrity in this process. Unfortunately, they only do analyses for 5 years. They rank income categories according to groups. Their analysis is a little different than the so-called Citizens for Tax Justice, a privately funded organization, which tends to do analyses in quintiles, rather than income brackets, like the Joint Tax Committee.
>
> According to the Joint Tax Committee, taxpayers with incomes of $200,000 or more—that is, the top 4 or 5 percent of taxpayers—do not receive 33.5 percent of the benefits of this bill as my good friend from North Dakota [Sen. Kent Conrad] says. Instead, they will receive 22.5 percent of the benefits of the bill. Those are the taxpayers who pay about 32 percent of all Federal taxes, not just income taxes.
>
> In fact, if you use the same analysis used by my good friend from North Dakota, the top 1 percent of taxpayers pay 26 percent of all Federal taxes and would receive 19 percent of the tax cuts in the bill if you take out the estate tax provisions.[17]

A Very Misleading Report

In fact, of all the reports I read about the Bush tax cuts, the most misleading was the one written by perhaps the most liberal writer to address the subject. This was Paul Krugman's May 27, 2001, column in *The New York Times*.[18] Here is how he described the distributive aspects of the tax cut:

> [T]he top 1 percent of taxpayers will still receive about 37 percent of the total tax cut once the plan is fully implemented; the bottom 60 percent of taxpayers will receive only 15 percent of the cut.

Krugman did not cite the source for the above statistics, but as I argue above, it must have been Citizens for Tax Justice. By not giving the source, Krugman misleads his readers into thinking that the statistics might have come from a nonpartisan source such as the Joint Tax Committee. Instead, if Krugman had reported that the source was Citizens for Tax Justice, then readers, just by seeing the name of the group, would have suspected that it was a liberal advocacy group. Further, Krugman failed to note any of the questionable assumptions on which the statistics were based.

Krugman's column also noted that—to make federal budgets balance over a ten-year period, as Senate rules required—Congress had added a sunset provision to the bill that required rates to return to their pre-cut levels at the beginning of 2011. This allowed anti-tax conservatives to cut rates lower for the first nine years for which the bill would apply. But the downside for conservatives was that it meant taxes would rise in the tenth year, and it also meant that the tax cut might be temporary. Although conservatives, perhaps in the ninth year, might introduce a new bill to make the cuts permanent, such a bill would fail if a majority of either house opposed it *or* if the new president decided to veto it.

Krugman called the sunset provision a "scam," and he noted, "Need I point out that absolutely nobody who supports this tax bill thinks of it as a temporary measure, to be canceled at the end of nine years?"

The latter statement indicates more speculation than truth. The only way he could know if that statement was true is if he had asked *all* of the congressional supporters of the bill if they thought it was a temporary measure. We can be certain that he did not do that, as the day before Krugman wrote his column, Sen. Dianne Feinstein, a Democrat from California, contradicted his claim. As she explained, part of her motivation for voting for the tax cut was the sunset provision—the provision that deemed the tax cut temporary:

> Some of my colleagues, for example, have raised concerns that the size of this tax package may threaten to undermine future fiscal stability. I share these concerns. But I would remind my colleagues

> that, although this bill may be larger than some on our side contemplated at the beginning of the year, it is also far smaller than the proposal put forward by the President. *And I would also remind them that this bill contains "sunset" provisions—critical to my decision to support this legislation* [my emphasis]—which allow us to revisit the components of this bill in the future, and make adjustments if and as need be.[19]

Most people would probably forgive Krugman for such truth-stretching if he hadn't, in the same column, directed so much vitriol toward his ideological opponents. He wrote, for instance:

> Throughout the selling of this tax cut, its advocates have engaged in a disinformation campaign unprecedented in the history of U.S. economic policy . . . Indeed the pretense that taxes can be sharply cut without undermining the fiscal integrity of the nation has been maintained via financial fakery that, if practiced by the executives of any publicly traded company, would have landed them in jail. . . .
>
> We should call in the Securities and Exchange Commission, and send the whole crew—Democrats like Senator John Breaux and Senator Max Baucus as well as their Republican partners in crime—to a minimum security installation somewhere unpleasant.[20]

17. The Media Mu

HERE IS A statement that sounds reasonable and true, yet is not: "Although some media, such as NPR and *The New York Times,* are biased left, other media, such as Fox News and talk radio, are biased right; thus, if we examine U.S. media outlets on net and in totality they are very balanced."

The purpose of this chapter is to evaluate that statement—to determine whether U.S. media outlets, *in their entirety,* are actually balanced, and, if not, to determine the extent to which they are unbalanced.

To do this, we need a measure of the average slant quotient of the news as a whole. Unlike previous chapters, we cannot just count the number of outlets that lean right or lean left. We also need to measure the *extent* to which they lean right or left. Further, we need to weight the news outlets according to the number of people watching, reading, or listening to them.

This measure—the average slant of all news outlets, weighted by the audience of those outlets—I call the Media Mu. The word *mu* comes from the Greek letter, which social scientists often use to represent averages.

The media mu is a number that I will estimate in this chapter. Specifically—to give away the punch line—my estimate is 58.5. Thus, it says that the U.S. news, in its entirety, has a slant that is approximately 8 points more liberal than the PQ of the average U.S. voter (50.4).

Constructing the Media Mu: Where Do People Get Their News?

To estimate the media mu, I first need to determine where people get their news. I need to know, for instance, what percentage of the average person's news comes from *CBS Evening News*, what percentage comes from *The New York Times*, what percentage comes from talk radio, and so on.

One way to do this is to use audience ratings of news outlets. However, a problem with audience ratings is that they often don't reflect the time or attention that people devote to the specific outlets. For instance, audience ratings tell us that, in 2005, approximately 2.5 million people watched *The O'Reilly Factor* each night, while approximately 1 million people subscribed to *The New York Times*. This does not necessarily mean, however, that when we compute the average slant of the news, we should weight *The O'Reilly Factor* 2.5 times as much as *The New York Times*.

One problem is that newspaper subscriptions—and just about any other measure of audience ratings—do not tell us the amount of time that the average person spends reading the newspaper. Similar issues arise with audience ratings of television shows, radio shows, and Web sites.

In addition, readers and viewers do not always devote equal *attention* to two different news outlets, even if they devote the same amount of time to them. For example, the average O'Reilly viewer might watch the show while washing dishes or putting kids to bed, while the average newspaper reader probably devotes nearly his full attention to reading.

Ultimately, we want a measure that reflects the time a person devotes to a news source, *weighted by the attention that he devotes to the news source*. The best way to measure this, I believe, is to use surveys that ask people to recall where they get their news. The average person, I believe, is more likely to recall consulting a news source if he spends a lot of time on the source *and* devotes a lot of attention to it.

For this reason I use a survey by the Gallup organization. Specifically, in December 2002, Gallup asked a random set of people to indicate "how often you get your news from" ten listed sources (such as local television news, local newspapers, nightly network news, etc.). Gallup recorded responses for Republicans, Independents, and Democrats. Since I am most interested in how the average voter responds to news, I focus only on the Independents.

As Gallup found, for instance, 52 percent of Independents said that they get their news from local television every day. Among the same respondents, 45 percent said they get their news from local newspapers; 41 percent said they get their news from nightly network news;[1] and 38 percent said they get their news from cable news networks. Those were the most frequently listed news sources. The two least frequently listed sources were the internet (14 percent) and "national newspapers (such as *The New York Times, USA Today*, or *The Wall Street Journal*)" (11 percent).

There are surely lots of ways to criticize Gallup's data. For instance, I strongly doubt that 45 percent of people actually read a local newspaper every day. (For instance, fewer than a million people subscribed to the *Los Angeles Times* in 2002. At the time about thirteen million people lived in the Los Angeles metropolitan area. If the 45 percent figure were true, then the average *Los Angeles Times* subscriber would have had to share his newspaper with approximately five people every day.)

Nevertheless, I believe that the numbers are still good at expressing the *relative* frequencies of where people get their news. For instance, although the people who read a local newspaper might be less than 45 percent, and the people who read a national newspaper might also be less than 11 percent, it might still be the case that the ratio of the two groups is still 45 to 11. That is, people might exaggerate the two activities by equal degrees.

If so, then we should expect that the numbers from the survey are roughly proportional to the amount of news that people get from each source. Consequently, the Gallup data imply that the mix of news for the average person is as follows: 52 parts local television, 45 parts local newspapers, 41 parts nightly network news, and so on. This means that—when we add up all the parts—the news has a total of 315 "parts," and that, for the average person, 16.5 percent of his news comes from local television (52 ÷ 315), 14.3 percent comes from local newspapers (45 ÷ 315), and so on. I list these percentages in column 2 of Table 17.1.

Slant Quotients of News Sources

Next, to compute the media mu, we need to know the slants of the various news sources. That is, we need to know the average slant of national newspapers, local newspapers, local television, talk radio, etc. I have computed such slants, and I list them in Table 17.1. In the next section, I give some of the details of how I computed the slants.

TABLE 17.1

Slant Quotients of Various Forms of News

News Source	% of the Total News It Comprises	Slant Quotient
Local television	16.5	65.4
Local newspapers	14.3	63.7
Nightly network news (ABC, CBS, or NBC)	13.0	65.4
Cable news networks (such as CNN, Fox, or MSNBC)	12.1	47.9
Public television news	9.8	55.8
Morning shows on national networks	9.8	62.2
National Public Radio	7.3	66.3
Radio talk shows	9.2	32.1
News on the Internet	4.5	60.4
National newspapers (such as *The New York Times, USA Today,* or *The Wall Street Journal*)	3.5	62.6

Given these numbers, I can now estimate the media mu. To do this, I simply calculate the weighted average of the slant quotients in the table, where the weight for each SQ is the percentage listed in the second column. Thus, the media mu is:

$$\begin{aligned}\text{Media Mu} = {} & 0.165(65.4) + 0.143(63.7) + 0.13(65.4) \\ & +0.121(47.9) + 0.098(55.8) + 0.098(62.2) \\ & +0.073(66.3) + 0.092(32.1) + 0.045(60.4) \\ & +0.035(62.6) \\ = {} & 58.46\end{aligned}$$

Details Behind the Calculation of the Media Mu

On my Web site www.timgroseclose.com/media-mu-details.pdf, I discuss the details behind these calculations. In this section I give a taste of some of those details.

For instance, to calculate the average SQ of the nightly network news, I used the SQs that I estimated in chapter 13, for *ABC World News Tonight, CBS Evening News,* and *NBC Nightly News.* Those were, respectively, 61, 73.7, and 61.6. They give an average of 65.4, which is the number I use in the media-mu calculation.

In general, when making assumptions, I tried to err on the side of working against the main conclusions of the book. That is, for instance, if two assumptions seemed equally reasonable, I chose the one that would make the media appear more conservative.

For example, consider my method for calculating the average SQ of national newspapers. When Gallup asked its respondents how often they got their news from national newspapers, it specifically asked, ". . . such as *The New York Times, USA Today,* and *The Wall Street Journal.*" To calculate the average SQ, I used the SQs of these three newspapers, which I estimated in chapter 15—the chapter that used the loaded-phrase method. Those estimates were 67.3, 68.6, and 55.1, which gives an average of 63.7. Recall, however, that in chapter 13 (which used the think-tank-citations method) I estimated more liberal SQs for the three newspapers. If I had instead used the latter estimates, then the average would have been 74.1. Thus, the former method makes the newspapers appear approximately ten points more *conservative* than does the latter method.

Another example where an assumption caused estimates to err on the conservative side involved talk radio. When I constructed a sample of radio shows, I assumed that if a show clearly leaned right, then its SQ was 16.1, which is the average PQ of Republicans in Congress. Likewise, if the show clearly leaned left, then I assumed its SQ was 84.3, the average PQ of Democrats in Congress. In contrast, however, I believe that many of the left-leaning shows were much more liberal than the average congressional Democrat. For instance, many Air America hosts often complained that congressional Democrats were not liberal enough. In contrast, this rarely happened with conservative radio shows. For instance, Rush Limbaugh and Sean Hannity, in my judgment, are no more liberal or conservative than Sen. Mitch McConnell, whose PQ, 9, is only a tiny bit more conservative than the average Republican's PQ. Further, my sample included a large number of shows—such as those hosted by Dennis Miller and Dr. Laura Schlessinger—which clearly lean right, but are clearly not as conservative as the average Republican speech in Congress.

The one possible exception to my rule involved my coding of moderate talk radio shows. To create a sample of talk radio shows, I performed a Google search of the term "talk radio" plus the name of various cities that I used to construct the sample. Often the search would produce shows that were clearly apolitical or that did not clearly lean left or right. For instance, consider Jacksonville's WFOY radio station. It broadcasts the shows of Rush Limbaugh, Laura Ingraham, and Fred Thompson, who are clearly conservative. But it also broadcasts shows such as *J.D.'s "Ride to Live" Motorcycle Radio Show* and *The Dave Ramsey Show* (which offers "life-changing advice on how to beat debt"). For the latter type shows, which have no clear political slant, I assumed that their SQ was identical to the PQ of the average voter, 50.4. According to this method, 57.2 percent of the talk radio shows were conservative, 39 percent were moderate or apolitical, and 3.8 percent were liberal. This gave an average slant of 32.07.

I am confident that the conservative-to-liberal ratio that I found, 57.2 to 3.8, is approximately accurate—indeed, if anything I think it overstates the true ratio. However, I question whether talk radio actually contains so many moderate shows. That is, if you had asked the Gallup respondents what shows they were thinking of when they said they got some of their news from "radio talk shows," then I suspect that less than 39 percent would have named moderate shows. If, however, the true number were, say, 19.5 percent (i.e., half of 39 percent), while the ratio of conservative to liberal shows remained 57.2 to 3.8, then this would mean that the true average SQ of talk radio would be 26.2, which is 5.87 points more conservative than I estimated. Since talk radio, according to my estimates, comprised approximately 9.2 percent of the average voter's news, this would cause my estimate of the media mu to drop by 0.54 points (5.87 × 0.092)—i.e., from 58.46 to 57.92.

Nevertheless, I am confident that, on net, my assumptions have caused me to significantly *underestimate* the true media mu. The main reason is because I completely ignored my estimates from chapter 16, which analyzed the Bush tax cuts. The estimates from that chapter, on average, were approximately 15.9 points higher than the estimates from chapters 13 and 15.

Thus, if you believe that the method from chapter 16 is the appropriate method to judge media bias, then the true media mu is approximately 15.9 points higher than my estimate, or approximately 74.4 (= 58.5 + 15.9).

Alternatively, if you believe the methods from chapters 13, 15, and 16 are all *equally* appropriate, then you should weight the estimates from each chapter by one third. Most important, this means that you should weight the estimates from chapter 16 by one third—instead of the zero weight I actually used. If so, then the true media mu is approximately 5.3 (i.e., 15.9 ÷ 3) points higher than my actual estimate, or approximately 63.8 (= 58.5 + 5.3).

PART IV

Effects of Media Bias

18. Measuring the Influence of the Media I

MANY METHODS FALSE AND SPENT, AND ONE THAT'S NOT

SO FAR, THIS book has made two major claims: first, that the main vehicle of bias in the media is a distortion method, not a lying method; and second, that this bias is significantly liberal.

The remainder of the book argues a third point: that the bias really matters. Scholars call this the "media effects" question. It asks whether the information that the media reports really can affect the thoughts and behavior of people. I give evidence that it does, and unlike most previous studies, I construct a way to describe precisely the *extent* to which it does.

Media Effects and "Rational Choice"

Before I explain why media effects are real and significant, let me first explain something that may surprise many people. There are strong theoretical reasons to believe that media effects should not exist at all.

Here is an example why. Suppose you were a moderate voter, unsure whether to vote for Obama or McCain. Suppose one day you heard Rush Limbaugh describing several bad characteristics of Obama. Naturally, this would push you off the metaphorical fence and toward McCain, right?

Not so fast. Instead you might think, "Well, of course Limbaugh is going to say negative things about Obama. He's a conservative, and he wants me to vote for McCain. Yet despite that, he really didn't have *that* many negative things to say about Obama, nor anything I found too terribly damning." Indeed, you might conclude, "If that's all the criticism Limbaugh can level at Obama, maybe Obama isn't so bad."

Note that this hypothetical example produced a very unintuitive result: When you listened to Limbaugh, it caused you to become more liberal, not conservative. The key principles were that you, as a rational voter, (i) understood Limbaugh's conservative bias and (ii) discounted the conservative bias from the message he delivered.

When you think in this rational—some might say, hyper-rational—way, Rush Limbaugh's bias does not necessarily make you more conservative. You become more conservative only if Limbaugh is more conservative than you *expected* him to be.

The same principle, applied in the opposite direction, may describe the influence of the media as a whole. That is, the average voter may understand that the media, as a whole, are biased left. Now suppose that he discounts this bias from the news reports he sees. If so, then to make him think and vote more liberal, the media must adopt a slant that is more liberal *than he expects.* Not only that, if the media's slant is less liberal than he expects, then this will make him more *conservative.*

The final point in this chain of logic is that, eventually, voters will learn the biases of the news media. Consequently, the bias they expect will, on average, equal the bias that the media actually report. This means that the net effect will be zero: the bias will sway the average voter neither to the left nor the right.

Until about a half dozen or so years ago, I was persuaded by this logic. That is, I was largely a media effects nonbeliever. Like many other "rational choice" social scientists, I found it difficult to believe that voters could be systematically fooled into thinking and voting against their natural tastes and values.

I have since abandoned those views.

What changed my mind? It was three pathbreaking studies, which I describe in this and the next chapter.

The First Step in My Media Effects Conversion

The first step toward my conversion occurred in March 2004, when I presented my research at a conference on the media at Stanford. During a break between sessions, over a tray of bagels and orange juice, I met a bright and enthusiastic young scholar who introduced himself as Stefano. Judging from his looks, I thought he was probably a graduate student; however, later I would learn that he had recently been hired as an economics professor at UC Berkeley.

"That topic is especially relevant in my home country of Italy," said Stefano, after I mentioned that I was working on media bias. "The prime minister owns a large number of the media outlets, and I think that that was part of the reason his party was able to retain power."

I was a little preoccupied with the presentation that I would give later that day, so I really wasn't really listening to Stefano. But then he piqued my attention.

"It turns out that Fox News entered only about twenty percent of the cable markets in the late nineties. We're going to test if Fox caused those neighborhoods to vote more Republican."

"But isn't there an endogeneity problem?" I asked.

In a few paragraphs, I'll explain what an *endogeneity problem* is. For now, however, please take my word that such problems are significant and nearly omnipresent in studies of media effects. Worse, most media scholars, even some at the very top universities, don't really understand what such a problem is, much less recognize how such a problem taints their research.

I thought Stefano probably fell into this camp. So I was about to explain to him, "That is, wouldn't you expect Fox News to enter the most conservative markets? Consequently, even if you see people in the Fox News markets voting more conservatively, it might be that the conservativeness of the market caused Fox to enter—not the reverse."

Before I could say this, however, Stefano interrupted, "Because we use differences in differences, that's not a problem. We *do* have to worry if the trend in voting conservative is correlated with the entry. But we test for that and find no correlation."

Later in the chapter I'll explain Stefano's jargon. For now, let me say that it was clear that he was a few steps ahead of my thinking and that he intimately understood what an endogeneity problem is. Not only that, as I began to talk to him more, I could see that his study might be the Rosetta Stone of media effects, the one study, not affected by endogeneity problems, that would tell us the true extent to which the media can influence opinions and votes.

"What was your last name again?" I asked.

"DellaVigna," he said.

Endogeneity Problems

Before our conversation ended, Stefano promised to send me a draft of his paper as soon as he and his coauthor, Ethan Kaplan, had finished one.

While the rational choice scholar in me made me a media effects agnostic, I vowed to myself that this was *the* study. If Stefano and his coauthor could find significant media effects, then I would become a media effects believer.

They indeed found significant effects, and I indeed became a believer. And it was not just me. Several months later, the study was published in the *Quarterly Journal of Economics*.[1] The economics field, like me, recognized the talents of DellaVigna and Kaplan. The publication helped cement their reputations as two of the brilliant young minds in the economics profession.

In January 2007, *The New York Times* echoed this sentiment about DellaVigna. It described him (along with Justin Wolfers [see chapter 3] and Matthew Gentzkow and Jesse Shapiro [see chapter 15]) as one of the thirteen young "economists to watch." As the article noted, he is "doing work that is both highly respected among experts and relevant to the rest of us." As the article suggested, he and the other twelve are "the future of economics."

Before I describe the study, however, let me first explain some of the jargon from our conversation. Most important is what precisely is an "endogeneity problem."

IN SCIENCE SOME effects are *exogenous*, that is, outside the system, while others are *endogenous*, that is, inside the system. An endogeneity problem occurs when a researcher treats an effect as if it is exogenous, when it is actually endogenous.

If you are currently thinking, "Well, that didn't tell me much," you should congratulate yourself for being a critical thinker. So far my explanation is extremely superficial and vague. A proper explanation requires some mathematical concepts. I'll skip those, but, as best as I can, I'll try to substitute a verbal explanation for the mathematical concepts.

This means that the next few paragraphs will be a little dry. At the same time, however, they may be the most rewarding paragraphs of the book. As I explain to my undergraduate students, "In your college career, if you gain nothing else besides a genuine understanding of what an endogeneity problem is, then you'll have a first-rate education." Most undergraduates—even those at top universities such as Harvard or Stanford—never fully grasp the concept of "endogeneity problem."

The best way to understand the terms "exogenous" and "endogenous" is to consider a medical example. Suppose, as a researcher, you suspect that if people take an aspirin each day, then this will decrease their chances of developing heart disease.

The easiest and cheapest way for you to test this is to commission a survey, asking people if they have or have ever had heart disease and also asking if they take an aspirin each day. The test seems simple. If the aspirin takers have lower rates of heart disease than the non-aspirin takers, then this seemingly would show that aspirin had a causal effect, that it really lowered people's chance of developing heart disease.

But here's the problem. There are *other factors* besides aspirin that affect heart disease, including diet, exercise, genetics, job stress, and so on. Now suppose that people who are vulnerable to heart disease from the "other factors" are the ones who are most likely to take aspirin. This taints your survey with a selection effect: aspirin takers are not a cross section of the population; rather they are ones who think they are more susceptible to heart disease.

As a consequence, in your survey, aspirin will have two effects: (i) a causal effect reflecting the possibility that it makes a person *less* likely to develop heart disease, and (ii) a selection effect that makes a person *more* likely to have heart disease. Because of the selection effect, your survey will understate the true causal effects of aspirin.

As any biologist will tell you, the problem was that you let your subjects choose whether they took aspirin. Instead, in a proper biology experiment the researcher should choose for them. Best of all, the researcher should randomly choose, say by flipping a coin, the subjects who receive the treatment (aspirin) and those who do not.

But in this example—where the subjects were allowed to choose whether they'd take the treatment—the treatment choice was *inside (i.e. part of) the system*. Most problematic, their choice might have been related to the "other factors" that cause heart disease. When this happens we say that the choice is *endogenous* and that, therefore, the study has an *endogeneity problem*.

Now, before I explain how endogeneity problems plague social-science studies, I want you to consider a different way that you, the researcher, in the aspirin example could have divided your subjects into a treatment and a control group. Suppose, instead of flipping a coin, you divided subjects according to whether they were born on an odd or even day of the month.

This method of dividing subjects, it is reasonable to believe, is not related to the "other factors" that cause or prevent heart disease. (For example, there is no reason to believe that people born on odd days of the month tend to have worse diets, exercise habits, or genetic factors than people born on even days.) Accordingly, the odd/even selection method, although it is not random, shares the main benefit of the random method: it is not related to the "other factors" that cause or prevent heart disease. Accordingly, we say that this method, like random selection, is exogenous—i.e., it is outside the system of factors that cause heart disease. Therefore, the method does not have an endogeneity problem.

One of the key principles of the odd day/even day selection method is that the subjects themselves cannot choose whether they take aspirin or not—that is, they cannot *self-select* into the treatment or control group. Instead, *nature* chooses for them—i.e., nature chooses whether they are born on an odd or even day.

This principle, to allow nature to choose treatment and control subjects, is important. Keep this in mind when I explain endogeneity problems in the social sciences. If you are a social-science researcher, the secret to avoiding an endogeneity problem is to conduct a *natural experiment.*

An Ingenious Natural Experiment

Now let's examine one of the most clever natural experiments ever devised in the social sciences.

Almost everyone would agree that police help deter crime. That is, for instance, if a town doubled its number of cops, then crime almost surely would decrease. However, it turns out that if you collected data across cities, you'd find the opposite correlation. The cities with the most police per capita tend to have the most crime per capita.

If you like brain teasers, put down the book and try to think of a story—one that uses your new knowledge about endogeneity problems—to explain how this perverse correlation could occur. That is, assume that police actually do deter crime. However, try to think of reasons why the raw data might show the opposite: that more cops lead to more crime.

Here's one story, the one that I believe best explains the puzzle. There are lots of factors that aid or prevent crime. One, of course, is the size of a town's police force. But others include unemployment, education, citizens' willingness or reluctance to aid the police, and demographic factors such as the percentage of twenty-something males who reside in a town.

Next, consider the fact that the size of a town's police force is not chosen exogenously. Instead, the town's politicians choose it, and their choice surely is affected by the "other factors." For instance, if your town has high levels of unemployment, low levels of education, and so on, then the crime rate will likely be higher than average. If you are a political leader of the town, then you will probably respond by hiring more police.

Here again, we have an example of a selection effect that masks an opposite-acting causal effect. If the selection effect is greater than the causal effect, then the data will show the perverse correlation.

If you wanted to test the true effect of police on crime, then you'd need to do something like a biology experiment. For example, you might choose a set of towns and randomly require some to increase their police force while requiring others to maintain their police force at a constant level. This, however, would be virtually impossible. How do you persuade the mayors and city councils of such towns to go along with your experiment?

"But isn't every variable in social science determined by 'other factors'?" asked one of my very bright students one day. "Accordingly," she continued, "isn't every social-science study plagued by an endogeneity problem?"

"It's not as hopeless as it appears," I replied. "Here's one way you could avoid the endogeneity problem." Then I explained an ingenious solution, proposed by Steve Levitt, to the police-and-crime example that I've just described.[2] Although Levitt is now world famous as the coauthor of *Freakonomics* and the winner of the John Bates Clark Medal, when he thought of the solution, he was a virtually unknown PhD student at MIT.

Levitt's key insight came when he discovered that towns tend to hire extra cops when the town leaders face reelection. Specifically, in mayoral election years, towns tend to increase their police force by about 2 percent more than they do in non-election years.

Levitt used this fact to conduct a natural experiment. That is, like the odd day/even day device in the aspirin experiment, Levitt noted for each year in his data set whether a town held a mayoral election, and he used this fact to assign the town to a treatment or control group.

It is reasonable to believe that this selection mechanism is truly exogenous. That is, it is doubtful that an election could affect the "other factors" that cause or prevent crime. If you wanted to claim otherwise, you would need to spin a fairly fanciful story. For instance, you might claim that when there is a mayoral election people are so busy learning about the candidates that they have less time to commit crimes. Or you might argue that when there is a mayoral election, candidates bribe disadvantaged citizens so much, that such citizens feel less need to steal, murder, and rape.

As you can see, it is hard to imagine a way in which mayoral elections are related to the "other factors" that cause or prevent crime. If you agree that they are not, then you agree with me that Levitt found a truly exogenous way to place towns into a treatment and control group. In social-science parlance we say that Levitt found a truly exogenous *instrument*.

"That's what Poterba always drills into us," said Koleman Strumpf. "If you can just come up with two or three good instruments over your life, sometimes even one, then that will make your career."

Strumpf is currently the Koch Professor of Economics at the University of Kansas School of Business. However, when he said that, in 1995, he was a PhD student in the MIT economics program. Like Levitt, he wrote his dissertation under the direction of James Poterba, who is currently the chair of the MIT economics department and president of the National Bureau of Economic Research.

"The other thing that Poterba always drills into us," continued Strumpf, "is that you've got to think of the instrument first, *then* think of the problem that it would solve—not the other way around. As Poterba tells us, if you do it the other way, you probably didn't find a real instrument."

Levitt verified to me that that's what happened with his mayoral-elections-and-crime project. "I noticed one day," he said, "that mayoral elections are staggered. They're not like House elections, which always occur every two years. Some towns have them every four years. Some even hold them in odd years.

"So I started thinking," he continued, "this has got to be a good instrument for something. Then I heard about how sociologists have struggled with the effect-of-police-on-crime problem. It seemed like my instrument might solve it."

It did, and Levitt soon became world famous as a specialist in the economics of crime. However, his specialty, I warrant, might have been completely different if he hadn't discovered the staggered-mayoral-elections fact that one fateful day.

The final step of Levitt's study was simply to note how many crimes occurred in a year in which towns held mayoral elections, and to compare this to the number that occurred in years when towns didn't hold mayoral elections. His results showed, for instance, that for each additional cop that a town hires, this prevents between 3.2 and 7 violent crimes per year.[3] Because his instrument was truly exogenous, we can say that this effect is truly causal—that is, that an extra cop *causes* crime to decrease by that amount.

Endogeneity Problems and Academic Studies on Media Effects

While economists such as Levitt (and, as I will argue in a moment, Stefano DellaVigna and Ethan Kaplan) have a fantastic understanding of endogeneity problems, most media scholars do not.

In an episode of *The Simpsons,* Homer, while driving a float in a football halftime show, accidentally runs over the leg of the star kicker, Anton Lubchenko. In the locker room Dr. Hibbert attends to Lubchenko:

DR. HIBBERT: Son, I'm afraid that leg is hanging by a thread.
LUBCHENKO: Lubchenko must return to game!
DR. HIBBERT: (chuckles) Your playing days are over, my friend. But you can always fall back on your degree in . . . [reads chart] communications?! Oh, good Lord!
LUBCHENKO: I know! Is phony major. Lubchenko learn nothing. Nothing! [cries][4]

While *The Simpsons* characterization of the communications field is a little harsh and exaggerated, if we apply it to the state of research in the subfield of "media effects," the characterization, I believe, is only slightly exaggerated.

One example involves a study by Steven Kull, Clay Ramsay, and Evan Lewis, all researchers at the University of Maryland's School of Public Affairs. It examined misperceptions that the public held about the Iraq War.

For example, as the study found, a significant fraction of the respondents in their survey believed that "weapons of mass destruction have been found in Iraq."[5] Another finding—which scores of journalists were gleeful to report—was that the respondents who watched Fox News were most likely to hold misperceptions about the war.

There are a number of problems with the study, and to the credit of the peer-review process in political science, the study was *not* published in a top-tier journal. For instance, the journal in which it was published, *Political Science Quarterly,* was ranked forty-ninth by an assessment published in *PS*, a journal published by the American Political Science Association.[6] Indeed, before I read about the study in the press, I had never heard of *Political Science Quarterly.*

In a moment I'll address the most significant weakness of the study—the endogeneity problems that plague it—but for now let me address one of its more minor weaknesses: it basically was nothing more than a hit piece on Fox News and conservatives.

With any fact, almost never will it be the case that 100 percent of the public has correct beliefs about it. For instance, approximately 8 percent of Americans believe that Elvis Presley is still alive, and another 11 percent are unsure if he's alive.[7] Related, survey respondents often don't devote their full attention to the questions they are asked, and even when they do, they often don't think very carefully about their answers. Consequently, their answers are often mistakes or random guesses. Sometimes their answers reflect more what they wish or hope is true than what they actually believe is true.

As a consequence, consider that proponents of the Iraq War, more so than opponents, tended to hope and wish that U.S. soldiers would find weapons of mass destruction. Consequently, proponents of the war were more likely to give a wrong answer to the survey questions that Kull et al. asked.

Now consider that proponents of the war were more likely to watch Fox News than were opponents of the war. As a consequence, this self-selection factor would make Fox News viewers, relative to viewers of other news shows, more likely to give a wrong answer to the survey. *And this would happen even if Fox never reported wrong or misleading information about the war.*

Now, here's why I believe the study is a hit piece. There were lots of other misperceptions, which were commonly held by liberals. If the study had asked questions that tried to demonstrate those misperceptions, then it would have found a very different result.

That is, suppose instead the study had asked questions such as:

- Was there evidence that Iraq had had *contact* with Al Qaeda prior to the war (as opposed to "working closely with Al Qaeda," as the study asked)?
- Was there evidence that before the war, Iraq harbored ambitions to use weapons of mass destruction?
- Before the war, did Iraq refuse to comply with the demand of the United Nations that it prove that it had destroyed its previously demonstrated WMD programs and stockpiles?

Many opponents of the war, if they had answered according to their hopes and wishes, would have given wrong answers to each of the above questions. Next, since they would tend *not* to watch Fox News, if a study used the above questions, then it would have found that viewers of Fox News were *the least likely* to hold misperceptions about the war.

The actual study asked none of the latter-type questions. This stacked the tables toward making Fox viewers appear more misinformed than non-Fox viewers. For this reason, I believe, the article is a hit piece.

Related to all this, and more important for my analysis, is the endogeneity problems that plagued the study. Note that, unlike a biology experiment, the respondents in the study *chose* whether they would watch Fox News or not. That is, it was not the case that, for example, the researchers randomly assigned half their subjects to watch Fox News and the other half to watch other news shows.

As a consequence, the study is plagued by the self-selection factors that I describe earlier. Consequently, the statistical correlation that the researchers found—that Fox News viewers tended more often to give wrong answers to their questions—does not necessarily reflect causality. Further evidence of this is that the researchers never cited any Fox reporter stating untrue facts about the war.

Consequently, the results of the study do not estimate the true media effect. Only an experiment, including possibly a natural experiment, can do that.

Although I have singled-out the Kull et al. study, a similar criticism can be applied to nearly all studies of media effects that have been conducted by political scientists or communications scholars.

It is only recently that researchers have begun to design media-effects studies that are not tainted by endogeneity problems. Almost always, such studies have been conducted by economists or other social scientists who have received significant training in economics.

Two such researchers are Stefano DellaVigna and Ethan Kaplan.

DellaVigna and Kaplan's Study

As I mentioned, the DellaVigna-Kaplan study begins by noting that in the late 1990s, Fox News was available to only approximately one fifth of the cable markets. This means that the mix of news in those markets was slightly more conservative than the mix of news in other markets. If media effects are real, then people in the Fox News markets should have voted more conservatively those who were not.

That's exactly what DellaVigna and Kaplan found. Specifically, they examined two different versions of a model that contained a full set of control variables. The average effect of the two versions showed the following: in the 2000 election, George W. Bush's vote share was 0.43 percent higher in Fox markets than it was in non-Fox markets.[8]

If, however, you've been paying close attention, your first thought should be "But why isn't their study plagued with an endogeneity problem? That is, Fox News *chose* which markets to enter, and maybe Fox chose markets that tended to have more conservative voters. Accordingly, when we see people in the Fox News markets voting more conservatively, it's not necessarily because Fox News *caused* them to vote more conservatively."[9]

That was exactly my thought when I first talked to DellaVigna. But it is now clear to me that (i) DellaVigna and Kaplan completely understand what an endogeneity problem is, (ii) their paper forthrightly addresses the possibility of an endogeneity problem, and (iii) it convincingly makes the case that the results are not tainted by any endogeneity problems. Accordingly, I am convinced that the 0.43 estimate truly reflects the *causal* effect of Fox News.

But just in case you're skeptical, here are some more details. First, it was not quite true that Fox decided which markets to enter. During the late 1990s, Fox negotiated deals with a few cable providers. When it made such deals, it had to broadcast to all of the markets that the provider served or none of the markets. It couldn't pick and choose according to the political views of those markets. Further, when Fox made the deals, the providers had already chosen the markets in which they would broadcast. There is little reason to believe that the providers chose markets based on the political views of voters in those markets.

Second, the key predictive variable in the DellaVigna-Kaplan study was not how conservative a market voted. Rather the variable was *the change* in how conservative the market voted. Specifically, for each region in their sample, they noted the difference in (i) the percentage of people voting for George W. Bush in 2000, and (ii) the percentage of people voting for Bob Dole in 1996. They then noted how the differences of (i) and (ii) differed between Fox regions and non-Fox regions. Note that they compared how *the differences differed*. That's what DellaVigna meant when he told me, "we examine differences in differences."

Now, although you could perhaps make an argument that Fox would search for conservative markets, it is harder to make the argument that Fox would search for markets that were *trending* conservative.[10] At any rate, DellaVigna and Kaplan, using additional data from the 1992 elections, tested this and found no evidence of it.

For these reasons, I (and the editors and reviewers at the *Quarterly Journal of Economics*) became convinced that the study is a bona fide natural experiment. It is as if nature chose markets for Fox, instead of Fox choosing the markets (based on the political views of the markets).

The results helped convert me and many others into media effects believers.

19. Measuring the Influence of the Media II

TWO MORE GROUNDBREAKING EXPERIMENTS

BEFORE I SAW the results of the DellaVigna and Kaplan study—and became a media-effects believer—my personal journey took two detours. Both involved additional experiments that tested media effects.

Unlike the DellaVigna-Kaplan experiment, these were not natural experiments, but real experiments, like the ones biologists and chemists conduct. Their results largely echoed those of DellaVigna and Kaplan: they showed a very strong influence of the media.

The Yale Revolution in Political Science

"But how did you pay for all the newspaper subscriptions?" I asked Yale political scientist Alan Gerber, as we sipped coffee in a New Haven bookstore one day.

For approximately a decade, Gerber and his colleague Donald Green had been leading a revolution of sorts in political science, showing that social scientists really can act more like biologists and chemists and conduct genuine experiments. In the New Haven bookstore, Gerber was telling me about his latest experiment, which he was conducting with fellow Yale researchers Dean Karlan and Daniel Bergan.

The research team was impressive. Bergan had just obtained his PhD from Northwestern University, and he had won a highly competitive selection process to become a postdoctoral fellow at Yale's Institution for Social and Policy Studies.

Karlan, who received his PhD from MIT, was a rising-star professor in the Yale economics department. *The New York Times* would later describe him as one of thirteen young "economists to watch." As the article noted, he is "doing work that is both highly respected among experts and relevant to the rest of us."[1]

Gerber, like Karlan, received his PhD from the economics department at MIT. Like Koleman Strumpf and *Freakonomics* author Steve Levitt, Gerber's dissertation advisor was James Poterba, who is now the head of the MIT economics department. (See the previous chapter for a discussion of Levitt, Strumpf, and Poterba.) While working on the project, Gerber was inducted into the American Academy of Arts and Sciences. Such an honor is usually the pinnacle of a scholar's career. Except for a Nobel Prize, few awards are more prestigious. He was inducted at age forty-four. As far as I am aware, no other political scientist has ever been inducted at such a young age.

For their project, Gerber, Karlan, and Bergan recruited hundreds of subjects in the Northern Virginia suburbs of Washington, D.C. They bought them subscriptions to *The Washington Post* or *The Washington Times* (and randomly chose which subjects would receive which subscription). Their plan was to test if the *Times* subscribers would vote more conservatively than the *Post* subscribers.

"That's one of the great things about Yale," said Gerber, answering my question about paying for the newspaper subscriptions. "There are lots of piles of money just kind of floating around here to pay for research, especially if you want to do an experiment. And it actually didn't cost that much. We called the *Post* and the *Times,* and both allowed us to buy something like a ten-week trial subscription for our subjects. It cost only like thirty dollars per subject."

When Gerber and Green began their revolution, many of us had been toiling in the salt mines of social science, trying to think of new and clever "instruments"—variables such as Levitt's staggered-mayoral-elections idea—that would form the basis for a natural experiment, a variable that would allow us magically to solve endogeneity problems.

Although biologists and chemists might accuse us of not doing "real" science, only social science, we patted ourselves on the back, since our work was actually *more* difficult than that of biologists and chemists. To test one of our hypotheses, we had to think of a clever natural experiment. We couldn't just "go to the lab" and run an actual experiment.

"Not so fast," Gerber and Green effectively told their fellow social scientists. "Maybe we *can* do actual experiments."

Gerber and Green's first major experiment tested if campaign advertising actually caused more people to vote. Although prior data suggested it did, most of us believed that that data was tainted by endogeneity problems. That is, for instance, maybe candidates advertise more when they see they are in a close race. And maybe people are more willing to vote when they see that the race is close. Thus the apparent causal relationship between advertising and voter turnout might be spurious—both might simply be *effects* of a close race.

To test their hypothesis, during the 1998 election, Gerber and Green gathered a sample of approximately thirty thousand citizens of New Haven.[2] Of these, they randomly selected approximately six thousand to be their "treatment" group. For each member of the treatment group, they instructed one of their research assistants to knock on his or her door, ask him or her to vote, and remind him or her of the date of the upcoming election.

As the study found, the effects of such personal canvassing were large: turnout among the treatment group was 9 percent higher than that among the control group. Further, because the study was a real experiment, we can interpret the effect as causal—that is, Gerber and Green's research assistants *caused* the treatment group to vote at higher rates.

The results of their study not only changed political science, they changed *politics*. After learning about the Gerber-Green results, Karl Rove, during the 2004 presidential campaign, decided to devote more resources to turnout—that is, to get-out-the-vote efforts for the Republican base—and less resources to traditional methods, which focused more on trying to convert fence-sitters into Bush supporters.[3] Many believe that the 2004 record turnout in swing states—especially Ohio, which was 61 percent in 2004 but only 54 percent in 2000—was a result of Rove's decision.

Yet, while impressed and intrigued by Gerber and Green's revolution, some of us were a little resentful. It was as if we'd been trying to run a mile-long stretch of road in four minutes, when Gerber and Green had came along and said, "Hey, look, we can *drive* it in one minute."

Their solution for solving social-science problems felt a little like cheating. "It shouldn't be that easy," some of us thought. But at the same time many of us also thought, "Why didn't I think of that?"

Results of the Gerber et al. *Washington-Post*-versus-*Washington-Times* Experiment

"Well, please send me a draft of the paper as soon as you finish one," I said to Gerber. "I'm kind of an agnostic on the media effects question. But I've just decided that your experiment is going to determine my beliefs."

What I didn't tell him was that I had made the same vow a few months earlier after talking to Stefano DellaVigna. Fortunately, however—as I'll explain in the next chapter—the two studies found very similar results. That is, both found extremely large media effects. In fact, as I'll explain in the next chapter, the results of both studies were closer to finding *impossibly large* effects than to finding nil effects.

Gerber and his coauthors found that in the gubernatorial race that they examined, their *Washington Post*–subscribing subjects voted 3.8 percentage points higher for the Democratic candidate than did their *Washington Times*–subscribing subjects.[4] Given that the *Post* adopts a more liberal slant than the *Times*, the result suggests that newspapers really do influence the way people think and vote.

"Signaling Games" and Their Relation to Media Bias

"Weird. But it has potential," said my colleague John Zaller when I described a research idea to him.

My idea was to use a highly theoretical model from economics—the Crawford-Sobel game of "strategic information transmission," which I briefly describe in chapter 5—as a method to analyze the effects of media bias.

My plan was to simulate the model in a laboratory, where I would pay human subjects to play the game. Data from the game, according to my idea, would provide evidence about the true strength of media effects.

As you may recall from chapter 5, the Crawford-Sobel model is highly abstract. Here, for instance, are some of its technical details:

> Play begins with Nature, which chooses a "state of the world." The latter is a number, which the Sender gets to see. The Sender reports a "message," which is also a number. Her message, if she desires, can be "truthful"—i.e., equal to the state of the world. However, if she desires, she can make it higher or lower than the true state of the world.
>
> The Receiver sees the Sender's message. He then tries to use it to infer the state of world. Next, he chooses a policy. He wants the policy to be as close as possible to the state of the world. Indeed, his "payoff" is higher according to the degree that this is true.
>
> Meanwhile, the Sender has preferences that differ from the Receiver's preferences. Specifically, she wants policy to be *d* units higher than the state of the world. That is, the Sender wants to fool the Receiver into choosing a policy that is *d* units higher than the policy he would choose if he were fully informed.

As you can see, the details become esoteric very fast. What my colleague John Zaller thought was so weird was how I was contorting this "game" into a model of media bias.

"But just think of the 'Sender' as a media outlet or a journalist," I replied, "who has more information about a topic than the median voter. And think of the 'Receiver' as the median voter, who ultimately decides policy after seeing the information that the 'Sender' sends to him."

When I talked with Zaller, my plan was to conduct the experiment myself. But then I learned (through correspondence with Vincent Crawford—the "Crawford" of the Crawford-Sobel model) that two rising-star economists, Hongbin Cai and Joseph Wang, had already conducted such an experiment.[5] (However, Cai and Wang focused on the *amount* of information that players transmitted in the game; whereas, my plan was to focus on *how biased* the information was and the extent to which it could fool subjects. Although Cai and Wang's paper didn't address my question, it turns out that their data could answer it.) I asked Cai and Wang for their data, and they graciously gave it to me.

As I conceded to Zaller that day, for several reasons, the game *is* artificial, and I further conceded that it is not clear that it accurately portrays how real news consumers react to real journalists. For instance, in contrast to real news consumers, the Receivers in the Crawford-Sobel model are very aware that the Senders have an incentive to report biased information.

But all those reasons suggest that the experiment should *understate* the true effect of the media. Despite this, the data showed large effects. As I'll discuss in the next chapter, the effects were about a third as large as the effects implied by the study by DellaVigna and Kaplan, the Berkeley economists; and they were about one fifth as large as the effects implied by the study by Gerber, Karlan, and Berger, the Yale researchers.

Although media scholars have not fully recognized it yet, this experiment, I believe, provides some of the most important evidence ever about media effects.

Results of the Cai-Wang Experiment

One of the main contributions of Cai and Wang was to show that when real humans play the Crawford-Sobel game, the Senders (journalists) indeed send informative messages. That is, their messages are correlated with the truth (i.e., the state of the world). More remarkable, the messages were even more informative than the Crawford-Sobel model predicts.

In general, Cai and Wang found that their results were consistent with a common finding from behavioral economics: The typical person tends to underestimate the degree to which other people are strategic. Consistent with this principle, the Receivers (similar to news consumers) in the experiment were more "trusting" than the Crawford-Sobel model predicts.

Here, for instance, are the main results from one version of the experiment (a version that was average in terms of the media effects that it implied). The Senders in the experiment, on average, sent a message of 5.894. In contrast, the average "state of the world" was 5. Thus, on average their message was biased by 0.894 units from the truth.

The Senders in this version of the experiment were indeed successful at fooling the Receivers. Namely, the Receivers—even though they knew that on average the state of the world would be 5—chose an average policy of 5.282. That is, they were fooled, on average, into choosing a policy that was 0.282 units higher than the policy they would have chosen had they been fully informed.

The latter number, 0.282, is remarkable. All rational-choice theories (and, accordingly, all "Nash equilibria" of the Crawford-Sobel game) predict that it should have been 0. The results show that even in a very artificial environment, where subjects are on guard for bias in the information they receive, the bias still distorts their beliefs. The Receiver subjects were indeed fooled in the direction that the Sender subjects wanted to fool them.

As the next chapter shows, the same thing happens, when real-world news consumers receive biased messages from real-world journalists.

20. The Media Lambda

THE FOLLOWING ARE six claims about the *effects* of the media:

I) During his 2008 campaign, Barack Obama told a reporter, "I am convinced that if there were no Fox News, I might be two or three points higher in the polls."[1]

II) Just prior to the 2004 election, on PBS's *Inside Washington*, *Newsweek* editor Evan Thomas noted that "The media, I think, wants Kerry to win. . . . I'm talking about the establishment media, not Fox . . . [T]hey're going to portray Kerry and Edwards as being young and dynamic and optimistic and all this. There's going to be this glow about them . . . [T]hat's going to be worth maybe 15 points."[2]

III) Three months later, Howard Kurtz, the host of CNN's *Reliable Sources,* asked Thomas to clarify his "15 points" remark:[3]

> THOMAS: Stupid thing to say. It was completely wrong. But I do think that—I do think that the mainstream press—I'm not talking about the blogs and Rush and all that—but the mainstream press favors Kerry. I don't think it's worth 15 points. That was just a stupid thing to say.
>
> KURTZ: Is it worth 5 points?
>
> THOMAS: Maybe, maybe.

IV) UC Berkeley economists Stefano DellaVigna and Ethan Kaplan conducted a natural experiment to test the "Fox News Effect." They found that if Fox News was available to a region, then this raised the vote share for George W. Bush in 2000 by about 0.43 percentage points.[4]

V) In their field experiment Yale researchers Alan Gerber, Dean Karlan, and Daniel Bergan gave one group of subjects a subscription to *The Washington Post* and another group a subscription to *The Washington Times*. They found that in the next gubernatorial election, the vote share for the Democrat was 3.8 percentage points higher among the *Post*-subscribing subjects than among *Times*-subscribing subjects.[5]

VI) Professors Hongbin Cai and Joseph Wang conducted a laboratory experiment of the Crawford-Sobel model of "strategic information transmission." The "Senders" in their experiment sent biased "signals," which on average were 0.89 units greater than the truth. This fooled the "Receivers" into choosing policies that on average were 0.28 units greater than the truth.[6]

Here's an exercise: Try to order these six statements in terms of the media effects that they imply—that is, according to the degree to which they suggest that the media actually can influence people's beliefs and behavior.

Do any of the statements seem to imply that the media's influence is so small that it really doesn't matter if they are biased? Alternatively, does any statement seem to imply that the influence is so large that it makes you think that the claim is impossible?

The exercise is not as simple as it might seem. For instance, in statement (I) it appears that Barack Obama claims that the media has less influence than Evan Thomas claims in statement (III)—since statement (I) only asserts that the media distort vote totals by 2 or 3 percentage points, while statement (III) asserts that the media distort vote totals by 5 percentage points.

But note that Obama refers to only one outlet, Fox News, while Thomas refers to the entirety of "establishment" outlets. Now consider the following facts: As I show in a companion paper to this chapter, when Obama made the statement, the average voter received approximately 8.2 percent of his news from Fox and approximately 79.9 percent from the establishment media (all outlets, except Fox, the Internet, and talk radio).[7] Thus, the "reach" of establishment media is approximately ten times that of Fox News.

Accordingly, while Thomas claimed that the establishment media has about double the effect that Obama claimed about Fox, if we discount by "reach," then Obama actually claimed a much greater media effect than Thomas. Specifically, per audience member reached, Obama claimed a media effect approximately five times greater than that claimed by Thomas.

IN THIS CHAPTER I construct a framework to measure media effects in a precise and systematic way. My ultimate goal is to answer the question "To what degree has media bias distorted the political views of the average voter?"

In the next chapter I'll answer that question. But, for now, I concentrate on a less ambitious goal: simply to define the framework. The framework allows us to order the strength of the above six statements. Indeed, as I will show, the order is: (II), (I), (V), (III), (IV), (VI).

More important, perhaps, the framework shows the *degree* of strength of the six statements. It will show, for instance, that the media effect implied by statement (II) is 3.8 times the effect implied by statement (IV).

Finally, the framework will impose some natural *constraints* on the effect of the media. The framework will show, for instance, that statements (I), (II), (III) and (V) are so strong that they must be wrong—they imply that the effect of the media is impossibly large.

But before I describe the framework, let me first discuss why political science needs such a framework—if not my framework, at least *some* framework—to measure media effects in a precise and systematic way.

A Note to My Fellow Social Scientists on the State of Scholarly Research on Media Effects

"Will it take a long, medium, or short time?" asked my four-year-old daughter as we packed the car for a trip to San Diego.

"About two hours and ten minutes" was the most informative and accurate answer that I could give. The problem, however, is that "hours" and "minutes" don't mean much to a four-year-old. Instead, I said "medium" and continued to pack the car.

In the "media effects" subfield of political science, the language of the researchers is, at times, as imprecise as a four-year-old's.

Although nearly everyone believes that the media influence the views of voters, lots of scholarly studies, especially some of the very early ones, have not found that. Following Joseph Klapper and his pioneering book *The Effects of Mass Communication*, scholars of the 1940s and '50s generally concluded that the media tend only to have "minimal effects" on voters' beliefs.[8]

Such studies had a strong impact, and to this day, if you walk the halls of political-science conferences, you can hear scholars repeat the received wisdom: that the effects of the media are best described by the "minimal effects hypothesis."

Many later researchers, however, argued that media effects were not "minimal," some even claimed that they were "massive."

But then, in 1986, William McGuire wrote an influential essay arguing that any claims of "massive media impacts" were myths.[9]

But the pendulum swung once again in 1992. In a brilliant response, my colleague John Zaller explained why past methods often failed to detect large media effects. He argued that "the persuasive effect of [the media] is closer to 'massive'" than to minimal.[10]

Such conclusions, however, are a bit like claiming that a trip to San Diego takes a "minimal," instead of a "massive," amount of time. The problem is that such terms are never defined precisely. For instance, no media scholar has ever offered a definition of "minimal" that is precise enough to say which, if any, of the above six statements is consistent with a "minimal effects" hypothesis.

Definition of the Media Lambda

My framework begins with a simple assertion: The political views of the typical voter are a weighted average of two things: (i) his natural views—i.e., the political quotient that he would have if the media had no bias, and (ii) the average slant quotient of the news that he receives. The latter concept is the same as the media mu that I discussed in chapter 17.

Scientists often use the Greek letter *lambda* to define a weighted average. For instance, suppose you wanted to predict the temperature in Little Rock using only the temperatures in Oklahoma City and Memphis. If you researched past data, you'd find that the best prediction involves a mathematical formula something like the following:

Little Rock temp. = 0.3 × Oklahoma City temp. + 0.7 × Memphis temp.

In the formula, the temperature of Little Rock is a weighted average of the temperatures of Oklahoma City and Memphis—where 30 percent (0.3) is the weight placed on Oklahoma City's temperature and 70 percent (0.7) is the weight placed on Memphis's temperature. Since Little Rock is closer geographically to Memphis than it is to Oklahoma City, the formula naturally places a higher weight on Memphis than Oklahoma City.

Note that the formula is not a *simple* average of the temperatures of Oklahoma City and Memphis. A simple average would replace 0.3 and 0.7

with 0.5. The 0.7 that appears in the formula is sometimes called "the lambda" on Memphis's temperature. I will call it the "Memphis lambda."

My framework for measuring media effects uses a similar, weighted-average mathematical formula to express the current, *observed* views of the average voter.

Avg. voter's views = (1–media lambda) × (avg. voter's natural views)
+ (media lambda) × (avg. slant of media)

As I will calculate in this chapter, the media lambda is about 0.7.[11] As I will calculate in the next chapter, the average voter's natural views are about 31.5. Using these numbers, we can rewrite the equation as:

Avg. voter's views = 0.3 × 31.5 + 0.7 × [avg. slant of media]

Note that if we substitute 58.5 for the "[avg. slant of media]," the value that I calculated in chapter 17, then this implies that the average voter's views are 50.4—which happens to be the value that I calculated in chapter 5.

This equation can answer many "what if" questions about the effects of the media. For instance, what if the entire media became as liberal as *The New York Times*? By what degree would this change the views of the average voter? To answer this, you simply substitute 73.7—the slant quotient I calculated in chapter 13 for *The New York Times*—for the "[avg. slant of media]" in the equation. Once you do that, you see that the views of the average voter becomes 61—10.6 points more liberal than his current views of 50.4. As I calculated in chapter 12, this is approximately the difference between (i) the views of the average voter in Colorado, Iowa, or Nevada, and (ii) the views of the average voter in Delaware, Maine, or Washington state.

As another "what if" example, suppose that the entire media became as conservative as Fox News *Special Report,* which has a slant of 39.7. Then the equation predicts that this would cause the average voter to become 13.2 points more conservative—from 50.4 to 37.2. This is approximately the difference between (i) the views of the average voter in Colorado, Iowa, or Nevada and (ii) the views of the average voter in Arizona, Indiana, or North Carolina.

Another Illustration of the Weighted-Average Equation

In a moment I'll describe how I arrive at the 0.7 value for the media lambda. But before I do that, it is useful to describe one more analogy to illustrate the weighted-average equation.

FIGURE 20.1

Forces (Trucks) Influencing the Observed Views (Cone) of the Average Voter (Media Truck at a 59 SQ)

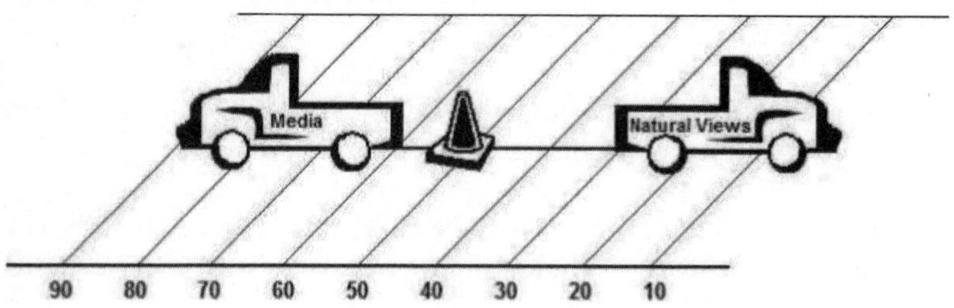

Imagine two trucks on a football field. One, which represents the natural (nondistorted) views of the average voter, is stationed at the 30-yard line. The other, which represents the average slant of the U.S. media, is stationed at the 59-yard line. (Instead of the usual football field, where the yard lines are numbered 0 to 50 then numbered backward to 0, on this one suppose they are numbered from 0 to 100.) Between the two trucks is a cone, which represents the (distorted) views of the average voter, the views we can observe.

The two trucks, each with an elastic rope attached to the cone, pull the cone in opposite directions. The ropes represent the fact that the views of the average voter are a product of a metaphorical tug-of-war: The media, because of their liberal bias, pull the average voter's views to the left. Meanwhile, the natural views of the average voter anchor him and prevent him from moving too far to the left.

If the two ropes had the same elasticity, then the equilibrium position of the cone would be at the midpoint of the two trucks—i.e., at the 44.5-yard line (the average of 30 and 59). However, if the elasticity of one rope is tighter than that of the other, then the cone will be pulled more in the direction of the tighter rope.

Suppose that the rope attached to the media truck has a tighter elasticity, just tight enough so that the equilibrium position of the cone is at the 50.3-yard line instead of the 44.5.

Now suppose you walked from the natural views truck, at the 30-yard line, toward the media truck, on the 59-yard line. You would walk a total of 29 yards. You would reach the cone after you had walked 70 percent of the distance (20.3 yards).

Now suppose that each rope behaves like a spring in a classic physics problem. (That is, suppose that the force exerted on the cone by either

FIGURE 20.2

Forces (Trucks) Influencing the Observed Views (Cone) of the Average Voter (Media Truck at 74 SQ)

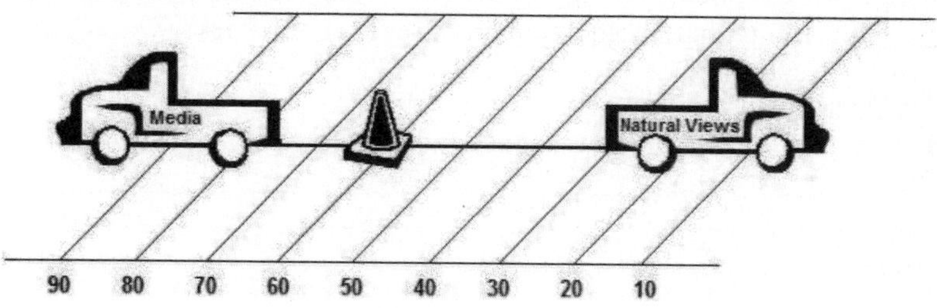

truck is proportional to the distance of the truck from the cone.) Suppose that the media truck moves away from the cone, in the direction of higher yard lines. Since the rope acts like a spring, the position of the cone will have a special property: no matter how far the media truck moves, the cone will always be positioned at 70 percent of the distance between the two trucks.

For instance, suppose the media truck moves to the 74-yard line. This would pull the cone to the 60.8-yard line. If you walked from the natural views truck to the media truck you would walk 44 yards (=74 – 30), and you would reach the cone after you walked 30.8 yards, which is 70 percent of 44.

The Marginality Principle: How This Allows Us to Measure the Media Lambda

A special property of the ropes involves *changes* in the positions of the trucks and the cone. Suppose you didn't know the position of the trucks or the cone; all you knew was that the media truck moved one yard, in the direction of higher yard lines, while the natural views truck remained stationary. By how many yards would the cone move? The answer is 70 percent of 1 yard, or 0.7 yards. This must be the case, otherwise the cone would not maintain its position at 70 percent of the distance between the two trucks.

I call this the *marginality principle*. If the natural views truck remains stationary and the media truck moves a certain distance, then the cone will move 70 percent of the latter distance, *regardless of where the cone and trucks were initially located and regardless how far the media truck moved.*

Another way to illustrate this principle is to use the temperature example. Suppose, as we assumed earlier, that the temperature of Little Rock is a weighted average of the temperatures in Oklahoma City and Memphis—where the weights, as before, are 0.3 and 0.7. Now suppose that the temperature of Oklahoma City stays constant at 30 degrees, while the temperature of Memphis rises from 40 to 60 degrees. In Table 20.1, I list the temperature that the equation produces for Little Rock:

TABLE 20.1

Temperatures, Weighted Averages, and the Marginality Principle

	Temperature in:		
Case	Okla. City	Memphis	Little Rock
1	30	40	37
2	30	50	44
3	30	60	51

The table illustrates how the change in Little Rock's temperature is consistent with the marginality principle. For instance, compare case 1 with case 2. As Memphis's temperature increases by 10 degrees, Little Rock's temperature increases by 7 degrees (from 37 to 44)—70 percent of the change in Memphis's temperature. Note that this is identical to the "Memphis lambda." Now compare case 1 to case 3. As Memphis's temperature increases by 20 degrees, Little Rock's temperature increases by 14 degrees. Once again, consistent with the marginality principle, the increase is 70 percent of the increase in Memphis's temperature.

Here's how the marginality principle helps us to measure the media lambda. Consider the temperature example, but suppose you didn't know that the Memphis lambda is 0.7. Suppose, however, that you knew that as (i) Oklahoma City's temperature remained constant, (ii) Memphis's temperature rose by 20 degrees, and (iii) Little Rock's temperature rose by 14 degrees. Because of the marginality principle, you'd know that the Memphis lambda must equal the latter temperature divided by the former: 14 ÷ 20, or 0.7.

Similarly, using the trucks-and-cone analogy, suppose you knew that as (i) the natural views truck remained in the same place, (ii) the media truck moved 20 yards, which caused (iii) the observed-views cone to move 14 yards. The media lambda must equal the second number divided by the first: 14 ÷ 20, or 0.7.

Estimating the Media Lambda

I use the marginality principle to measure the actual media lambda. For instance, consider the results from "The Fox News Effect." In this study, DellaVigna and Kaplan compared voting patterns between two different types of regions: (i) those in which Fox News was available, and (ii) those in which it was not.

In a companion paper that I have posted on my Web site, I calculate the overall media slant for the two types of regions.[12] I find that (i) in the regions where Fox News was available, the overall slant was 59.093, and (ii) in regions where Fox News was unavailable, the overall slant was 60.054. Note that the difference in these two numbers is 0.961. This is similar to the media truck moving 0.961 yards in the analogy world. This number forms the denominator for my estimate of the media lambda.

Now recall another result from the DellaVigna and Kaplan study. If Fox News was available to a region, then this aided George W. Bush's vote share by about 0.43 percentage points. As I show in the companion paper on my Web site, this corresponds to a decrease in the average voter's political quotient of 0.840.

Thus, to summarize, when Fox News becomes available to a region, it causes the slant quotient of the overall news to decrease by 0.961, and simultaneously it causes the average voter's political quotient to decrease by 0.840. These numbers imply that the media lambda is approximately 0.874 (=0.840/0.961).

Now consider again the six statements that I listed at the beginning of the chapter. I have conducted similar exercises for the other five statements—the ones that did not involve the DellaVigna-Kaplan study—calculating their implied value for the media lambda. Those values are:

I) Barack Obama claimed that Fox News caused his vote totals to decrease by 2 or 3 percentage points. => Media lambda = 2.44 or 3.66.

II) Evan Thomas claimed that the liberal bias of the establishment media gave John Kerry a 15-percent advantage in the 2004 presidential election. => Media lambda = 3.31.

III) Evan Thomas retreated from the 15-point claim, instead claiming that the establishment media gave John Kerry "maybe" a 5-point advantage. => Media lambda = 1.10.

IV) UC Berkeley economists Stefano DellaVigna and Ethan Kaplan found that when Fox News was available to a region, this raised the vote share for George W. Bush by 0.43 percentage points. => Media lambda = 0.87.

V) In their field experiment, Yale researchers Alan Gerber, Ethan Kaplan, and Daniel Bergan found that the vote share for the Democratic candidate was 3.8 percentage points higher among their *Washington Post*–subscribing subjects than among their *Washington Times*–subscribing subjects. => Media lambda = 1.73.

VI) In their laboratory experiment on "strategic information transmission," Professors Hongbin Cai and Joseph Wang found that the "Senders" sent biased "signals," which on average were 0.894 units greater than the truth. This fooled the "Receivers" into choosing policies, which on average were 0.282 units higher than they would have chosen if they had known the truth. => Media lambda = 0.32.[13]

Constraints on the Media Lambda

Note that four of the above statements produce a media lambda greater than 1.0. It is impossible for the media lambda to be that large.

Here's why. If the media lambda were really greater than 1.0, then, if you do the math, you can show that this causes the observed (distorted) view of the average voter to be *outside* the two forces that supposedly pull on it: (i) his natural views and (ii) the media slant.

In the trucks-and-cone analogy world, it would mean that at least one of the ropes *pushes* the cone instead of pulls it.

Further, if the media lambda were really greater than 1.0, then it would mean that when someone tried to persuade you of something, she would end up persuading you *too much*. That is, for instance, suppose you are conservative and your only source of news is speeches by Sen. Barbara Boxer (D-Calif.). Then, if the media lambda were greater than 1.0, this would cause you to become *more* liberal than Boxer. Even stranger, suppose that someone else had natural views that were more liberal than Boxer's. If he listened to the same speeches, and if the media lambda were really greater than 1.0, then this would cause him to become more *conservative* than Boxer.

For these reasons, you should be skeptical of statements such as (I), (II), (III), and (V), which imply that the media lambda is greater than 1.0.

Constructing an Estimate of the Media Lambda

It is easy to dismiss statements (I) and (II). Not only do they imply that the media lambda is much greater than 1.0, the claims—made respectively by Barack Obama and Evan Thomas—were based only on the speaker's intuition, not on any systematic data. Indeed, Thomas later dismissed his own statement.

It is not as easy to dismiss statement (V), which is based on statistical evidence by the Yale researchers. However, this seemingly anomalous result can be explained by sampling error.

Similar problems occur with any type of polling. For instance, suppose that shortly before the 2008 election, 53 percent of the people planned to vote for Barack Obama. If, however, you polled only, say, one thousand voters, then almost surely your poll would find Obama's support not at exactly 53 percent but at something slightly higher or slightly lower than 53 percent. This is the reason pollsters frequently report the "margins of error" for their polls.

Similar problems plague the Yale experiment. Its sample of *Washington Post* subscribers was 603, and its sample of *Washington Times* subscribers was 592. Recall that the experiment's researchers found that the *Post* subscribers voted for the Democrat at a 3.8 higher percentage rate than did the *Times* subscribers. However, if instead the researchers had adopted a much larger sample—say, 100,000 of each type of subscriber—then I'm confident that instead of a 3.8 difference, the researchers would have found a smaller difference—something in the range of a 1.1-to-1.8 difference (which would respectively have produced a media-lambda estimate in the 0.5-to-0.8 range).

The hard sciences have several "universal constants." For instance, one is *c*, which represents the speed of light. Another is *G*, which expresses the gravitational pull between any two bodies.

The media lambda, I propose, is a similar universal constant. That is—just as the same *G* appears in (i) the equation that describes an apple falling from a tree and (ii) the equation describing Earth's gravitational pull on the Moon—I propose that the same media lambda describes (i) the influence of Fox News, which DellaVigna and Kaplan examined, and (ii) the influences of *The Washington Post* and *The Washington Times,* which the Yale researchers examined.

If so, then why do the two studies produce two different estimates for the media lambda? The answer, again, involves sampling error. Indeed, the authors report fairly wide confidence intervals for the original parameters that they estimate (i.e., the 0.43 figure by the Berkeley researchers and the

3.8 figure by the Yale researchers).[14] It is therefore no surprise that the media-lambda estimates, which I have translated from these parameters, are not exactly alike.

Meanwhile, however, the same cannot be said about the media-lambda estimate, 0.32, that I derived from statement (VI) (which involved the laboratory experiment on "strategic information transmission"). This estimate is much smaller than the estimates from statements (IV) and (V). Further, the estimate was based on a very large sample, which produced tight bounds on its confidence interval. The discrepancy, therefore, cannot be explained by sampling error.

Instead, the main reason for the discrepancy, I believe, involves the artificial nature of the experiment on which it was based. For several reasons, the "signal receivers" of the experiment—if we compare them to real-world newspaper readers or real-world television viewers—were more *on guard* for biased messages from the "signal senders."

First, the signal receivers—because the researchers running the experiment told them—knew exactly the preferences of the signal senders. Translated to the real world, this would be as if all newspaper readers and all television viewers had detailed knowledge of the political views of the journalists they read and watched. In striking contrast, journalists rarely reveal their political views. For instance, when ABC News correspondent Martha Raddatz appeared on C-SPAN's *Washington Journal,* a viewer asked her to describe her political views, including the political party to which she belonged and if she had ever voted for a Republican. Raddatz refused to answer and noted that most other journalists would also refuse. "We don't talk about those things," she said.[15]

Second, the signal receivers were acutely aware of the signal senders' incentives to send biased messages. Indeed, the signal receivers were paid according to how well they could understand those incentives and, in turn, discount the biases from those signals.

Further, almost all the subjects in the experiment played both roles in the experiment. This means that almost all the signal receivers had earlier played the role of a signal sender. Translated to the real world, this would be as if every newspaper reader, at some point in his or her life, had held a job as a newspaper reporter.

For all these reasons, I believe, the experiment severely understated the true media lambda. Thus, the experiment should be interpreted not as estimating the media lambda at 0.32, but instead as estimating it as "significantly greater than 0.32."

Now let me use statements (IV), (V), and (VI) to construct an aggregate estimate of the media lambda.

First consider the estimate 1.73 from statement (V), produced from the Gerber et al. study. Since it is greater than 1.0, it is impossibly large. Accordingly, we should interpret the study as implying not an estimate of 1.73 but rather a "very high" estimate, one very close to 1.0. I will interpret the statement as producing a media-lambda estimate of 0.95.[16]

Now consider the results from the laboratory experiment. Again, let me err on the side of estimating too small a value for the media lambda. Instead of concluding that it produces an estimate "significantly greater than 0.32," I will treat the estimate as if it were exactly 0.32.

Finally, to obtain an aggregate estimate, I average these two estimates with the 0.87 estimate from the Berkeley study. *This gives an aggregate estimate of approximately 0.7 as the media lambda.* (More precisely, the estimate is 0.713 [=0.87+0.95+0.32]/3, which I round to 0.7.)

Let me admit that I consider this estimate rough and, at best, only an approximation of the true media lambda. The main problem is that there are only three studies of media effects that I trust enough to allow me to calculate an estimate. As you can see, those studies give a fairly broad range of values.

Nevertheless, I am confident that the media lambda is not too different from 0.7. For instance, given the results from the laboratory experiment, I am confident that the true value cannot be much less than 0.5. And given the theoretical upper bounds, I am confident that the true value cannot be much more than 0.8.

Some Final Thoughts on the Media Lambda: Why "Rational Choice" Theorists Should Not be Skeptical of Such a High Estimate

Recall my earlier discussion of "rational choice" and how it implies that news consumers should discount any biases of the media. Rational choice implies that the media lambda should be 0.

However, despite the theoretical plausibility of rational-choice arguments, I don't think that anybody actually believes them when they're applied to the effect of the media. Indeed, the rational-choice logic leads to some counterfactual, if not preposterous, conclusions.

The logic implies, for instance, that my children, whom my wife and I are raising to be Christian, will at some point think: "My parents want me to be Christian. Consequently, they have probably overstated the virtues of Christianity and understated the virtues of other religions. I should therefore consider converting to another religion." Carried to its full extent, the rational-choice logic implies that my children should be just as likely to become Muslim as Christian. Likewise, it implies that children of Muslims should be just as likely to become Christian as Muslim.

The rational-choice logic also implies that our court system would still be fair and just if we changed it so that instead of giving each attorney approximately equal time, we gave defense attorneys, say, only one tenth the time that we give prosecuting attorneys. Such a system, so goes the rational-choice logic, would produce convictions neither more, nor less, frequently than our current system, since jurors would adjust their beliefs to account for the prosecutors' extra time.[17]

These examples, I believe, expose the problems of rational-choice logic when applied to the media or any other area where humans try to persuade each other. The examples suggest, contrary to the rational-choice logic, that the media lambda is greater than 0.

Some other reasons—in addition to the statistical evidence I presented earlier—suggest that the media lambda is *much* greater than 0. One reason involves the fact that the media lambda is defined in terms of the *average* voter, which by my definition means that he has moderate political views. Some survey evidence suggests that moderates are less sophisticated than partisan voters. For instance, according to a 2004 survey conducted by American National Election Study, only 19 percent of moderate voters could correctly name Dennis Hastert's political office (Speaker of the House). In contrast, 60 percent of "strong Republicans" and 46 percent of "strong Democrats" could do so. Consequently, given their lack of political sophistication, it is reasonable to believe that moderates are not so savvy at discounting the bias of the media. This makes them easier to persuade, which produces a high media lambda.

Another reason involves a dubious assumption of the rational-choice logic, an assumption that seems to be contradicted by survey evidence. This assumption is that news consumers will eventually recognize any bias in the news. In contrast, however, surveys show that approximately 63 percent of moderate voters do not believe that there is any bias in the news.[18] Many of the same voters are unaware that journalists' political views are significantly different from their own. This has profound implications for media effects.

To see why, suppose that news consumers are rational in every way except that they think that journalists have political preferences identical to their own. Now consider the following well-established result from principal-agent theory, a subfield of economics: Suppose an agent (say, a journalist), who is more informed than you, is sending you (the principal) a message (say, a news report). Suppose also that you believe that she has preferences identical to yours. If so, then she is your "perfect agent." Your optimal response is to believe everything she says and to do any action that she suggests.

In this scenario, such a news consumer will be completely fooled by the bias of the journalist. His actions will reflect not just a very high media lambda, but one equal to 1.0.

On top of all this, three pieces of anecdotal evidence have further convinced me that the media lambda is very large—i.e., much closer to 1.0 than 0.0. One involves the *L.A. Times* article about UCLA admissions that I discussed earlier. My moderate friends, and even some conservative friends, completely bought the picture that the journalist painted. That is, they were convinced, as the article insinuated, that UCLA is slightly racist and that it had little desire to increase the number of black students it admitted.

Another anecdote involves the media's treatment of Sarah Palin during the 2008 election. Although the media frequently discussed stories that suggested that Palin was unqualified, they rarely did the same about Barack Obama. This happened even though Palin's level of experience in government was similar to Obama's, and many would reasonably conclude it was superior. By the time of the 2008 election, both had served twelve years in elected office. (Obama served four years as a U.S. Senator and eight years as an Illinois state senator. Palin had served two years as Alaska governor, six years as mayor of Wasilla, and four years as Council member of Wasilla.) In terms of executive office, Palin had eight years of experience, and Obama had none. Despite this, my moderate friends mirrored the media's treatment. That is, although many voiced concerns about Palin's qualifications, few voiced concerns about Obama's qualifications.

The third anecdote involves the Bush tax cuts. My moderate friends were completely unaware of the fact that the cuts made the tax system more progressive—that the rich would actually pay a greater share of the tax burden under the Bush plan. In contrast, the same friends were very aware of a different fact, which the media often mentioned, that in dollar terms, the rich would receive most of the benefits of the cut.

In all these cases, my moderate friends did not discount the reports of the journalists—as they would have if the media lambda really were less than 1.0. They did not say, for example, "Although the *L.A. Times* painted UCLA as a slightly racist institution, the writer probably exaggerated things, since she, like most journalists, is probably liberal and a supporter of affirmative action." Nor did they say, "Although Sarah Palin does not seem to be highly qualified, given that journalists strongly prefer Democrats over Republicans, I bet she is really more qualified than the media suggest."

The beliefs of my moderate friends didn't just move in the direction of the media reports, they became *identical* to the media reports. This implies not just a high value of the media lambda, but a maximally high value of 1.0. The anecdotes suggest that, if anything, my 0.7 estimate understates the true media lambda.

21. Rendezvous with Clarity

THE GREATEST POLITICAL speech ever, in my judgment, was Ronald Reagan's "A Time for Choosing." Given in 1964, when he was just an actor, Reagan urged Americans to vote for Barry Goldwater. In addition, he warned that Americans were slowly losing their freedoms and that the United States was creeping toward socialism.

"Somewhere a perversion has taken place," said Reagan. "Our natural unalienable rights are now considered to be a dispensation of government . . . [F]reedom has never been so fragile, so close to slipping from our grasp as it is at this moment."[1]

He discussed a Cuban refugee who had recently escaped the tyranny of Fidel Castro:

> And the Cuban stopped and said, "How lucky you are? I had someplace to escape to." And in that sentence he told us the entire story. If we lose freedom here, there's no place to escape to. This is the last stand on Earth.

And then Reagan concluded with the famous words:

> You and I have a rendezvous with destiny. We'll preserve for our children this, the last best hope of man on Earth, or we'll sentence them to take the last step into a thousand years of darkness.

Whereas Reagan discussed freedom and the perversion of rights, my concern is with truth and the distortion of facts. Whereas Reagan discussed America's rendezvous with destiny, in this chapter I discuss America's rendezvous with *Clarity.*

Clarity

Here's what I mean by Clarity. Imagine a world where journalists report the news as the average voter wants them to report it. In such a world the average journalist has the same political values as the average voter, or at least, when reporting the news, *acts* as if she has the same values. This means that she adopts a slant quotient equal to the political quotient of the average voter.

As I discussed in the preface, because of media bias, we currently see the world as if we are looking through a glass. Journalists, instead of presenting the world as it really is, distort it, shining more light on the facts that liberals want us to see and less on the facts that conservatives want us to see.

Clarity means removing the glass. It means seeing the world as it really is. It also means seeing how Americans would think and vote once their minds are no longer distorted by media bias.

My task in this chapter is to describe that world—specifically, to calculate the overall slant and political quotients that we would see in such a world.

Why It Takes a Journey to Achieve Clarity

The task is not as easy as it may seem. Here's why: Suppose the overall slant of the media became as moderate as the current views of the average voter. That is, suppose the overall SQ dropped from 58.5 to 50.4. At first glance, you might conclude that this would mean that the media had become perfectly unbiased, and that, consequently, we had reached Clarity.

But here's the problem. If the media really influence the thoughts and behavior of people—i.e., if the media lambda really is greater than 0—then such a change causes the views of the average voter to change.

Specifically, note that in this scenario the media's slant quotient changes by 8.1 points (=58.5–50.4). Because the media lambda is 0.7, this causes the PQ of the average voter to become 5.7 points (≈ 0.7 x 8.1) more conservative. Thus, if the media changed its slant to 50.4, this would cause the average voter's PQ to drop to 44.7.

But once the average voter changed his views, this means that the media, even after they changed their SQ to 50.4, would still be more liberal than the average voter. Thus, they would still have a bias. The magnitude would be less—before it was 8.1 points (58.5–50.4); while now it is 5.7 points (50.4–44.7)—but they would still have a bias.

To achieve Clarity, the media need to move once again to the right. Let us now repeat this exercise.

Specifically, let the media change their slant (again) to the PQ of the average voter, which is now at 44.7. This is a change of 5.7 points, which causes the average voter to change his PQ by 4 points (=0.7×5.7)—a decrease from 44.7 to 40.7. Note that, once again, after the voter responds to the change in slant, the media still have a bias.

Note that when you move the slant of the media toward the views of the average voter, that very act causes the average voter to move away from the media. The process is like chasing a small animal. You reach down to grab it, but that very act makes the animal move away from you.

At first it might appear that to reach Clarity you would need to repeat this analysis an infinite number of times. Consequently, it might appear that it is impossible to reach Clarity.

That, however, is wrong. The best way to explain why is through Zeno's Paradox. Zeno, an Ancient Greek philosopher, described a race between Achilles and a tortoise. Although Achilles is much faster, the tortoise has a head start, which, let's say, is one hundred yards. After the race begins, Achilles, at some point, will have run one hundred yards, and he will reach the point where the tortoise began. During this time, the tortoise will have run a much shorter distance, say, ten yards. But he will still have a lead on Achilles. Now let Achilles run an additional ten yards—that is, let him once again reach the point where the tortoise was. During this time, the tortoise will have run a much shorter distance, say one yard. Accordingly, he will still have a lead on Achilles.

Whenever Achilles reaches the point where the tortoise was, he still has to run farther to reach the point where the tortoise is. Consequently, because there are an infinite number of points that Achilles must reach where the tortoise has already been, he, according to the paradox, can never overtake the tortoise.

Of course, this wouldn't really happen in practice. In a real race Achilles would eventually pass the tortoise. The reason it might *seem* that Achilles can't overtake the tortoise is that Zeno uses an artificial construct: he requires Achilles and the tortoise to travel in a series of discrete periods of time, whereas in an actual race they would move continuously through time.

For the same reason, it only appears that the average SQ can't reach the average PQ. As I will show, if instead we imagine the SQ and PQ moving continuously through time—instead of through a series of discrete jumps—then we can solve the problem. It allows us to calculate Clarity, the point where the average SQ and average PQ are equal.

Dr. Rendezvous

Although all the astronauts in the Apollo program were very smart, one of them, Buzz Aldrin, floated on a smartness level above the rest. In the documentary, *In the Shadow of the Moon,* two of Aldrin's colleagues expressed their admiration for him. One was Mike Collins. Once called the "loneliest man in the universe," Collins piloted the command module for Apollo 11, while Aldrin and Neil Armstrong piloted the lunar module to the Moon's surface. The other was Alan Bean, a member of Apollo 12 and the fourth man ever to walk on the moon.

> BEAN: One thing I know about Buzz—he's one of these guys that's a lot smarter than most of us. He had a nickname, Dr. Rendezvous.
>
> COLLINS: He loves to talk about technical stuff, particularly rendezvous. I mean he'll get this orbit going this way and that orbit going the other way, and he really grooved on those things.
>
> BEAN: You didn't want to sit near him at a party. Because he would start talking about rendezvous, and you would be wanting to talk about that good-looking girl across the room. [Laughing]. He could care less. He wanted to talk about rendezvous, and he'd been talking to you about it all week long!

Aldrin earned his PhD from MIT in aeronautical engineering. His dissertation examined how two different bodies, like spacecraft, would behave when orbiting a large mass such as the Earth or Moon. His task was to calculate how, when, and where the two bodies would rendezvous. In terms of the complexity of his analysis, the following is a typical passage of his dissertation:[2]

> To find the pseudo intercept rendezvous parameters b', k', and the radial distance d' between circular orbits which correspond to the actual intercept described by b and k and the final target true anomaly f_{ft} with a_w, a_t, and e_t specified, one proceeds as follows:
>
> $$d = a_t - a_w - a_t e_t \cos f_{ft}$$
> $$d' = a_t - a_w - a_t e_t \cos (f_{ft} - \Delta f_i)$$

where:

$$\Delta f_i = f_f - f_i$$
$$= \cos^{-1}(-b/k) - \cos^{-1}([1 - b]/k)$$

The problem that I examine is similar to Aldrin's, albeit much simpler. For instance, (i) while the bodies in Aldrin's problem move in a three-dimensional space, the bodies in mine move in a one-dimensional space, i.e., a line; and (ii) while Aldrin's problem uses some very complex math, including trigonometry, calculus, and differential equations, mine uses only algebra.

My problem is similar to Aldrin's in another important respect: it examines two bodies (the SQ of the media and the PQ of the average voter) and calculates where they will rendezvous—i.e., where they become equal.

And Time Goes By

Another similarity is that to solve the problem, I borrow an insight from Aldrin. This is to think of the bodies as moving continuously, rather than as a series of discrete steps.

Specifically, suppose, like Aldrin's rendezvous problem, that the media and voter moved simultaneously—both in the direction of lower SQ and PQ scores. Suppose also, as the media lambda implies, that the average voter's PQ moved seven tenths as fast as the media's SQ. Given these assumptions, at what PQ/SQ score would the media and voter rendezvous?

Posed this way, the problem is identical to the classic algebra problem you might have faced in eighth or ninth grade:

> Suppose a red car and a blue car are positioned on a stretch of highway. Specifically, the blue car is at the 58.5-mile marker, and the red car is at the 50.4-mile marker. Suppose they begin traveling at the same time, both moving toward the 0-mile marker. Suppose the red car moves seven tenths as fast as the blue car. At what mile marker do they rendezvous?

The algebra works as follows. Let x be the mile marker where they rendezvous. Once they reach x, the red car will have traveled $50.4 - x$ miles, and the blue car will have traveled $58.5 - x$ miles. The red car will have traveled 70 percent of the distance of the blue car. Thus, $0.7(58.5 - x) = 50.4 - x$.

Once you do the math, you see that $x = 31.5$. This is my estimate of Clarity.

If journalists ever reached a point where they reported the news as the average voter wanted them to report it, then this would be the slant quotient that they would adopt. Further, this would be the political quotient that the average voter would hold.

The point, 31.5, is my estimate of the natural views of the average voter. Note that at this point, the media is pulling his views neither to the left nor the right. In the analogy world, at this point the media truck has met the cone, which has met the natural views truck. The ropes attached to the trucks would be completely slack: they are pulling the cone neither left nor right.

Why the True World of Clarity Is Probably More Conservative Than I Have Estimated

Recall that earlier I noted some caveats about my estimate of the media lambda—specifically, that I am not certain that the true value is 0.7, although I am confident that the true value is between 0.5 and 0.8.

Also recall that I believe that 58.5 probably understates the true overall slant of the media. The reason is because it was based on some assumptions that cause my estimate to be too conservative. Most substantially, when I calculated the estimate, I ignored results from the fact-based, Bush-tax-cuts method. If I had used more realistic assumptions, then I believe, I would have found an estimate closer to 63.8.

In Table 21.1, I show how my estimate of Clarity would change if instead I had used one of the alternative estimates of the media lambda or the overall slant of the media.

TABLE 21.1

Estimates of Clarity Under Alternative Assumptions

Media Lambda	Overall Slant of the Media	
	58.5	63.8
0.5	42.3	37.0
0.7	31.5	19.1
0.8	18.0	−3.2

Note that three of the estimates are less than 31.5, while only two are greater. Note also that the average of the six estimates, 24.1, is notably less. Thus, although earlier I report 31.5 as my estimate of Clarity, I believe that the true value is more likely in the low- or mid-twenties, and it might be near 0. In the next chapter I'll describe in more substantive terms what it would mean if the average American had a PQ as low as 25 or 30.

22. Walk a Mile in the Shoes of a Centrist . . . Whose Mind Has Not Been Distorted by Media Bias

HOW WOULD AMERICA look and feel if it achieved Clarity? That is, what if media bias suddenly disappeared, and, as the media lambda implies, the political quotient of the average American dropped to 25 or 30? How would he or she think and vote in such world?

In this chapter I try to answer those questions in a tangible way. Specifically, I transport you, metaphorically, to *regions of Clarity*: places where the average political quotient is approximately 25 or 30. As I'll show, such places include Orange County, California; Salt Lake County, Utah; and the state of Kansas.

But before I do that, let me begin by explaining a simpler way for you to experience Clarity: Watch a NASCAR race. As I show in a companion paper for this chapter (see www.timgroseclose.com/statistical-analysis-nascar-fans.pdf), the average PQ of people who follow NASCAR is approximately 24.

Drive a Mile in the Tornados Chevrolet Filled with Sunoco Fuel

On April 10, 2010, just after he won NASCAR's Subway Fresh Fit 600, Ryan Newman engaged in perhaps the most environmentally unfriendly victory celebration in all of sports: the burnout. After driving near the grandstand, he floored the gas, turned the steering wheel hard right, and spun out his tires for several seconds. The result was a large gray cloud of burned rubber, which enveloped his car and eventually drifted to the grandstand.

After the burnouts, Newman drove to "Gatorade Victory Lane," where Steve Burns, an announcer for Fox Sports, waited to interview him.

"Ryan, when this race started," asked Burns, "you talked about the car being on top of the track. Then it was tight. Did you think you had a shot to win the race?"

Newman, like most NASCAR drivers, would make an excellent politician. He quickly dispensed with the question and instead used the camera time to further his own agenda: to give free advertising to the companies that had sponsored him:

> Well, I thought we had a good car in practice. But, uh, I gotta thank Tornados for coming on board, helping us out, with, uh, what Tony Stewart and everybody at Stewart-Haas Racing, giving me an opportunity with. And, uh, I thank the fans. I gotta thank Sprint, Chevrolet, and, uh, Coca-Cola, U.S. Army—*man,* we've been working so hard for those guys to get into victory lane—and, uh, everybody at Haas Automation. Um, just, Kraft, everybody that helps us out, Gillette . . .[1]

Many progressives would be repulsed by Newman's corporate name-dropping. But such "corporatism" is a staple of NASCAR. In fact, the preferred term of NASCAR fans for such corporatism is "loyalty."[2]

If you're a progressive, then you would have been even more repulsed by the race's opening ceremony. It began with a prayer by the official chaplain of Phoenix International Raceway, and it ended with a flyover by four F-16 fighter jets, just as "The Star-Spangled Banner" finished its last note.

Although progressives might describe the ceremony as a display of jingoism, Christian intolerance, and American hegemony, a NASCAR fan would describe it as a show of patriotism, faith, and support for the troops.

Yet, while the attitudes of NASCAR fans may seem out of place to many people, according to my estimates, if the United States achieved Clarity, then such attitudes would be commonplace.

Regions of Clarity

Another way to experience Clarity is to visit a geographic region that has a political quotient near 25 or 30. The following are the U.S. states that have a PQ between 20 and 35:

TABLE 22.1

States That Illustrate Clarity	PQ
Alaska	20.4
Alabama	20.9
Kansas	24.3
North Dakota	26.4
Kentucky	26.8
Texas	27.5
Louisiana	28.5
Mississippi	28.5
South Dakota	29.8
Arkansas	30.4
Tennessee	30.5
South Carolina	32.1
West Virginia	32.2
Montana	33.5
Georgia	34.3

Recall that I have also estimated political quotients for U.S. counties. Table 22.2 lists all U.S. counties that (i) have a population of at least three hundred thousand and (ii) have an average PQ between 20 and 35.

TABLE 22.2

Counties That Illustrate Clarity

County	Description	PQ
Knox, Tenn.	Knoxville and suburbs	20.3
Oklahoma County, Okla.	Oklahoma City and suburbs	22.0
Lancaster, Pa.	Lancaster and suburbs	22.2
Gwinnett, Ga.	Northeastern exurbs of Atlanta	23.1
York, Pa.	York and suburbs	23.7
Sedgwick, Kans.	Wichita and suburbs	25.0
Ocean, N.J.	Jersey Shore, 40 miles S. of NYC	25.2
Tarrant, Tex.	Fort Worth and suburbs	26.1
Cobb, Ga.	Northwestern exurbs of Atlanta	27.6
Johnson, Kans.	Southwestern Kansas City suburbs	28.4

(continued)

TABLE 22.2 (continued)

County	Description	PQ
Allen, Ind.	Fort Wayne and suburbs	29.0
Lee, Fla.	Fort Myers and suburbs	29.2
Ada, Idaho	Boise and suburbs	30.1
Westmoreland, Pa.	Eastern exurbs of Pittsburgh	30.7
Hamilton, Tenn.	Chattanooga and suburbs	31.4
Mobile, Ala.	Mobile and suburbs	31.7
Brevard, Fla.	Eastern Orlando suburbs	31.9
Maricopa, Ariz.	Phoenix and suburbs	32.5
Morris, N.J.	Far western suburbs of NYC	32.5
Orange, Calif.	Southern suburbs of Los Angeles	32.8
Polk, Fla.	Eastern exurbs of Tampa	33.2
Salt Lake, Utah	Salt Lake and suburbs	33.4

Elections of Clarity

How would elections be affected if the U.S. achieved Clarity?

The answer is that the country would vote the way regions of Clarity currently vote. Table 22.3 lists all the states with PQs between 24 and 31. It also notes how they voted in the presidential elections of 2004 and 2008.

TABLE 22.3

Voting Behaviors of States That Illustrate Clarity

State	PQ	Bush–Kerry Vote	McCain–Obama Vote
Kansas	24.3	62–37	57–42
North Dakota	26.4	63–35	53–45
Kentucky	26.8	60–40	57–41
Texas	27.5	61–38	55–44
Lousiana	28.5	57–42	59–40
Mississippi	28.8	59–40	56–43

TABLE 22.3 (continued)

State	PQ	Bush–Kerry Vote	McCain–Obama Vote
South Dakota	**29.8**	**60–38**	**53–45**
Arkansas	**30.4**	**54–45**	**59–39**
Tennessee	**30.5**	**57–43**	**57–42**

As the table shows, in regions of Clarity the 2008 presidential vote was about 56–42 in favor of McCain. This contrasts with the actual election, in which Obama won 53–46.

In 2004, among regions of Clarity, the vote was about 59–40 in favor of Bush, whereas in the actual election Bush won by only 51–48.

Note that in both elections the Republican polled about 8 to 10 points higher in regions of Clarity than in the country as a whole.

Accordingly, this analysis illustrates the degree to which media bias aids Democratic candidates—about 8 to 10 percentage points.[3]

Tell the Folks Back Home This Is the Land of Clarity Calling

To illustrate Clarity in a tangible way, it is useful to describe the political views of a few of the above regions. In this final section, I describe the views of three regions: (i) Salt Lake County, Utah; (ii) Orange County, California; and (iii) the state of Kansas.

Salt Lake County, Utah

According to a joke, the Pope receives a call from his bishop, who tells him, "I have good news and bad news."

"What's the good news?" asks the Pope.

"Our Lord, Jesus Christ, has returned to Earth," says the bishop.

"That's wonderful," the Pope responds. "What could possibly be the bad news?"

"He's in Salt Lake City."

A common misconception, which is reflected in the joke, is that Salt Lake City, at least approximately, is the most Mormon place on Earth. Although the LDS Church is headquartered there, Salt Lake City has nearly the *lowest* percentage of Mormons in Utah.

Another misconception is that Salt Lake City is extremely conservative. Although Salt Lake County leans right, the city leans left. Here, for instance, is how the *2010 Almanac of American Politics* described Salt Lake City.[4]

> Interestingly, the Salt Lake City neighborhoods close to the church headquarters, with gracious old houses and a smaller street grid that attract academic and professional newcomers, have become the most heavily "gentile" (the Mormon term for non-Mormons) and politically liberal part of the state. Just as the Yankee hub of Boston filled up with Irish Catholic Democrats in the 1890s, so Salt Lake City has been getting secular liberal Democrats. Former Salt Lake City Mayor Rocky Anderson called President George W. Bush a "war criminal," and in 2004 the city voted 58% for Democratic presidential nominee John Kerry.

Meanwhile, as I mentioned, Salt Lake *County* leans right. First, it should be noted that even if Salt Lake *City* leans left, it comprises only 18 percent of the county's population. Second, although the county's Mormon population, 53 percent, is less than the rest of the state, that percentage is still much higher than the U.S. percentage, which is slightly less than 2 percent.

Third, Salt Lake County votes significantly more Republican than the rest of America. In 2008, for instance, John McCain received 50.3 percent of the county's two-party-vote share—4 percent more than he received in the entire country, 46.3 percent. In 2004, George W. Bush received 61.3 percent of the county's two-party vote—10.1 percent more than he received in the entire country, 51.2 percent.

Orange County, California

Recall from the preface my Hollywood acquaintance, who said to another Hollywood acquaintance, "Ah, don't cross the Orange Curtain." His point was that, for his tastes at least, Orange County is too conservative, family-friendly, and boring. Recall, also from the preface that the writers of *The Sopranos* considered Orange County similar to Purgatory.

The county, however, is not as conservative as it is sometimes perceived. As the *2010 Almanac of American Politics* notes:[5]

> Always Republican, Orange County became a symbol of conservatism, first in California and then nationally. This was a solid base for Ronald Reagan in his campaigns for governor and president. In 1988, the district's 317,000-vote plurality for George H. W. Bush was his largest in any county in the nation. Orange County's conservatism reflected a belief in technological progress and traditional values as unyielding as the mile-square grid that the county's founders imposed on most of its land, and a belief in market economies that produced wonders such as the area's advance military

> technologies. Over the years, Orange County has become racially and ethnically more diverse. Contrary to the images presented in the television series *The O.C.*, the all-white Orange County stereotype is now thoroughly out of date, exemplified by the election in 2007 of the county's first Vietnamese-American supervisor. In 2004, Orange County gave George W. Bush a 222,000-vote margin, well below his father's margin 16 years before. The GOP advantage dwindled significantly in 2008, when John McCain prevailed over Barack Obama by only 29,500 votes.[6]

A significant demographic trend in Orange County is the influx of Latinos. In 1990, Latinos comprised 23 percent of the County.[7] By 2008, the number had risen to 34 percent.[8] The trend caught at least one Orange County politician flat-footed. Republican Bob Dornan was first elected in 1984 to one of the six U.S. House districts that are at least partially contained in Orange County. He easily won five reelection bids, usually by margins greater than 15 percent. However, by 1996, when he flirted with a run for president, his district had become 50 percent Latino. That year, he lost his seat to Loretta Sanchez, a Latina Democrat. The district is now 69 percent Latino. Sanchez has since won reelection usually by safe margins. Even in 2010, a tidal-wave year for Republicans, she won her reelection bid by 14 percentage points.

Although Orange County may be trending left, at least for now it still leans right. Its airport is named after John Wayne. It is home to the Crystal Cathedral, one of the country's first mega-churches. The cathedral, famous for its weekly televised *Hour of Power*, is said to be the most watched Christian service worldwide. Orange County is also home to famed pastor Rick Warren.

In 2008, John McCain received 51.8 percent of the county's two-party vote—5.5 percent higher than the share he received from the entire country, 46.3 percent. In 2004, George W. Bush received 60.5 percent of the county's two-party vote—9.3 percent higher than the share he received from the country, 51.2 percent.

Although strongly Latino, two anecdotes reveal that even the most Latino congressional district in Orange County is not a cakewalk for Latino candidates—that is, they cannot stray too far from the wishes of non-Latino, conservative voters. In 2002, Loretta Sanchez's sister, Linda, won a seat to Congress in nearby District 39 (which is part of Los Angeles County). They became the first sisters ever to serve in Congress.

Linda, the Los Angeles representative, lists her last name with an accent mark on the "a." Loretta, the Orange County representative, does not.

In 2010, after Arizona passed its controversial immigration law, Linda charged that the law's promoters had ties to white supremacy groups. Loretta never made such a charge.

Kansas

As I noted earlier, the political quotient of Kansas is 24.8. The state has a strong tendency to vote Republican. For instance, in 2008 it voted for McCain 57–42, and in 2004 it voted for Bush 62–37. It has not elected a Democrat to the U.S. Senate since 1932. In 1964, when Barry Goldwater proclaimed, "Extremism in defense of liberty is no vice," and Lyndon Johnson subsequently demolished him in a landslide, Kansas was approximately split between the two candidates.

The state was the subject of Thomas Frank's bestseller *What's the Matter with Kansas?*. Frank's thesis was that Kansans don't seem to understand their own economic interests. That is, although they are poorer than the average American, and thus they would benefit on net from bigger government and higher taxes, they still vote Republican.

Frank's book contains some inaccuracies. For instance, as Steven Malaga noted in *The Wall Street Journal*, Frank attributes severe economic woes to the state (where "heaps of rusting junk and snarling Rottweilers blight the landscape"), and he blames these woes on the pro-capitalistic attitudes of the state's voters. However, by most measures, Kansas has outpaced the U.S. economy. For instance, during the 1990s its growth rate with regard to jobs was 24 percent, while the nation's growth rate was only 20 percent.

More problematic, like many left-wing writers, Frank does not grant Kansans the possibility that they are voting their economic values instead of their tastes. That is, maybe Kansans recognize that, yes, they would be better off personally if taxes were higher and government were bigger. But perhaps they also recognize that bigger government shrinks the total economic pie for others, even if it makes their own slice bigger. Maybe they also recognize the immorality in government's taking from people what they have produced honestly by their own labor.

Regardless of the reason *why* Kansans favor less government and lower taxes, no one can deny that they *do*. My results show that if the media weren't so successful at distorting political values, then the *average* American would hold similar views.

Thus, while Frank's book asks, "What's the matter with Kansas?" my results suggest that Kansans should ask, "What's the matter with the rest of America?"

Epilogue

SMALL STEPS TOWARD A BETTER MEDIA

THE GREATEST WEB log in the universe, in my judgment, is MarginalRevolution.com, run by Tyler Cowen and Alex Tabarrok, two economics professors at George Mason University. The blog's motto is "Small steps to a much better world." In that spirit, let me offer two small steps that I believe would help remedy problems of the media.

I spent the first ten years of my career as a congressional scholar. The more I studied politicians, the more I respected them. I spent the next eight years as a media scholar. The more I studied journalists, the less I respected them.

Both of the remedies that I suggest involve ways to make journalists more like politicians. I promise I'm not joking when I say that. Some useful norms and institutions govern the behavior of politicians. If the same norms and institutions governed journalists, then the news industry, I believe, would be more accurate, unbiased, and respected.

A Little *More* Conversation . . . with Conservatives

My first remedy is that journalists should interact more with conservatives. I'm not suggesting that government mandate this, only that journalists engage in some self-regulation and do this on their own.

They should consider that even the most liberal members of Congress interact very frequently with conservatives. For example, when Sen. John

Kerry goes to work in the morning, he knows that approximately half of his colleagues will be Republican. Further, when he interacts with constituents, again, he knows that a significant fraction will be conservative. For example, even though he represents approximately the most liberal state in the country, Massachusetts, 36 percent of his constituents voted for McCain. Unlike journalists, Kerry realizes that every day there is a high probability that he will encounter—and be forced to be polite to—conservatives.

This suggestion—that journalists interact with conservatives more—is not new. For instance, David Awbrey, the former editorial-page editor of *The Wichita Eagle*, noted:

> With their six-figure salaries, establishment journalists have little understanding of how hard it is to raise a family on a working-class paycheck. They are more likely to vacation in London or on Martha's Vineyard than in Branson or at Disney World. And from their gilded Manhattan and Georgetown ghettoes, many of them look contemptuously upon such towns as Wichita, Omaha, and Des Moines as little more than overgrown Gopher Prairies as depicted in Sinclair Lewis' *Main Street*.[1]

Bernard Goldberg, in his book *Bias*, gives the same advice and quotes the same passage from Awbrey.[2]

If, however, a journalist decided to follow the advice of Goldberg and Awbrey—that is, to visit places such as Branson and Wichita in order to balance her perspective from the newsroom—there's only one problem. Those places aren't conservative enough.

Recall that Washington correspondents vote about 93–7 for the Democrat. Meanwhile, the places that Awbrey and Goldberg mention are not nearly as conservative as Washington correspondents are liberal. For instance, Taney County, Missouri, which contains Branson, voted 69–31 for McCain. Sedgwick County, Kansas, which contains Wichita, voted 57–43 for McCain. Orange County, Florida, home of Disney World, actually voted for Obama. So did the counties that contain Omaha and Des Moines.

Instead, if you're a journalist and you want to balance your perspective, then you need to visit a place like King County, Texas, or Washington County, Utah, or one of the other thirteen counties that I listed at the beginning of chapter 11.

If you've seen *Mr. Smith Goes to Washington*, you may recall the bill that Jefferson Smith (played by Jimmy Stewart) tried to pass—the bill that angered the corrupt senators and led Smith to filibuster. It was a measure to bring boys out of the city and let them visit a camp in Smith's home state of Montana.[3] As Smith explained:

> It's a funny thing about men, you know. They all start life being boys. I wouldn't be surprised if some of these senators were boys once. And that's why it seemed like a pretty good idea to me to get boys out of crowded cities and stuffy basements for a couple months out of the year and build their bodies and minds for man-sized jobs. Because those boys are gonna be behind these desks some of these days. And it seemed like a pretty good idea, getting boys from all over the country, boys of all nationalities and ways of living, getting them together. Because I wouldn't give you two cents for all your fancy rules, if behind them they didn't have a little bit of plain ordinary everyday kindness, and a little lookin' out for the other fellow too.
>
> That's pretty important all that. [Smith slams a book on his desk.]
>
> It's just the blood and bone and sinew of this democracy that some great men handed down to the human race, that's all!

Following Jefferson Smith, let me suggest a specific way to implement my first remedy. I call it the "Mr. Journalist Goes to Washington County" program.

Remember Tom Seegmiller? He's the man who displays a picture of Jesus and George Washington in his office—the man I called "American exceptionalism personified."

Seegmiller loves to show Washington County to visitors. This includes, if the visitors desire, taking them hunting with him. Some of his favorite hunting companions, he said, were some of the "liberal friends" whom his son brought home from Yale when he went to school there.

For a small fee, Seegmiller is willing to host journalists who visit Washington County. Further, if the journalist is willing, Seegmiller will take him or her hunting with him. Also, if the journalist is willing, Seegmiller will take him or her to church with him. Any interested journalist should contact the Locker Room or Dixie Gun and Fish in St. George, Utah.

Open and Transparent, but That Was Just a Lie

As I mentioned earlier, a few years ago ABC correspondent Martha Raddatz appeared on C-SPAN's *Washington Journal.* A call-in viewer asked a pointed question:

C-SPAN VIEWER: I would like to know if your guest this morning—if she is a Republican, Democrat, or Independent?

RADDATZ: We don't talk about those things. We don't talk about those things at all. I'm an objective reporter. Uhh, we can't, uhh. We don't really talk about that. I wouldn't talk about that. I'd like you to find a reporter that does.

C-SPAN VIEWER: Well, you notice that when we call this program . . . we have to state whether we are Republican, Democrat, or Independent. And I think it is a little disingenuous that you would suggest that you are totally unbiased, or that if you were Democratic that you could not be objective, or if you were Republican you couldn't be objective. So could you tell me the last time that you voted for a Republican?

RADDATZ: I'm not going to tell you anything about how I vote, when I vote, and who I have ever voted for. I am here as a journalist. I'm not here as a political representative of either party. I am a journalist. And that is my job, to try to maintain objectivity. It is not . . . I'm not calling in on a call show to tell you what party I belong to. I'm a journalist.[4]

Now try to imagine Barack Obama, Nancy Pelosi, or John Boehner saying something like that. Suppose, for instance, one of them were asked, "How do you stand on partial-birth abortion?" and suppose he or she answered, "I'm not going to tell you anything about my position on that issue. If I did, it would compromise my ability as an objective lawmaker." Voters would laugh at such a response. And they would soon oust him or her from office.

Journalists, in contrast, are very secretive about their views and those of their colleagues. Responses like Raddatz's are common. For instance, when I asked Rebecca Trounson, the *Los Angeles Times* reporter I interviewed in chapter 6, about her political views, she similarly refused to answer.

Such secretiveness has become something of an institutional norm among journalists. Meanwhile, a contrasting norm of transparency exists among politicians.

ON NOVEMBER 7, 2009, as the U.S. House debated the "Obamacare" health bill, Bart Stupak (D-Mich.) proposed his famous amendment, which would disallow taxpayer money to pay for abortions. His amendment pitted (i) strongly pro-choice Democrats against (ii) Republicans and "Blue Dog" Democrats, such as Stupak. Indeed, many progressives were angry at Stupak for introducing the amendment and causing a division among Democrats.

After a specified time for debate, Speaker Pro Tempore Ed Pastor (D-Ariz.) banged the gavel and announced, "The question is on the amendment by the gentleman from Michigan, Mr. Stupak. Those in favor say aye. Those opposed, no."[5]

The legislators voiced their "ayes" and "noes." Pastor then declared, "The noes have it." However, that would not be the final verdict.

What occurred next was a magnificent legacy of the Constitutional Convention of 1787.

"Mr. Chairman," responded Stupak, "on that I ask for a recorded vote."

"Is the gentleman asking for the yeas and nays?" asked Pastor.

"Yes," said Stupak.

"The yeas and nays are requested," said Pastor. "Those in favor of a vote by yeas and nays will rise. A sufficient number having arisen, the yeas and nays are ordered."

At this point, James Madison, looking down from Heaven, smiled.

Although the Constitution allows the House and Senate to write their own rules for procedure, a particular clause limits that ability. As Article 1, Section 5 states: ". . . and the yeas and nays of the members of either house on any question shall, at the desire of one-fifth of those present, be entered into the journal."

When Pastor asked if Stupak was "asking for the yeas and nays," he was referring to this clause. When Pastor said, "A sufficient number having arisen," he meant, as the clause specifies, that at least one fifth of the chamber had risen (i.e., stood up).

Although I've treated this execution of the one-fifth clause as if it were rare and special to the Stupak amendment, it is not. Its execution is routine, and it occurs on nearly every major roll call vote in Congress.

Indeed, presiding officers in the House and Senate usually insist upon even more openness and transparency than the Constitution requires. For instance, as is common, Ed Pastor did not even count the standing members to see if they constituted one fifth of those present. He decided, I believe, that even if they were less than one fifth, it would be improper even to appear to oppose a recorded vote.

The main purpose of the clause is to prevent politicians from conspiring against the people. That is, although the Founding Fathers allowed members of Congress to vote against their constituents, they made it very difficult for them to hide those votes from their constituents.

When journalists refuse, as did Raddatz, to disclose their personal views, I suggest they are conspiring against the people. We news consumers, like the C-SPAN caller, should demand an end to this practice. Here are some particular things we can do.

First, we should stop believing the fiction "I report the news as it is. My political opinions do not influence how I report it."

As I have spent several chapters arguing, when you examine bias from a distortion theory, the reporting by journalists is *very* susceptible to their political opinions. Namely, such opinions can easily influence—sometimes without the journalists' realizing it—the topics they cover, the experts they choose to quote, the language they use, and the facts they include or omit from their reports.

When journalists try to hide behind such "I only report the news as it is" language, we should respond simply: "That doesn't fool us anymore."

Second, we should reward news outlets that *are* transparent about the personal opinions of their journalists. One shining example is talk radio—both from the left and the right. For instance, although Rush Limbaugh and Alan Colmes are near opposites in terms of their political views, they are near clones in terms of their openness about those views. The same can be said about basically every other talk radio host in the United States.

Another shining example is the online magazine *Slate*. Recall that then-editor Michael Kinsley asked his reporters and staff to reveal whom they support for president. Sixty-two employees accommodated the request.

But while talk radio and many *Slate* reporters are near paragons of openness, the opposite is true of Martha Raddatz and nearly every other mainstream reporter. We should shift our viewing, listening, and reading habits away from the latter and toward the former.

Third, news outlets can aid in this pursuit. What if a news outlet, say, on its Web site, listed a detailed description of the political views of all of its journalists? Perhaps the outlet might even list the political quotients of its journalists.

If just a few outlets did this, I believe the practice would snowball. For instance, suppose Fox News did this. Then, I believe, many liberal news consumers would be surprised about the views of the journalists at Fox. That is, although right-leaning, I believe their views would prove to be more centrist than many people think. More important, Fox could claim, "We disclose our reporters' opinions. Why don't the other news outlets?" Once viewers showed their appreciation for the practice—by watching Fox News more—the other outlets would be pressured to follow.

Such disclosure does not even require a news outlet to implement it—individual journalists can do that on their own Web pages or on sites such as Twitter or Facebook.

On top of all this, I have begun a program to aid this pursuit: If you are a journalist and you'd like to disclose your political quotient, just email me, and I will post it on my Web site, as well as your answers to the survey I use to construct the PQ.

If such disclosure and transparency snowball, however, not all journalists will be happy. For instance, if you are a "progressive" journalist and have, say, a very high political quotient, then you might prefer to keep that fact to yourself. However, if all the other journalists are disclosing their PQs and you do not, then news consumers will suspect that you are trying to hide something. You will feel pressured—you might even feel like you are being "forced"—to disclose your views.

Let me anticipate a potential criticism to this call for greater openness and transparency. Many such progressive journalists will call it "McCarthyism." They will say they are being "outed" for their political views and that this could put their jobs in jeopardy.

However, if a journalist feels this way, then she should consider that she has built her career partly on deception. That is, many of her readers or viewers will assume that she is a centrist, and part of their trust in her is based on that belief. When she refuses to disclose her true views, she insists upon fooling those readers or viewers who assume she is centrist.

HERE'S A FINAL thought that any such progressive journalist should consider: On the day that the House considered the Stupak amendment to the "Obamacare" bill, a few Democrats voted nay, even though they knew that such a vote would jeopardize their jobs.

One such Democrat was Frank Kratovil, a freshman representative from Maryland's First District. Kratovil had won his seat by the slimmest of margins: 50.4 percent to 49.6 percent. He had surely benefitted from Obama's coattails, which would not exist in the 2010 election.

In the 2008 election, he had also benefitted from a brutal Republican primary: state Sen. Andy Harris had narrowly defeated incumbent Wayne Gilchrest. Gilchrest was so bitter that he endorsed Kratovil rather than his fellow Republican. Kratovil surely knew this factor would be gone in 2010—or at least be severely diminished.

Kratovil also surely knew that his nay vote would be a blessing for his opponent. Indeed, after he cast it, a consultant for Andy Harris (who ran against Kratovil again in 2010) told me, "Oh, this one's a gem."

For Kratovil, life would have been easier if the Stupak amendment could have been decided by secret ballot—or perhaps more realistically, by a voice vote. It would have allowed him to vote according to his values *without* having to jeopardize his job.

Yet after Stupak asked for the yeas and nays, after more than one fifth of the House supported the request, and after the House Clerk actually recorded the yeas and nays, Kratovil did not complain. Although the process forced him to make his view transparent to his constituents, he did not call it "McCarthyism."

Nor did any other member of Congress.

ACKNOWLEDGMENTS

Although writing this book began as a fun and exciting experience, after about three years, the task became tedious, sometimes even agonizing. Completing the book took a total of eight years, which is a long time for any project. Imagine, for instance, trying to stick to one hobby—and no others—for eight years.

So let me begin my thank-you list with two very unlikely people: Jim Lehrer and Ellen DeGeneres. Because of Lehrer's memoir, I learned the first rule for being a good writer: "Keep butt on chair." Because of DeGeneres, while writing the book, I often would repeat a line that her character, Dory, sang in *Finding Nemo:* "Just keep swimming, swimming, swimming." Except I would replace "swimming" with "writing."

One person, more than any other, helped give me the determination and persistence necessary to complete the book—my late father, Joe Groseclose. Most important were his lessons about hard work, including the example he set. I remember the many times he would brew coffee after dinner, spread blueprints across the big table in our laundry room, and work late into the night, as my mom, sisters, and I watched TV or slept.

Also important was the obvious admiration he showed for fellow hard workers. When I was in second grade, the fastest person on our town's swim team was Steve King, who at the time was in eleventh or twelth grade. King knew that to be an Olympic swimmer you had to practice twice a day. The problem was that our team did not hold morning sessions.

As a solution, the town's YMCA gave him a key and allowed him to work out, alone, in its pool at 5:30 AM each morning. My father told me, "Now watch Steve King. There's a hard worker. That's how you succeed at life."

In October 2002, as my father lay in a hospital bed, I told him that I was thinking of writing a book, directed toward a popular audience, about media bias. "I think that's a great idea," he responded. That began a conversation about what would become this book. The conversation turned out to be one of the last of my father's life. Although it was nothing like a deathbed promise, the conversation did much to inspire me. Whenever I'd have thoughts of abandoning the book and starting a new project, the sentence, "I think that's a great idea," did wonders for my resolve.

Also deserving much gratitude is my mother. In addition to the life lessons she taught me, she was a great reviewer. To avoid academic jargon yet to write in a way that would appeal to educated laypersons, I often wrote as if I were talking to her.

My best friend, Jeff Milyo, also deserves many thanks. The book began with the article that we wrote together. He is a fantastic coauthor and even better friend. He also happens to be the funniest social scientist on the planet. One point of this book is to illustrate how unpleasant life must be for conservative journalists to be surrounded by such a monolithically progressive environment. The same is true for conservative academics. Progressive professors really can be annoying at times. (See, for instance, the email I describe on page 4.) Without Milyo and his humor, I suspect that long ago I might have left academia for another line of work.

It was a joy and honor to work with Phil Revzin, my senior editor at St. Martin's. I am extremely grateful that he agreed to take a chance on a first-time book author. He was tireless in his help. A number of times, for instance, I would send him chapters at the end of a Friday workday. By Saturday morning, he would email me comments about the chapters. I suspect that if my father had met Phil, he would have said, "Now watch Phil Revzin. There's a hard worker."

While I normally strive to be modest and humble, when it comes to describing my ability to hire excellent research assistants, I cannot. I truly might be the best person on Earth at hiring talented, hard-working RAs. One technique is simply to note the students who do very well in my class. Another is to offer a job to the guy (Elmer Membreno) working in the student cafeteria who has a fantastic attitude and seemed to have memorized all the prices on the menu. A third is to note the student (Katherine Estrada) who refused to reschedule her test, even though she was ill with a 103-degree fever, who also requested to take the test in the hall outside the classroom so her classmates would not catch her illness. The following people, who were spotted by the best RA-talent-spotter in the world, helped tremendously to make this a better book: Aviva Aminova, Jose Bustos, Anya Byers, Evan Davidson, Kristina Doan, David Lee, Pauline Mena, Orges Obequiri, Byrne Offutt, Mathew Patterson, Darryl Reeves, Susie Rieniets, Thomas Rosholt, Michael Uy, Diane Valos, Michael Visconti, Margaret Vo, Rachel Ward, Andrew Wright, Daniel Bogatz, Katherine Estrada, Dayna Garwacki, Stefanie Ju, Elmer Membreno, John Scheerer, Wesley Hussey, Brian Law, David Primo, and Flori So. The latter four, all PhD students when they worked for me, in addition to being outstanding research assistants, are on their way toward being outstanding scholars.

My wife, Victoria, deserves the most gratitude of anyone. She is not just a great wife, mom, and the love of my life, she is also a great editor and coach. The early versions of the book were, frankly, very bad. She, however, saw some promising aspects—while also giving some constructive feedback about the not-so-promising aspects. I used to think that Elina, my daughter's ice-skating coach, was the world's champ at striking the balance between praise and constructive criticism. I now realize that my wife holds that title.

Approximately tied with my daughter's ice-skating coach, and almost as good as my wife at praise and criticism, is my literary agent, Teresa Hartnett, the founder and president of the Hartnett Agency.

Hartnett usually represents more famous people than I. She, for instance, represented Jack Kemp and Jeane Kirkpatrick. Despite that, she took a gamble on me. Included in her gamble was devoting a huge amount of time toward helping me write the proposal for this book. Her help not only aided me in finding a publisher, it helped me organize the argument for the book. The preface and first chapter of the book grew out of conversations with her. Also, she is the one who perceived that people might be interested in the "Political Quotients" that I discuss in the book. She, in fact, is largely responsible for coining that phrase.

I am also very grateful for the help of Marinka Peschmann, one of the agents at the Hartnett Agency. Peschmann was instrumental in helping me find a publisher. Once I began to shop around the proposal, I received only mild interest. Even the publishers who showed some interest understood that since I was not a big name—and only a rookie at book writing—none of the other publishers would act quickly in signing me to a contract. Consequently no publisher felt an urgency to read my proposal thoroughly. I was thus in a catch-22. Publishers would not read my proposal thoroughly because they felt no urgency to do so. And publishers felt no urgency to read my proposal, because they surmised that no other publisher would do that.

Enter Peschmann . . . and Ronald Reagan. Peschmann decided to shop my proposal at CPAC, the annual conference for the Conservative Political Action Committee. CPAC was becoming known as a great place for conservatives to shop their book proposals. Even better, Peschmann told publishers that she would shop my proposal at CPAC. One of those publishers was St. Martin's Press. Shortly before the conference, some of its representatives, including Phil Revzin, asked to have an "exclusive" on the proposal for a few days. That is, St. Martin's would promise to take an urgent look at the proposal, while we would agree not to shop it with any other publisher for a few days. Thus, Marinka and CPAC broke the catch-22. Just before the CPAC conference began, St. Martin's agreed to be my publisher.

Of course, none of this would have happened—or it would have at least been significantly delayed—if CPAC didn't exist. Meanwhile, many people believe that CPAC wouldn't exist if Ronald Reagan hadn't decided to attend its conference multiple times during his presidency.

So a final word of gratitude goes to Ronald Reagan. Not only did he end communism and make three hundred million people more free and prosperous, he helped me find a publisher. It's hard to thank him enough.

NOTES

PREFACE

1. In later chapters I will explain my statistical method for computing a person's PQ. Although I asked Ben Stein to complete the survey that would have allowed me statistically to compute his PQ, he did not grant my request. My claim, that his PQ is approximately 25, is based mostly on anecdotal research I have conducted. That research suggests that on contentious political issues, Stein agrees with the liberal position approximately 25 percent of the time. My claim is also based on an interview with Phil DeMuth, who coauthored approximately ten books with Stein. When I told DeMuth that Stein's PQ "seems to be about 25, which would put him approximately at the midpoint between Michele Bachmann and Ben Nelson," the moderate Democratic senator from Nebraska, DeMuth responded, "That sounds about right."

2. Neither O'Reilly nor Miller agreed to complete my survey, which would have allowed me statistically to compute their PQs. My estimate is based on anecdotal research, which suggests that on contentious political issues they seem to agree with the liberal position about 25 percent of the time. For instance, although O'Reilly usually agrees with conservatives, on many issues he does not, including (i) the death penalty; (ii) whether global warming is caused by humans; (iii) investigating oil companies for price gouging; and (iv) gun control. Dennis Miller similarly agrees with conservatives on most issues, perhaps especially Mideast foreign policy and getting tough on Muslim terrorists. However, on many issues he agrees with liberals, including (i) repealing "Don't Ask, Don't Tell" ("[W]hether it's Lee Liberace or Lee Marvin in the fox hole, they don't need a cadaver like that [Sen. Harry Reid] showing up a year before and saying the war is lost."); (ii) abortion ("[I]f men were the ones getting pregnant, abortions would be easier to get than food poisoning in Moscow."); and (iii) gay marriage ("You know, a lot of this seems to be an actual tug-of-war over the word *marriage.* Well, how's this? We'll give you the word *marriage,* if you give us back the word *gay.* I mean, how many years now have I stood silently by unable to accurately convey when I'm merry and full of fun?").

INTRODUCTION

1. See www.americanprogress.org/issues/2006/01/b1347483.html.
2. Saul Alinsky, *Rules for Radicals*, New York: Vintage Books, 1989, p. 130.

1. What Are PQs and How Do They Reveal Media Bias?

1. I chose the ten questions from a set of forty roll call votes chosen by the Americans for Democratic Action (ADA). Twenty of the ADA's roll calls occurred in the House, and twenty in the Senate. All forty took place in 2009. In deciding which ten to choose, I faced a significant constraint. Namely, the ten questions had to produce PQ scores comparable to those I computed for politicians. That is, the scale set by (i) the ten questions above, had to be the same as the scale set by (ii) the twenty roll calls the ADA chose from the 1999 House. More specifically, I needed the following to be true: Define the *liberalness* of a question as the degree to which it is difficult for a typical person to vote on the liberal side of the question. (For instance, the question "Should morning-after birth control pills be legal?" has a lower level of liberalness than "Should partial-birth abortions be legal?") I need the average liberalness of the two sets of questions, (i) and (ii), to be roughly the same.

To ensure this, I conducted the following exercise (which, I apologize, requires some technical jargon to explain): First, with each of the sixty roll calls (the twenty that the ADA chose for the 2009 House, the twenty the ADA chose for the 2009 Senate, and the twenty the ADA chose for the 1999 House), I conducted a probit analysis, where the dependent variable was the yea or nay vote cast by the politician, and the only independent variable was the politician's average PQ. The probit produced an estimated intercept, a, and an estimated coefficient for the independent variable, b. I next computed the *cut point* for each roll call. (This indicates the liberalness of the roll call.) This is the predicted PQ that would make a legislator equally likely to vote yea or nay on the roll call. It can be shown that it equals $-a/b$. The average cut point for the twenty roll calls the ADA chose for the 1999 House was 45.85. From the forty questions available to me, I chose ten so that their average cut point would be as near to 45.85 as possible. The ten I chose produced an average cut point of 45.83. It is also important that the standard deviation of the two sets of cut points be similar. Again, part of my criteria when choosing the ten questions was to achieve this goal. The standard deviation from set (i) was 15.17, and the standard deviation from set (ii) was 14.16.

2. For the vote totals on each issue, I count Vermont senator Bernard Sanders and Connecticut senator Joe Lieberman as Democrats. Both are considered officially as Independents; however, both caucus with the Senate Democrats, and are treated as Democrats for purposes of committee assignments.

3. Note that some of the politicians served in the executive branch. I based their PQ on only the votes they cast while serving in the legislative branch. While Barack Obama served as a senator for four years, 2005–08, during his final two years he was campaigning for president, and as a consequence, was absent for several roll calls. I used only the 2005–06 period to calculate his PQ. A similar issue arose when I computed the PQs of John McCain and Hillary Clinton.

The scores above differ slightly from those listed in the *QJE* article that I wrote with Milyo. The main reason is that the earlier article used only roll call votes cast during the 1995–99 period.

An argument can be made that my choice to calculate Arlen Specter's PQ from all the votes he cast in 2009 causes his Democratic PQ to be biased downward, since he cast some of those votes while he was a Republican. However, it appears that in early 2009, while he was still a Republican, he was planning to switch parties, or at least to adopt a more liberal voting record. Of the nine votes he cast *before* April 29, 2009, seven (77.8 percent) agreed with ADA's position. Of the eleven votes he cast on or after April 29, 2009, eight (72.7 percent) agreed with ADA's position. That is, in 2009, Specter agreed with ADA more as a Republican than as a Democrat.

Note that some politicians have PQs below 0 or above 100. I give more details for this in chapter 4, but here is a brief explanation. In each year, I calculate a PQ for each member of Congress. Those yearly PQs are based on twenty or so roll call votes chosen by the ADA. The roll calls are similar to exam questions a student might face. That is, just as a student might score higher on an exam when the questions are easier, a politician's yearly PQ might be higher if the ADA happened that year to choose roll calls for which it was easy to vote the liberal side. (For instance, suppose the roll call is (i) whether morning-after birth control pills should be legal, or (ii) whether partial-birth abortions should be legal. If you are, say, a moderate, it is easier to vote the liberal side on the first than on the second.) Just as a teacher sometimes "curves" grades so that two tests are comparable, I adjust yearly PQs so that they can be placed on a common scale. The scale to which I convert PQs is based on the twenty roll calls the ADA chose for the 1999 House. To convert PQs to that scale, in some years I needed to add a number to each yearly PQ, and in some years I needed to subtract a number. For this reason, depending on the years the politician served in Congress, his average PQ could be above 100 or below 0.

2. Caught in a Trap: Problems in Judging Media Bias

1. Walter Lippmann, *Public Opinion,* New York: Penguin, 1922/1946, p. 59. I learned of the quote from John Zaller's *Nature and Origins of Mass Opinion,* New York: Cambridge University Press, 1992, p. 6.

2. See www.youtube.com/watch?v=qhjt6hsuCQ0.

3. "Is Newspaper Coverage of Economic Events Politically Biased?" Revised October 18, 2004, available at www.ssrn.com/abstract=588453.

3. But I've Been to Oklahoma

1. Gingrich, Gramm, and Armey earned PhDs—Gingrich in history, and Gramm and Armey in economics. All three began their careers as professors. Although Cheney was never a professor, nor obtained his PhD, he was once enrolled in the political-science PhD program at the University of Wisconsin. Unlike 66 percent of the political-science professors in the Ivy League, and 56 percent of the political-science professors at Harvard, Cheney has published in the top academic journal in political science, the *American Political Science Review.* Another academic credential of Cheney is the fact that he has an Erdös number. Named after the great mathematician, Paul Erdös, who was famous for his prolific scholarship and his numerous coauthors—an Erdös number is calculated as follows. All of Erdös's coauthors have an Erdös number of one. Anyone who has coauthored with one of Erdös's coauthors has an Erdös number of two. Anyone who has coauthored with a coauthor of one of Erdös's coauthors has an Erdös number of three. And so on. Cheney's Erdös number is no more than seven. He wrote his *American Political Science Review* article with Aage Clausen, who has coauthored with Greg Caldeira, who has coauthored with me, who has coauthored with Keith Krehbiel, who has coauthored with John Ferejohn, who has coauthored with Peter Fishburn, who has coauthored with Erdös.

2. David Leonhardt, "The Future of Economics Isn't So Dismal," *New York Times,* January 10, 2007, C1.

3. Joseph Price and Justin Wolfers, "Racial Discrimination Among NBA Referees," NBER working paper, 2007, available at http://bpp.wharton.upenn.edu/jwolfers/Papers/NBARace.pdf.

4. See www.nytimes.com/2004/07/25/opinion/the-public-editor-is-the-new-york-times-a-liberal-newspaper.html.

5. Bernard Goldberg, *Bias: A CBS Insider Exposes How the Media Distort the News,* Washington, D.C.: Regnery Publishing, Inc., 2002, p. 43.

4. *Ps* and *Qs* of PQs

1. More specific, the *absolute value* of the correlation coefficient was always greater than 0.7. For instance, as you might expect, the correlation coefficient between the scores by (i) the Americans for Democratic Action and (ii) the American Conservative Union was highly *negative*.

5. Defining the "Center"

1. John Samples, "Statement on the Motor Voter Act and Voter Fraud Before the Committee on Rules and Administration, United States Senate," available at www.cato.org/testimony/ct-js031401.html.

2. See www.c-spanvideo.org/program/MediaIssues10.

3. Strictly speaking, in the Crawford-Sobel model the "Senders" with extreme preferences don't exactly *exaggerate*. More proper would be to say they *obfuscate*. Again, to explain why, one must resort to the mathematics of the model.

4. Duncan Black, *The Theory of Committees and Elections*, New York: Cambridge University Press, 1958.

6. Lies, Damned Lies, and Omitted Statistics : A Case Study in Distortion Theory

1. To read the entire article, see, for example, http://articles.latimes.com/2006/jun/03/local/me-ucla3, www.aapf.org/focus/UCLA.pdf, or http://aad.english.ucsb.edu/docs/06-03-06trounson.htm.

2. See www.nytimes.com/2008/07/06/magazine/06Limbaugh-t.html. Zev Chafets, "Late-Period Limbaugh," *New York Times*, July 6, 2006, p. 30.

3. See www.freerepublic.com/focus/f-news/1614041/posts.

4. My source for the 22 figure, the increase in expected enrollment by transfers, is a document that the admissions staff gave me when I was on the oversight committee. UCLA's official name for expected enrollment is "stated intention to register" (SIR). It is calculated by noting the number of students who pay a deposit fee and the number of students who have declined admission. Between spring admissions and fall registration, the number changes from day to day. In the same document I received (which reported that the SIR among transfers had increased by 22), the SIR for freshmen was 103, a decrease by 23 from the year before. Note that this differs slightly from the 96 figure that Trounson quoted. Thus, according to that document the net black expected enrollment (i.e., transfers and freshmen) had decreased by 1 from the year before. At any rate, the important point is that while freshmen expected enrollment dropped in 2006, transfer expected enrollment rose by approximately the same amount. Further, in fairness to Trounson, I should mention that, according to most admissions staff to whom I spoke, UCLA released the transfer statistics only a few days before her article was published, and some think that the data might have been released a few days after. Either way, it is almost certain that Trounson did not know these statistics when she wrote her article. Nevertheless, she never wrote any follow-up article noting the transfer numbers, nor did she ever write that on net the *total* number of incoming black undergraduates (i.e., freshmen *and* transfers) was about the same as the prior year. In an interview, Trounson told me that she did not write about transfer statistics because one of her colleagues wrote about them. In my Lexis-Nexis search I found two articles that mentioned statistics about minority transfer students to UCLA. Neither article mentioned, however, that the increase in black transfers was approximately as large as the decrease in black freshmen, nor that the net total of black students was approximately the same as the year before. Neither article mentioned that, without the data on transfer students, Trounson's original article gave a misleading picture about whether UCLA was discriminating against black students in its admissions decisions.

5. Prop. 209 passed in November 1996. African American admissions for that year and the four previous years were 606, 661, 699, 633, 596 respectively, giving an average of 639. In 1997 the new law was not fully implemented, partly because of a court challenge. In

1998, after the law was fully implemented, and the four subsequent years, African American admissions was 294, 313, 325, 326, and 337, giving an average of 319. See www.ucop.edu/news/factsheets/flowfrc_09.pdf.

7. Hidden Under a Bushel

1. James Varney, "City Spurned Offer of Cash for Cars; Abandoned Vehicles Can Be Hauled Away," *Times-Picayune* (New Orleans), March 19, 2006, p. 1.

2. James Varney, "Price No Object in N.O. Car-Removal; City Appears to Choose Top-Dollar Contract," *Times-Picayune* (New Orleans), March 22, 2006, p. 1.

3. *Glenn Beck* (Fox News), August 13, 2009. See www.youtube.com/watch?v=RvMbeVQj6Lw&feature=related for a video of the speech. The link is sponsored by Wright's Church, Trinity United Church of Christ Chicago. It contains the above passage plus the prior six or so minutes of the sermon. The video is entitled "Tell the Whole Story FOX! Barack Obama's Pastor Wright." Indeed, the video gives some context to the passage—namely, before saying the passage, Wright notes that slavery existed in the United States before the Civil War, Jim Crowe laws existed until only a few decades ago, the country treated Native Americans wrongly, it bombed Japan, and it is guilty of other shortcomings. In my judgment, however, the context hardly mitigates the inflammatory passage. Almost all voters, I believe, who have a PQ less than 75 will find the passage, even after seeing the full video, distasteful. And after seeing the video most such voters, I believe, would lower their opinion of Obama, knowing that he once attended the church.

4. Bob Von Sternberg, "Inside Campaign 2008; Obama Condemns Pastor's Remarks," *Minneapolis Star Tribune*, March 15, 2008, p. 6A.

5. "ABC's Charles Gibson Talks to Barack Obama," *ABC News*, March 28, 2008.

6. Jonathan Strong, "Documents Show Media Plotting to Kill Stories about Rev. Jeremiah Wright," *The Daily Caller*, July 20, 2010, www.dailycaller.com/2010/07/20/documents-show-media-plotting-to-kill-stories-about-rev-jeremiah-wright/.

7. Ibid.

8. *Anderson Cooper 360°* (CNN), March 13, 2008.

9. See Jodi Kantor, "Pastor's Words Still Draw Fire," *New York Times*, March 14, 2008, p. 18. The article contains six sentences, but two of the six discuss not Obama and Wright but the fact that earlier in the week Hillary Clinton had denounced Geraldine Ferraro's claim that Obama's success in the polls was partly due to his being black.

10. Jim Rutenberg, "An Old Hand at State Politics Re-emerges as a Vocal Foe of Obama's Health Plan," *New York Times*, September 5, 2009, p. A10.

11. *Glenn Beck* (Fox News), August 31, 2009. See also www.eastbayexpress.com/eastbay/the-new-face-of-environmentalism/Content?oid=1079539.

12. *Glenn Beck* (Fox News), August 25, 2009. Beck read from p. 51 of the book, *Reclaiming Revolution: History, Summation, & Lessons from the Work of Standing Together to Organize a Revolutionary Movement (STORM)*. See http://ia700109.us.archive.org/2/items/ReclaimingRevolution/ReclaimingRevolution-Storm-Spring2004.pdf.

13. *Glenn Beck* (Fox News), September 1, 2009. See www.youtube.com/watch?v=o3Zb0EVKOkY for the video.

14. See www.foxnews.com/politics/2009/09/02/white-house-green-jobs-adviser-apologizes-calling-republicans-assholes/.

15. See www.911truth.org/article.php?story=20041026093059633.

16. Garance Franke-Ruta and Anne E. Kornblut, "White House Says Little About Embattled Jones," *Washington Post*, September 5, 2009, p. A03.

17. Ibid.

18. Ibid.

19. John Broder, "White House Official Resigns After Flood of G.O.P. Criticism," *New York Times*, September 7, 2009, p. A1.

20. At the time of the Van Jones saga, CNN's *NewsNight with Aaron Brown* was no longer on the air. However, at least three CNN programs covered parts of the saga: *Lou Dobbs*

Tonight, The Situation Room, and *CNN Newsroom.* Although ABC News did not cover it on television, it did cover some aspects on its blog.

Stangely, MSNBC's Keith Olbermann *did* cover Van Jones that week. It was part of a segment about Glenn Beck's "paranoia" and "factual errors." Olbermann showed a clip of Beck discussing communism; then he showed another clip of Beck announcing that the Rockefeller Foundation had given an award to Jones. Although Beck did not literally say it, Olbermann insinuated that Beck called the Rockefeller Foundation a "hotbed of communism." Olbermann then called this insinuation about Beck "factual error number 2." Olbermann's report aired the day that Representative Pence and Senator Bond called on Jones to resign. Olbermann did not mention this fact, nor that Jones signed the 911Truth petition, nor that he had issued two public apologies that week, nor that White House spokesman Robert Gibbs had given him such a faint endorsement that day. On the following Monday, Olbermann reported that Van Jones had resigned. "At Yankee stadium last night," Olbermann began his report, "a goober actually shouted at me from the safety of twenty thousand feet and one story away that Van Jones is just the first and now dominos will fall." The remainder of Olbermann's report was a discussion with Chris Hayes of *The Nation.* It focused mainly on what a bad person Glenn Beck is and how the attack on Van Jones was "racist." Olbermann and Hayes never mentioned any of the following facts: (i) that Jones signed the 911Truth petition, (ii) that he claimed white people are "steering poison into the people-of-color communities," (iii) that he was a founding member of STORM, or (iv) that he was at one time a self-avowed communist.

21. Although it did not focus on her, a *Newsweek* story devoted a sentence to McCaughey and her false statement. Also, six days before Jones resigned, Keith Olbermann devoted six sentences to the false statement by McCaughey. It was part of his segment awarding her the "bronze medal" for the "Worst Person in the World."

22. "Meaning Beyond Measure?: Separating the Effects of Obama's Race from the Effects of Racial Prejudice," manuscript. See web.me.com/vavreck/Lynn_Vavreck/Working_Papers .html.

23. For the seminal "list experiment" article, see Kuklinski, Cobb, and Gilens, *Journal of Politics* 59, no. 2 (1997): 323–49.

24. Although I list the six characteristics in a specific order, when the study interviewed respondents, it randomized the order.

25. That said, however, a number of caveats should be noted. First, although Jackman and Vavreck did not report it, my own calculations show that the difference between the two numbers (20 percent and 0 percent) was not statistically significant. Second, as Jackman and Vavreck suggest, the 0 percent number might have been artificially low. Specifically, they note that 8 percent of the Obama-opposing treatment group "topped out" in their answers. That is, they said that all six of the factors were important in their decision not to vote for Obama. Consequently, for this group "He's black" necessarily is one of the factors that they report as important for their voting decision. Therefore, some people will claim that "at least 8 percent" of white McCain voters—not 0—opposed Obama partly because "He's black." Accordingly, so goes the claim, the proper analysis should compare the 20 percent estimate with the latter, "at least 8 percent" estimate. However, for at least three reasons this is inappropriate. First, such an analysis does not compare "apples with apples." Namely, the 20 percent figure comes from noting the difference in answers between the control and treatment groups. The 8 percent figure does not—that is, the data for the 8 percent figure come only from the treatment group. Second, and related, such a comparison stacks the deck toward finding more evidence of people voting *against* Obama because he is black. Namely, recall that the Jackman-Vavreck analysis analyzes two samples of voters: (i) whites who voted against Obama, and (ii) whites who voted for Obama. Through the list-experiment method, the analysis essentially runs a horse race to see if the traditional racism of (i) is greater than the reverse racism of (ii). However, if one uses the 8 percent figure, while rejecting the 0 percent figure, then this is akin to requiring group (i) to run two races (where the researcher chooses the race that shows more racism by

group (i)), while requiring group (ii) only to run one race. Third, with survey data, it is well known that subjects often pay little attention to the questions, and they sometimes give answers, which, instead of reflecting the truth, require the least thought. For instance, it is well known that survey respondents disproportionately give the last answer in a multiple-choice question. For this reason many of the respondents may have simply said "Yes" to each of the six factors (that is, that each was important to their voting decision), not because "Yes" was the true answer, but because it required the least thought. If so, then many of the 8 percent did not really vote against Obama because "He's black."

26. Jonathan Strong, "Documents Show Media Plotting to Kill Stories about Rev. Jeremiah Wright," *The Daily Caller,* July 20, 2010, www.dailycaller.com/2010/07/20/documents-show-media-plotting-to-kill-stories-about-rev-jeremiah-wright/.

27. Ibid.

8. An "Alien" Conservative Injected into a Liberal Newsroom and the Topics She Might Cover

1. See "How the Imams Terrorized an Airliner," *Washington Times,* November 28, 2006, www.washingtontimes.com/news/2006/nov/28/20061128-122902-7522r/.

2. See http://archives.secretsofthecity.com/magazine/reporting/features/one-woman-solution.

3. See www.c-spanvideo.org/program/205575-1, July 9, 2008.

4. Katherine Kersten, "The Real Target of the 6 Imans' 'Discrimination' Suit," *Star Tribune,* March 15, 2007, p. 1B.

5. *Congressional Record,* March 27, 2007, p. H3147.

6. Ibid., pp. H3147–48.

7. See www.c-spanvideo.org/videoLibrary/clip.php?appid=595569856. (This is the C-SPAN version of the House proceedings, beginning approximately 7:00 p.m. EST, March 27, 2007.)

9. Political Views in the Newsroom: Viva Homogeneity

1. Richard Feynman, *Six Easy Pieces: Essentials of Physics by Its Most Brilliant Teacher,* New York: Basic Books, 2005, p. 4.

2. Two percent voted for Perot, and 2 percent voted for other candidates. See www.mrc.org/biasbasics/biasbasics3.asp for more details of the study. Using a standard 95 percent confidence level criterion, one can show that the 7 percent figure has a margin of error of 4.2 percent.

3. "Finding Biases on the Bus," *New York Times,* August 1, 2004. Tierney polled 153 journalists, "about a third of them based in Washington." Using a standard 95 percent confidence level criterion and assuming that Tierney polled 51 Washington-based journalists, one can show that the 8 percent figure has a margin of error of 7.4 percent.

4. For details, see www.mrc.org/biasbasics/biasbasics3.asp. Using a standard 95 percent confidence level criterion, one can show that these percentages respectively have margins of error of 3, 4.4, 5, and 5 percent.

5. For details, see www.mrc.org/biasbasics/biasbasics3.asp. Using a standard 95 percent confidence level criterion, one can show that both percentages have a margin of error of 5 percent.

6. For instance, in 2005, *The New York Times* published a special advertising supplement entitled, "Leading with Diversity." One section focused on the New York Times Company itself. At the top of the section is a drawing of a balding, gray-haired white man, a younger black man, and a younger Asian woman. The text stated that "We want a diversity of background, thought, and opinion." However, when it discussed recruiting efforts, it noted "[T]he company works with a variety of external groups, including the National Society of Hispanic M.B.A.'s, the National Society of Black M.B.A.'s, and the Black Journal ists' Association." It did not mention working with any conservative groups. See www.nytimes.com/marketing/jobmarket/diversity/nyt.html.

7. Indeed, the phrase, "choking on gnats, while swallowing camels," illustrates the benefits of a diverse set of political viewpoints. I have conducted an informal poll of my colleagues. Most of my conservative colleagues knew who the author of the phrase was, while the vast majority of my liberal colleagues did not.

8. The author of the phrase is Jesus. See Matthew 23:24.

9. See www.timgroseclose.com/corporate-media-theory-debunked.

10. *Scarborough Country* (MSNBC), June 19, 2003.

11. Eric Alterman, *What Liberal Media?,* New York: Basic Books, p. 20.

12. Op. cit, pp. 21, 24.

13. See, respectively, http://people-press.org/2000/04/30/self-censorship-how-often-and-why/2/ and http://www.fair.org/index.php?page=2447.

14. Alterman does not cite his evidence that "most social scientists" would reject a survey with a response rate of 43 percent, nor, as he told Joe Scarborough, that "no responsible social scientist would ever use" such a survey. In contrast, I am not aware of any bona fide social scientist—one with a PhD in a real social-science discipline and who, at least occasionally, publishes in top peer-reviewed social-science journals—who would reject, out of hand, a survey just because its response rate was 43 percent. Indeed, Alan Gerber, Dean Karlan, and Daniel Bergan, all researchers at Yale University, note, "Response rates of 30 or 40 percent are typical in the public opinion literature." See "Does the Media Matter? A Field Experiment Measuring the Effect of Newspapers on Voting Behavior and Political Opinions," *American Economic Journal: Applied Economics* 1, no. 2 (2009): 41.

Meanwhile, although actual social scientists prefer to see high response rates in a survey, more important is that the event—whether a person responds or not—be orthogonal to the answer that he gives. That is, what is important is that (i) his choice to respond or not, be statistically independent of (ii) the preference factors that determine his answer.

I see no reason to believe that this orthagonality condition was violated in the Freedom Forum poll (nor for the other two surveys that Alterman cites in his chapter 2). Nor does Alterman give any reason why he thinks the Freedom Forum poll might violate the orthagonality condition. Nor does he even discuss the orthagonality condition or any similar condition.

15. See Alterman, *What Liberal Media?,* p. 20.

16. "Polling Games and Information Revelation in the Downsian Framework," *Games and Economic Behavior* 51 (2005): 464–89.

17. In contrast, however, there are plausible reasons to believe that conservatives are more honest than liberals. First, if Larry Greenfield's claim is true (see preface)—that leftists worship the god of Equality—then their principles allow them to lie, as long as the lie works to make society more equal. I do not know of a similar principle that conservatives would tout. Second, and related, suppose that among all virtues conservatives and liberals are equal at following them. Suppose, however, that in terms of advocating government redistribution to the poor, conservatives are more stingy—that is, they are inferior at this virtue. But if conservatives and liberals are indeed equal on the *total* set of virtues, then this means that conservatives must be superior on some other virtue, possibly honesty. The idea is similar to the fact that a blind person often develops superior abilities for senses other than sight. Third, conservatives are generally more religious than liberals. To a nonreligious person taking the survey, the survey is anonymous—no one will learn the answers that he or she provides. However, to a religious person, the survey is not quite anonymous—God will learn the answers. This gives the religious person an additional incentive to reply honestly.

18. Let x be the true fraction of journalists who voted Republican. Thus $0.95x$ is the fraction who voted Republican and truthfully reported that they voted Republican. Meanwhile, $0.05(1-x)$ is the fraction who voted Democratic but reported that they voted Republican. The fraction who reported they voted Republican, 0.145, must equal the sum of these two fractions. Thus, $0.145=0.95x+0.05(1-x)$. After simplifying, we get $0.095=0.90x$, which implies that $x=0.1056$. That is, the true percentage of journalists who voted Republican is 10.56 percent, and the true percentage of journalists who voted Democratic is 100 percent −10.56 percent, or 89.44 percent. Thus, the percentage of journalists who voted

Republican and said they voted Republican is 0.95 × 10.56 percent, or 10.03 percent. The percentage of journalists who voted Democratic but said they voted Republican is 0.05 × 89.44 percent, or 4.47 percent.

19. For results of the study, see David Brooks, "Ruling Class War," *New York Times,* September 11, 2004; or Thomas B. Edsall, James V. Grimaldi, and Alice R. Crites, "Redefining Democratic Fundraising," *Washington Post,* Saturday, July 24, 2004, p. A01.

20. William Tate, "Putting Money Where Mouths Are: Media Donations Favor Dems 100–1," *Investor's Business Daily,* July 23, 2008.

21. Jennifer Harper, "ABC Employees Donated Heavily to Obama," *Washington Times,* June 19, 2009.

22. Bill Dedman, "Journalists Dole Out Cash to Politicians (Quietly)," June 25, 2007, available at www.msnbc.com/id/19113485.

23. "Slate Votes: Obama Wins This Magazine in a Rout," *Slate,* October 28, 2008, available at www.slate.com/id/2203151/?from=rss.

24. Ibid.

25. *The O'Reilly Factor* (Fox News), January 5, 2007.

26. For a transcript and video, see http://isaacweatherspersonal.blogspot.com/2009_10_01_archive.html.

27. The survey, conducted in December 2008, was designed by Zeljka Buturovic. She and Daniel Klein give details of the survey in their article "Economic Enlightenment in Relation to College-going, Ideology, and Other Variables: A Zogby Survey of Americans," *Econ Journal Watch* 7, no. 2 (May 2010): 174–96, available at www.journaltalk.net/articles/5671. The Web site contains a link that allows users to access their data. The poll had a counterfactually high number of McCain voters. Specifically, of those who reported that they voted for or preferred one of the two main candidates, 53.42 percent said they voted for or preferred McCain. In contrast, among actual voters, McCain's share was 46.31 percent. Thus, the Zogby result was 7.11 percentage points larger than the true number. One way to correct for this problem is to place a higher weight on the Obama-preferring respondents. Another way is simply to discard some of the McCain voters. I did the latter. Specifically, the Zogby poll contained 2,080 people who indicated that they preferred Obama in the 2008 election. Meanwhile, it contained 2,385 people who indicated that they preferred McCain. I omitted the first 591 of the latter observations. Note that this leaves 2,080 Obama respondents and 1,794 McCain respondents. Most important, note that of these 3,874 remaining respondents (= 2080 + 1794), exactly 46.31 percent preferred McCain. Thus, by omitting the 591 McCain observations, I can make the sample exactly reflect the true percentages of the actual election. Note that this choice—to discard McCain-voting respondents—works against my main conclusions. That is, it makes the liberal groups (union members, nonreligious people, etc.) vote for Obama at higher rates. Accordingly, this causes Washington correspondents to look *less* liberal relative to the liberal groups. In other words, if I hadn't discarded the 591 McCain observations, this would have caused the media to look even more liberal. I repeated the analysis where, instead, I deleted the second 591 observations (that is, observations 592 to 1,182 of those where the respondents indicated that they preferred McCain). The results were nearly identical to the results that I report. The same thing happened when I instead omitted the third, fourth, or final 591 observations.

28. Approximately 18 percent of the respondents said they were members of a labor union. With this group and the other liberal demographic groups, I report the two-party vote shares of the group.

29. The survey asked how often the respondent attends religious services. The possible answers were: more than once a week, once a week, one or two times a month, only on holidays, rarely, or never. I label the respondent "nonreligious" if he or she answered "rarely" or "never."

30. If the respondent listed his or her income as less than $50,000, I labeled him or her as a "low-income" person. These comprised approximately the poorest 24 percent of the respondents.

31. Approximately 22 percent of the respondents said that they never shop at Walmart. My label "anti-Walmart refusenik," assumes that the reason was an ideological aversion to Walmart and not, for instance, that no store was located near them. However, one of the responses available to the survey participants was that they shop at Walmart "one or two times per year." Given the ubiquity of Walmarts, and the likelihood that respondents will travel away from home at least one or two times a year, I do not see how many people could completely avoid Walmart without an ideological aversion to the store.

10. The Second-Order Problem of an Unbalanced Newsroom

1. Christopher F. Cardiff and Daniel B. Klein, "Faculty Partisan Affiliations in All Disciplines: A Voter-Registration Study," *Critical Review* 17, nos. 3–4, (2005): 237–55.

2. See Goldberg, *Bias*, p. 24.

3. David Shaw, "Abortion Foes Stereotyped, Some in the Media Believe," *Los Angeles Times*, July 2, 1990.

4. Ibid.

5. Howard Kurtz, "Suddenly Everyone's a Critic," *Washington Post*, October 3, 2005, Style section, p. C01.

6. Deborah Howell, "Remedying the Bias Perception," *Washington Post*, November 16, 2008, p. B06.

7. See "Slate Votes," *Slate*.

8. As I have observed, members of the far left are often guilty of seriously overestimating their numbers. Especially within elite intellectual circles, far-left individuals often believe that a majority of Americans share their view: that the Democratic Party is not left-wing enough. A recent Gallup poll, however, refutes this. It found that 46 percent of Americans think the Democratic Party is too liberal, and 42 percent think it is "about right." Only 8 percent think the party is too conservative. In contrast, members of the far right would be more justified in holding the mirror view about the Republican Party. As Gallup found, 17 percent of Americans think the Republican Party is too *liberal*. (See Jeffrey M. Jones, "More Americans See Democratic Party as 'Too Liberal,'" June 30, 2009, available at www.gallup.com/poll/121307/More-Americans-See-Democratic-Party-Too-Liberal.aspx.)

9. *The O'Reilly Factor* (Fox News), August 27, 2008.

10. William Greider "Past and Future," *The Nation*, November 24, 2008, available at http://www.thenation.com/doc/article/past-and-future.

11. See www.twilightpines.com//index.php?option=com_content&task=view&id=19&Itemid=67.

12. Specifically, she said, "We know there were numerous warnings of the events to come on September 11th. Vladimir Putin, President of Russia delivered one such warning. Those engaged in unusual stock trades before September 11th knew enough to make millions of dollars from United and American Airlines, certain insurance, and brokerage firms' stocks. What did this administration know, and when did it know it? Who else knew, and why did they not warn the innocent people of New York?" She also noted, "What is undeniable is that corporations close to the administration have directly benefitted from the increased defense spending arising from the aftermath of September 11th." See Juliet Eilperin, "Democrat Implies Sept. 11 Administration Plot," *Washington Post*, April 12, 2002, p. A16. Also see http://www.youtube.com/watch?v=c2QoQml27NI.

13. "Census Bureau Drops ACORN from 2010 Effort," Associated Press, published on *The New York Times* Web site. See http://www.nytimes.com/2009/09/12/us/politics/12acorn.html?r=2&scp=3&sq=census%20bureau&st=cse.

14. Clark Hoyt, "Tuning in Too Late," *New York Times*, September 27, 2009.

15. David Shaw, "'Rally for Life' Coverage Evokes an Editor's Anger," *Los Angeles Times*, July 3, 1990.

16. Ibid.
17. Ibid.
18. Ibid.
19. Ibid.

11. The Anti-Newsroom, Washington County, Utah

1. The 61 percent figure comes from the *Salt Lake Tribune*, "Rise and Fall: Mormon Majority is Slipping Away," available at http://extras.mnginteractive.com/live/media/site297/2005/0726/20050726_101404_DTTTRB24A10.PDF. I used the study's latest figures, which were from 2004. The Mormon population in Washington County is trending downward, mainly because of so much immigration to the county. In 1989, 75.5 percent of its residents were Mormon.

2. *Jim Slinsky Presents: The Outdoor Talk Network*, February 2006. The topic was "Bias in the Media." The host, Jim Slinsky, interviewed me.

3. Jeffs was convicted; however, the Utah Supreme Court reversed the conviction because of incorrect jury instructions, and it ordered a new trial.

4. See "Hands Are Shaky and Knees Are Weak? Are Journalists Really Dupes of their Corporate Bosses?" available at www.timgroseclose.com/corporate-media-theory-debunked.

12. Walk a Mile in the Shoes of a Centrist

1. Lieberman explained his stance at a debate at Pace University on September 25, 2003. See www.ontheissues.org/2008/Joseph_Lieberman_Tax_Reform.htm.

2. John F. Harris and Dan Balz, "Delicate Moves Led to Tax Cut," *Washington Post*, May 27, 2001, p. A01.

3. Jerome L. Sherman, "How a Lifelong Hawk Became a Dove, Too," *Pittsburgh Post-Gazette*, June 24, 2007, p. A1.

4. David S. Cloud, "Lawmaker Returns Home, A Hawk Turned War Foe," *New York Times*, November 22, 2005, p. 14.

5. More precisely, Suffolk County voted 49.46–48.52 for Kerry. With each vote total I rounded up (to preserve the approximate one-percentage-point difference).

6. This analysis gives: [Predicted 2004 PQ] = −58.22 + 2.192 × [Kerry vote percentage].

13. "Wise Men from the Center on Budget and Policy Priorities Say . . ."

1. Michael Kinsley, "Gore Carries *Slate*," *Slate*, November 7, 2000. See www.slate.com/id/92782/.

2. Kathleen Hall Jamieson, *Everything You Think You Know About Politics . . . and Why You're Wrong*, New York: Basic Books, 2000, p. 188.

3. See Goldberg, *Bias*, p. 20.

4. Timothy Crouse, *The Boys on the Bus*, New York: Ballantine Books, 1973, p. 116.

5. We provide a cursory explanation of those details in our article ("A Measure of Media Bias," *Quarterly Journal of Economics* 120, no. 4 (November 2005): 1191–237.

6. See www.wheretodoresearch.com for a list of the two hundred groups.

7. My expectation does not necessarily agree with the "corporate media" theory. The latter theory asserts that—assuming the bosses of News Corp. are indeed more conservative than the previous bosses of the *Journal*—the SQ of the *Journal* should drop immediately after the ownership change. That is, because the new bosses can pressure liberal journalists at the *Journal* to adopt a conservative slant, the *Journal*'s SQ should drop *before* News Corp. replaces liberal journalists with conservative ones. My expectation, in contrast, asserts that the change should be much more gradual. Almost all of the change should occur *after* News Corp. has hired new journalists.

8. Reed Irvine and Cliff Kincaid, "Post Columnist Concerned About Media Bias," September 17, 2001, available at www.aim.org/media-monitor/post-columnist-concerned-about-media-bias.

9. WorldNetDaily, June 25, 2002, available at www.worldnetdaily.com/news/article.asp?ARTICLE_ID=28078.

10. See www.people-press.org/reports/display.php3?ReportID=215 for a description of the survey and its data. See also Howard Kurtz for a summary of the study: "Fewer Republicans Trust the News, Survey Finds," *Washington Post,* June 9, 2004, p. C01. See also www.washingtonpost.com/wp-dyn/articles/A26345-2004Jun8.html.

11. Sometimes even liberals consider NPR left wing. As Bob Woodward notes in *The Agenda* (New York: Simon and Schuster, 1994, p. 114), "[Paul] Begala was steaming. To him, [OMB director, Alice] Rivlin symbolized all that was wrong with Clinton's new team of Washington hands, and represented the Volvo-driving, National Public Radio-listening, wine drinking liberalism that he felt had crippled the Democratic Party for decades."

12. Indeed, one of the left-wing blogs, www.brendan-nyhan.com/blog/2005/12/the_problems_wi.html, agrees with this assessment. It noted, "Technocratic centrist to liberal organizations like Brookings and the Center on Budget and Policy Priorities tend to have more credentialed experts with peer-reviewed publications than their conservative counterparts." Although I agree that the Brookings Institution has many scholarly experts, my and Milyo's method found this think tank to be very centrist. If journalists are citing Brookings because of its scholarly experts, this causes our method to spuriously make news outlets appear more centrist than they actually are, not necessarily more liberal.

13. It is important to note that to judge our method, all that is relevant is whether (a) it is true *among the think tanks in our sample.* If, for instance left-wing think tanks outside our sample are more scholarly than right-wing think tanks outside our sample, yet within our sample left-wing and right-wing think tanks are equally scholarly, then this will pose no problem for our method.

14. The Language of Journalists and the Special Case of Partial-Birth Abortion

1. David Crary, "'Monumental Day' or 'A Very Sad Day'?", Associated Press, *Bismarck Tribune,* October 23, 2003.

2. Will Lester, "Abortion Vote Casts Spotlight on Presidential Candidates," Associated Press State and Local Wire, October 22, 2003.

3. Crary, op. cit.

4. Lester, op. cit.

5. *Special Report with Brit Hume* (Fox News), October 22, 2003.

6. *Congressional Record,* October 21, 2003, p. S12916.

7. See, for instance, http://medical-dictionary.thefreedictionary.com/partial+birth+abortion.

8. Some argued that "intact dilation and extraction," a term widely used in the medical literature, should be the term that journalists use to describe the procedure. However, "intact D&X," as medical textbooks define it, is *not* the same thing as "partial-birth abortion" as the Senate bill defined it. That is, some intact D&X abortions would not legally be called partial-birth abortions; and some abortions that would legally be called partial-birth would not be called intact D&X. "Intact D&X" means that (i) a doctor dilates the mother's cervix; (ii) he pulls the fetus from the uterus, through the cervix, until part of the fetus, but not the head, is outside the mother's body; and (iii) he punctures the skull and suctions the "cranium matter" from the fetus. This allows the fetus to be delivered intact, albeit dead, through the vagina. "Partial-birth," as defined by the Senate bill, occurs when (i) the doctor pulls the fetus from the uterus until either its entire head or entire lower trunk (defined in the Senate bill as the fetus's body from the navel to the toes) is outside the mother's body; and (ii) the doctor knowingly and willingly kills the fetus. Thus, suppose a doctor pulls the lower trunk of the fetus outside the mother and then, rather than puncturing the skull, completely cuts the head from the body. Then this would legally be called "partial-birth," but it would not be called "intact D&X." In contrast, suppose a doctor performs all the steps of the "intact D&X" procedure, yet pulls the fetus only enough so that the lower legs, but not the navel, are outside the mother's body. Then this is called

"intact D&X" but not "partial-birth." Similarly, suppose a doctor injects a fatal drug to the fetus while it is still in the uterus. He can then perform all of the steps of an intact D&X procedure, but it would not legally be called a partial-birth abortion.

9. Frank Luntz, *Learning from 2004 . . . Winning in 2006*, Luntz Research Companies, 2005. I first learned of the quote from Gentzkow and Shapiro's working paper "What Drives Media Slant? Evidence from U.S. Daily Newspapers," *Econometrica* 78, no. 1 (January 2010): 35–71.

10. See Amy Fagan, "Senate Target Abortion Method; OKs bill to Ban Partial Birth," *Washington Times*, October 22, 2003, p. A1.

11. Like voters, the U.S. House was slightly more conservative than the Senate. In the House 66 percent of the members voted for the bill.

12. For details, see note 8.

13. *NBC Nightly News*, October 21, 2003.

14. *CNN NewsNight with Aaron Brown*, October 21, 2003.

15. *Congressional Record*, October 21, 2003, p. S12927.

16. Ibid., p. S12942.

15. The Language of Journalists and the Gentzkow-Shapiro Measure of Media Bias

1. See Gentzkow and Shapiro, "What Drives Media Slant," *Econometrica*.

2. Gentzkow and Shapiro, before doing their text analysis, removed "extremely common" words such as "a," "an," "the," "to," and "from."

3. One small difference, however, is that Gentzkow and Shapiro's method estimates not the most likely PQ of the politician, but the most likely ideology of his district, as measured by George W. Bush's two-party vote share in the district from the 2004 election. However, it is easy to convert (i) the vote share of a district for George W. Bush, into (ii) the predicted PQ of the district's representative. I do this through a regression analysis, a statistical technique commonly used by social scientists. Specifically, I regressed the average PQ of a politician upon the share of the two-party vote that George W. Bush received in the politician's district. The results of the regression gave the following equation: $PQ = 160.9 - 2.1914 \times$ [Bush's vote percentage in the district]. Using this formula, I have converted all of Gentzkow and Shapiro's results—expressed in Bush vote shares—to SQs. Another difference is that although I interpret an SQ differing from 50.4 as a bias, Gentzkow and Shapiro do not. For instance, on pages 36–37, they note, "The resulting index allows us to compare newspapers to one another, though not to a benchmark of 'true' or 'unbiased' reporting."

4. Circulation data comes from www.burrellesluce.com/top100/2007_Top_100List.pdf.

5. Because Gentzkow and Shapiro did not compute an estimate for the *San Jose Mercury News*, I did not include data for San Jose in my averages.

16. Facts About the Bush Tax Cuts: Another Way to Measure Media Bias Objectively and Quantitatively

1. David E. Rosenbaum, "Doing the Math on Bush's Tax Cut," *New York Times*, March 4, 2001. See www.nytimes.com/2001/03/04/us/doing-the-math-on-bush-s-tax-cut.html.

2. Steven E. Landsburg, "Bush's Tax Cuts Are Unfair . . . to the Rich," *Slate*, October 21, 2004. See www.slate.com/id/2108201.

3. For the congressional data, I used speeches about (i) the House and Senate versions of the bill, which respectively occurred on May 16, 2001, and May 17–23, 2001, and (ii) the final compromise bill, written in the House-Senate Conference Committee, which occurred in the House on May 25, 2001, and in the Senate on May 26, 2001.

4. Jospeph Curl and Dave Boyer, "Bush $1.6 Trillion Tax-Cut Proposal Goes to Congress," *Washington Times*, February 9, 2001, p. A1.

5. Frank Bruni, "The President's Budget: The Promotional Campaign; Bush Takes His Tax Proposal on Tour," *New York Times*, March 1, 2001, p. 23.

6. Fred Barnes, on *Special Report with Brit Hume* (Fox News), March 22, 2001.

7. Carl Cameron, on *Special Report with Brit Hume* (Fox News), February 27, 2001.

8. See Jospeph Curl and Dave Boyer, "Bush $1.6 Trillion Tax-Cut Proposal Goes to Congress," *Washington Times.*

9. The maximum possible score is actually slightly greater than 100. The reason involves some technical issues that I explained in chapters 1 and 4. My article with James Snyder and Steve Levitt ("Comparing Interest Group Scores Across Time and Chambers," *American Political Science Review* 93 (March 1999): 33–50) gives more details. However, to keep the presentation simple, in this chapter I treat the minimum and maximum PQs as if they were 0 and 100.

10. For instance, on page 104 he writes, "The key question to ask is not whether examples of bias can be found, but exactly where is bias pervasive and what is its effect on the news and American public life? Though the evidence is sketchy, I tend to believe that on many social issues, conservatives have a case."

11. For instance, on page 122 he notes, "Contempt for the questioning of the fundamentals of globalization and free investment is of a piece with the media's total embrace of corporate values in virtually all matters of political economy."

12. Just as Milyo and I did for the think-tank method, and just as Gentzkow and Shapiro did for the loaded-phrase method, for this chapter's analysis I excluded magazine and newspaper editorials, as well as letters to the editor.

13. The calculation ignores the fact that the 39.6 and 35 percent rates are marginal, not average, rates. However, for the very highest-earning taxpayers, these rates very closely approximate average rates.

14. David E. Rosenbaum, "Balance of Power: The Tax Vote; Senate Approves Cut in Income Tax in Bipartisan Vote," *New York Times,* May 24, 2001, Section A, p. 1.

15. Glenn Kessler and Juliet Eilperin, "Congress Pass $1.35 Trillion Tax Cut; Lawmakers Hand Bush a Big Legislative Victory," *Washington Post,* May 27, 2001, Section A, p. 1.

16. A notable exception, where a journalist *did* explain some of the tenuous assumptions by Citizens for Tax Justice, was Richard W. Stevenson. See his article, "The 2000 Campaign; Sorting It Out: Tax Cuts and Spending," *New York Times,* October 6, 2000.

17. *Congressional Record,* May 17, 2001, p. S5048–49.

18. Paul Krugman, "Reckonings; The Big Lie," *New York Times,* May 27, 2001, Section 4, Editorial Desk, p. 9. Since the essay was an opinion piece, it was not included among the data for my statistical analysis.

19. *Congressional Record,* May 26, 2001, p. S5785–86.

20. Krugman, op. cit.

17. The Media Mu

1. See www.gallup.com/poll/7507/republicans-more-likely-than-democrats-use-talk-radio-news.aspx.

18. Measuring the Influence of the Media I: Many Methods False and Spent, and One That's Not

1. Stefano DellaVigna and Ethan Kaplan, "The Fox News Effect: Media Bias and Voting," *Quarterly Journal of Economics* 122, no. 3 (August 2007): 1187–234.

2. See Steven Levitt, "Using Electoral Cycles in Police Hiring to Estimate the Effect of Police on Crime," *American Economic Review* 87 (June 3, 1997): 270–90.

3. It turns out that Levitt's study had a minor problem. Namely, his computer code did not weight observations properly. UC Berkeley economist Justin McCrary discovered the error and reported results once the weighting error had been corrected. He concludes that Levitt's estimates—the effect of an extra cop on violent crimes—were approximately double the correct estimates. See McCrary, "Using Electoral Cycles in Police Hiring to Estimate the Effect of Police on Crime" Comment, *American Economic Review* 92 (September 4, 2002): 1236–43.

4. See www.snpp.com/episodes/BABF06.

5. Steven Kull, Clay Ramsay, and Evan Lewis, "Misperceptions, the Media, and the Iraq War," *Political Science Quarterly* 118, no. 4 (2003-4): 569–98.

6. Michael W. Giles and James C. Garand, "Ranking Political Science Journals: Reputational and Citational Approaches," *PS* (October 2007): 741–51.

7. See www.foxnews.com/story/0,2933,60353,00.html.

8. DellaVigna and Kaplan, op. cit.

9. Unlike with the Kull et al. experiment, DellaVigna and Kaplan do not have to worry about a self-selection problem by voters. That is, a voter is a member of their treatment group if Fox became available to the market in which he lived. It did not depend on whether he chose to watch Fox News or not. That is, if Fox entered the market in which the voter lived, yet he chose not to subscribe to Fox (or chose not to watch Fox even if he subscribed) he was placed in the treatment group—just like a voter who lived in a market in which Fox entered and chose to watch Fox.

10. That is, suppose market A voted 80 percent Republican but the prior election voted 81 percent Republican. Suppose market B voted 20 percent Republican, but the prior election voted 19 percent Republican. If I were Rupert Murdoch, I would prefer market A. Although market B, if trends continue, might eventually become more conservative than market A, I would wait until this occurred before choosing market B.

19. Measuring the Influence of the Media II: Two More Groundbreaking Experiments

1. David Leonhardt, "The Future of Economics Isn't So Dismal," *New York Times*, January 10, 2007, p. C1.

2. For details, see Alan S. Gerber and Donald P. Green, "The Effects of Canvassing, Telephone Calls, and Direct Mail on Voter Turnout: A Field Experiment, *American Political Science Review* 94, no. 3 (September 2000): 653–63.

3. See David Frum, "Bush's Secret Canadian Weapon," available at www.aei.org/article/22941.

4. The 3.8 number comes from table 4 of the Gerber et al. article. As column four of the table notes, if the subject was placed in *The Washington Post* treatment group, then his probability of voting for the Democrat was 0.112 units higher than if he had been placed in the control group. If he was placed in *The Washington Times* treatment group, then his probability of voting for the Democrat was 0.074 units higher than if he had been placed in the control group. Note that 0.112 minus 0.074 is 0.038, or 3.8 percent.

5. Hongbin Cai and Joseph Wang, "Overcommunication in Strategic Information Transmission Games," *Games and Economic Behavior* 56 (2006): 7–36.

20. The Media Lambda

1. Matt Bai, "Working for the Working-Class Vote," *New York Times Magazine*, October 19, 2008.

2. The show appeared on July 10, 2004. The quote comes from the transcript that the Media Research Center provided at www.mrc.org/notablequotables/bestof/2004/bestquote.asp#bias.

3. CNN's *Reliable Sources*, October 17, 2004.

4. See DellaVigna and Kaplan, "The Fox News Effect."

5. Alan S. Gerber, Dean Karlan, and Daniel Bergan, "Does the Media Matter? A Field Experiment Measuring the Effect of Newspapers on Voting Behavior and Political Opinions," *American Economic Journal: Applied Economics* 1, no. 2 (2009): 35–52.

6. See Cai, and Wang, "Overcommunication in Strategic Information Transmission Games," *Games and Economic Behavior.*

7. See www.timgroseclose.com/estimating-the-media-lambda.pdf.

8. Joseph T. Klapper, *The Effects of Mass Communication*, New York: Free Press.

9. William J. McGuire, "The Myth of Massive Media Impact: Savagings and Salvagings," *Public Communication and Behavior* 1 (1986): 173–257.

10. John Zaller, "The Myth of Massive Media Impact Revived: New Support for a

Discredited Idea," chapter 2 in Diana C. Mutz, Paul M. Sniderman, and Richard A. Brody, eds., *Political Persuasion and Attitude Change*, Ann Arbor: University of Michigan Press, 1996, pp. 17–78.

11. The concept of the media lambda is somewhat similar to the persuasion rate that (i) DellaVigna and Kaplan discuss in their "Fox News Effect" article, and (ii) DellaVigna and Matthew Gentzkow discuss in their article "Persuasion: Empirical Evidence," *Annual Review of Economics* 2 (2010). One major difference between the two concepts, however, is that the persuasion rate is calculated from discrete outcomes—whether individuals are persuaded to do something or not. Meanwhile, the media lambda is calculated from continuous outcomes—namely, the *degree* to which the average voter changes his political views. Similarly, unlike the media lambda, persuasion rates do not analyze how extreme the message is—that is, the degree to which a person is being asked to change his views.

12. See www.timgroseclose.com/estimating-the-media-lambda.pdf for this paper.

13. Cai and Wang actually ran four different sets of experiments. I discuss each set in my paper "Bias in a Laboratory Simulation of a Signaling Game with Implications for the Influence of the News Media." From the four sets of experiments, I have calculated media lambdas of 0.510, 0.325, 0.315, and 0.271. The median of these four estimates is approximately 0.32.

14. Indeed, Gerber et al. note that the 3.8 result is not statistically significant—thus, the 95 percent confidence interval for the result includes 0. Further, the authors do not focus on the result as one of the main conclusions of their study. The 0.43 result from the DellaVigna-Kaplan article is the average of two estimates from two different versions of their basic model. The two estimates were 0.37 and 0.48. The standard errors of the two estimates were 0.21 and 0.19.

15. See the epilogue of this book for a transcript of Raddatz's exchange with the C-SPAN caller.

16. Although we know that the media lambda cannot be greater than 1, if we want an unbiased aggregate estimate, then we should still use 1.73 and not alter it to 1 or a smaller number. Thus, when I make this adjustment, I err on the side of estimating a media lambda smaller than its true value. To see why, consider the following example. Suppose that the true media lambda is 0.95, and that N studies are designed to estimate the media lambda. Suppose that each study will produce an estimate of 0.75, 0.95, or 1.15, each with one-third probability. Thus, in expectation each study produces the true media lambda, 0.95, as an estimate. However, suppose that after seeing the estimates from the N studies, we alter each 1.15 estimate to 1. Then, in expectation our aggregate estimate will be 0.9 (i.e. [0.75 + 0.95 + 1]/3), which is biased downward from the true value, 0.95.

17. I owe this insight to Peter DeMarzo, Dimitri Vayanos, and Jeffey Zwiebel. See their article, "Persuasion Bias, Social Influence, and Uni-Dimensional Opinions," *Quarterly Journal of Economics* 118, no. 3 (2003): 909–68.

18. See, for instance, James Hamilton's *All the News That's Fit to Sell*, Princeton, N.J.: Princeton University Press, 2004, p. 106. He reports the results of a survey where respondents were asked if the "coverage of the presidential race by news organizations shows: a Democratic bias, a Republican bias, or no bias. As the survey reported, 62.8 percent of Independents said, "No bias," while 48.7 percent of Republicans and 66.1 percent of Democrats said, "No bias."

21. Rendezvous with Clarity

1. See, for example, www.nationalcenter.org/ReaganChoosing1964.html.

2. Edwin Eugene Aldrin, *Line-of-Sight Guidance Techniques for Manned Orbital Rendezvous*, pp. 80–81, available at http://dspace.mit.edu/handle/1721.1/12652.

22. Walk a Mile in the Shoes of a Centrist . . . Whose Mind Has Not Been Distorted by Media Bias

1. See http://www.youtube.com/watch?v=u_C5ZySBUOg.

2. See, for example, the discussion by legendary driver Mark Martin with Beth Tuschak, *NASCAR for Dummies*, 2nd ed., Indianapolis, Ind.: Wiley Publishing, Inc., 2005, pp. 24–25.

3. The above analysis solves the following thought experiment: What if we could eliminate the liberal bias of the media and rerun the previous two elections, *while keeping everything else the same.* Most important, the latter phrase means *constraining the candidates to keep the same policy positions that they held in the actual elections.* However, if we could truly eliminate media bias, and the average voter, accordingly, really became 20 or 25 points more conservative, then I don't believe that the candidates would keep the same policy positions. That is, if the country really became 20 or 25 points more conservative, then, I believe, the typical Republican and Democratic presidential nominees would adopt policy positions that were about 20 or 25 points more conservative. If I'm correct, then—although expected policies would indeed become more conservative—the expected vote share of Republican candidates would not increase. Anthony Downs (*An Economic Theory of Democracy,* New York: Harper and Row, 1957) and Harold Hotelling ("Stability and Competition," *Economic Journal* 39, no. 153 [March 1929]: 41–57) give excellent theoretical explanations why this would be true.

4. Michael Barone with Richard Cohen, *2010 Almanc of American Politics,* Washington, D.C.: National Journal Group, p. 1491.

5. Ibid., 240–41.

6. See www.en.wikipedia.org/wiki/Orange_County,_California.

7. See http://quickfacts.census.gov/qfd/states/06/06059.html.

EPILOGUE

1. David Awbrey, "The Media Elite's Inside Job," *Pittsburgh Post-Gazette,* June 23, 1996.

2. See Goldberg, *Bias,* p. 25. Indeed, I became aware of Awbrey's passage through reading Goldberg's book.

3. The movie never mentioned Smith's state. However, the movie was based on an unpublished novel called *The Gentleman from Montana.*

4. *Washington Journal,* May 11, 2007. See www.c-spanvideo.org/program/USPolicy inIraq58. The following occurs at approximately the 34:28 point in the video.

5. See www.c-spanvideo.org/videoLibrary/clip.php?appid=595085887. (This is the C-SPAN version of the House proceedings, beginning approximately 8:12 p.m. EST, November 7, 2009.)

INDEX